An Unexpected Everything

the cage family

CARRIE ANN
NEW YORK TIMES BESTSELLING AUTHOR
RYAN

An Unexpected Everything

THE CAGE FAMILY
BOOK TWO

CARRIE ANN RYAN

An Unexpected Everything

An Unexpected Everything
By: Carrie Ann Ryan
© 2025 Carrie Ann Ryan

Cover Art by Sweet N Spicy Designs

This book is a work of fiction. Names, characters, places, and incidents either are products of the author's imagination or are used fictitiously. Any resemblance to actual events, locales or persons, living or dead, is entirely coincidental.
No part of this book can be reproduced in any form or by electronic or mechanical means including information storage and retrieval systems, without the express written permission of the author. The only exception is by a reviewer who may quote short excerpts in a review.

All content warnings are listed on the book page for this book on my website.

NO AI TRAINING: Without in any way limiting the author's [and publisher's] exclusive rights under copyright, any use of this publication to "train" generative artificial intelligence (AI) technologies to generate text is expressly prohibited. The author reserves all rights to license uses of this work for generative AI training and development of machine learning language models.

Praise for Carrie Ann Ryan

"Count on Carrie Ann Ryan for emotional, sexy, character driven stories that capture your heart!" – Carly Phillips, NY Times bestselling author

"Carrie Ann Ryan's romances are my newest addiction! The emotion in her books captures me from the very beginning. The hope and healing hold me close until the end. These love stories will simply sweep you away." ~ NYT Bestselling Author Deveny Perry

"Carrie Ann Ryan writes the perfect balance of sweet and heat ensuring every story feeds the soul." - Audrey Carlan, #1 New York Times Bestselling Author

"Carrie Ann Ryan never fails to draw readers in with passion, raw sensuality, and characters that pop off the page. Any book by Carrie Ann is an absolute treat." – New York Times Bestselling Author J. Kenner

"Carrie Ann Ryan knows how to pull your heartstrings and make your pulse pound! Her wonderful Redwood Pack series will draw you in and keep you reading long into the night. I can't wait to see what comes next with the new generation, the Talons. Keep them coming, Carrie Ann!" –Lara Adrian, New York Times bestselling author of CRAVE THE NIGHT

"With snarky humor, sizzling love scenes, and brilliant, imaginative worldbuilding, The Dante's Circle series reads as if Carrie Ann Ryan peeked at my personal wish list!" – NYT Bestselling Author, Larissa Ione

"Carrie Ann Ryan writes sexy shifters in a world full of passionate happily-ever-afters." – *New York Times* Bestselling Author Vivian Arend

"Carrie Ann's books are sexy with characters you can't help but love from page one. They are heat and heart blended to perfection." *New York Times* Bestselling Author Jayne Rylon

Carrie Ann Ryan's books are wickedly funny and deliciously hot, with plenty of twists to keep you guessing. They'll keep you up all night!" USA Today Bestselling Author Cari Quinn

"Once again, Carrie Ann Ryan knocks the Dante's Circle series out of the park. The queen of hot, sexy, enthralling paranormal romance, Carrie Ann is an author not to miss!" *New York Times* bestselling Author Marie Harte

For the ones who fight for their family and are called ice queens for it.
For the ones who are call critical and domineering when they are merely breathing the same air as a man who looks down on them.
For the ones who love this genre and still feel the need to hide their love because the patriarchy tells them to.
This one is for you.
This genre is for you.
Never forget that.

Chapter One
WESTON

"Every time I drive, I hear a whomping sound. I think it's the rear axle. It has to be. I looked it up on this one website. They were very informative. They even told me about that special air I need for the tires. You know the one I told you about last time? And how I need to change my filter every month. So I think I need a whole new rear axle and thingy." She then proceeded to make the whomping sound her car currently made, complete with hand motions.

I nodded along as Diedre continued to talk about her sedan's apparent rear axle problems. She had multiple notes on her phone, as well as various links to random websites since she'd done her research.

And since Diedre had babysat me as a kid and I'd had a crush on her when I was eight, it hurt me to hold back the biting words such as—her car didn't have a rear axle. And that I hadn't charged her to put air in her tires—special air or not.

"I've got your notes, Diedre. Thank you for all of your hard work. Now let me go take a look. Your car is in my team's hands. I promise."

"Oh, Weston. You're the sweetest. Drew told me he'd get to it when he finished his big project, but he's been so busy." Her eyes tightened at the sides.

I fisted my hands, doing my best not to show any other reaction.

Drew barely worked on his construction crew for some of the new builds in town, and when he wasn't working, he was drinking. The Lake Bar wouldn't let him run a tab anymore and that place was the only so-called seedy area of Cage Lake. I wasn't even sure if Drew remembered the names of two of the five of his kids. The kids who either hung out with *my* kids or my kids watched hers when Diedre couldn't get Drew to take care of them on his own.

I wasn't surprised Drew hadn't had a chance to look at the tires. And frankly, if the man touched this car, then it would most likely end up with a worse issue later. Not that I'd tell Diedre that.

I grunted in response at Drew's name, not in the mood to speak about him, then looked down at her notes. "You popped two of your tires?" I looked up at her, confused. "Hell. How did that happen?" Visions of exactly how she could have done that slammed into me and a sweat nearly broke out on my forehead.

"Yes." Diedre bit her lip when I looked up. "I went off the road on...well on *the bridge*. I mean...after it, but I slid on the bridge itself." Regret covered her face, and my heart kicked that familiar beat, but I ignored it.

"I'm glad you didn't get hurt. Kids okay?"

Relief that I didn't want to go into detail or that I didn't react to her perceived slip up covered her features, and she nodded. "Yes. Thankfully. And then well...we should have come here right after it happened, but Drew said he'd handle it. He got a good deal on the replacement tires and took care of it himself."

I held back a curse and nodded, having a clearer idea as to what the issue was with her car. Because Drew was a damn idiot and hadn't put the tires on correctly. She's lucky she hadn't been run off the road again—this time hurting herself or someone else.

"I'll take care of it, Dee."

"Thank you, Weston. Just...thank you."

I turned at the pleading in her eyes and made my way back to the shop. She was never going to leave Drew and his wasteful ways. No matter how hard people in our small town tried. After all, Cage Lake was all about that small town feel. People got into their business and tried to do what was best for others. Even if that meant constantly being in the way or taking steps that could make things worse. They ignored the ugly sides of things, though, and I was pretty sure most people forgot that key detail.

I owned the only mechanic shop in the area so people from town and a few towns over would come to me for help. Meaning this family run place always had business. My uncles had opened the place and had taught me everything I knew. Dad had been the small-town lawyer with Mom working with him, but he'd stood by my side when I'd wanted to learn how to hold a wrench and then later, when college had called my name—at least until the world changed. Caldwell's was a staple in Cage Lake, much like many of the places that dotted the town but actually brought in tourists.

Cage Lake was a small town in the Rocky Mountains a couple hours west of Denver. It had nearly everything someone needed to stay and never leave—not that I hadn't tried. There was one main road leading to the town and two large bridges that connected the area to other towns and the main highway that cut through the Rockies. And like most small towns, there was one main road that bisected the area. Most of the business, restaurants, and historical areas were located there. Then each of the lanes branching off the main road led to mostly residential and forested areas. There were a few other businesses—like Doc Henry's clinic—that popped up around them as well. Then the road curved to either lead to the lake or the resort the Cages owned. There were other houses lining the lake and the road that circled back to the main road.

In other words, it was hard to get lost and everyone knew everyone. And there was no escaping the constant need to be in everyone's business. It's why I'd tried to get out of the place all those years ago.

And then a single deer on that lone bridge with just enough rain on the road had changed everything.

I quickly got to work and by the time my shift ended, the rest of my crew was ready to head out or start on a couple custom pieces after hours. I wasn't closing today so I grabbed the endless paperwork that came with being an owner, and decided to head to Rise and Cage, the main bakery in town. I was in the mood for sugar and caffeine, though a beer sounded damn good too.

However, the moment I took a step outside of my truck, I knew I'd made a mistake. If I wanted to be alone with my paperwork, running into the mayor's wife who looked to be in the mood to gossip—which was most hours of the day—wasn't a good choice. I was a permanent Cage Lake resident, so listening to Ms. Patty talk about her husband and his choices as mayor was par for the course. Practically rote at this point.

"Like I was saying. When those girls of yours graduate you're going to find yourself with an empty nest. With Lance off at business school and Sydney and Sam ready to start their new lives, you'll have so much time on your hands you won't know what to do with yourself. Believe me. I was the same way back in the day when the boys moved to Denver and Cheyenne and decided to stay there after college. Not that it's too far away, but I do miss being able to see my babies and *their* babies often. But it's not as if Mr. Mayor and I could truly leave town and move to be near them. Cage Lake is our home. You would know that, after all. This is your home and you're never going to leave. It's what we do as Cage Lake Lifers. It's everything we need even with so many new transplants. Like the other Cages. I'm sure you heard about the *other* Cages, of course."

I nodded along, letting Ms. Patty continue to ramble because I knew from experience that if I spoke aloud or asked a question, I'd relegate myself to another ten minutes of this. For one moment, I let myself think the terrible thought of her calling her husband Mr. Mayor. I didn't want to know when else she used that title. Ever.

Then the rest of her question that wasn't a question

finally slid through the mud that was my thoughts and I blinked. "The other Cages are moving here?"

That's all we needed. More drama because Daddy Cage couldn't keep his pants zipped. I might be friends with Hudson, one of the original Cages, but I had no desire to learn about the rest of them.

Especially one of them in particular.

Ms. Patty tittered but there wasn't any harm in it. There never was with her. She might gossip like nobody's business, but she was also one of the first to call Drew out to his face. And she'd been at my house the day after the funeral with casseroles and cookbooks so I'd know how to feed the kids. "Oh, I don't think so. I know a couple of them have visited, but I don't know all of the details yet."

I knew that had to be killing her.

"Anyway, since the patriarch of the Cages decided to keep both families secret from each other, I can only imagine the dynamics over those family dinners they are forced to have. You heard about that, right? They must have dinner once a month in order to keep their inheritance. And considering this *town* is part of inheritance, I sure hope they find a way to break bread. Could you imagine what would happen to Cage Lake if the Cage assets were divided and dissolved? Why, they own over eighty percent of this town—including the homes around the lake itself and the resort that brings in the town tourism budget. In other words: No Cages. No town."

I ground my teeth at that. Hudson didn't like talking about what his father had done and I had no desire to learn the details. If he needed to talk, I'd be there like he'd been there for me when I'd been forced to raise my three siblings and was so out of my depth it wasn't even funny. But if he made me talk about it beyond the superficial, I'd be required to think about the one person and time in my life I'd done my best to forget.

Not that I could truly forget.

After all, she survived in my dreams, my memories, and my waking regrets every day.

"That gives you something to think about for sure." I cleared my throat before she could continue. "I'm headed out to the lake to catch up on something. You have a nice day, Ms. Patty."

"Oh yes, my mouth and I have kept you for too long. Be safe, Weston. This town needs you."

And without waiting for her to say another word, I headed out to my truck. I needed air and I knew the best place to do that wasn't going to be on the primary street with everyone watching me. They might not know my past, but they always knew when something was beneath the surface.

AN UNEXPECTED EVERYTHING

The problem—one of many—with a small town.

I drove down Main Street and turned toward my favorite thinking spot. Right on the edge of the mountain itself, it had a great view of the town and the beauty that was the Rocky Mountains. The best part of Cage Lake was that most of the views were breathtaking. It was hard to find a shitty spot of town—something the residents and Cages who didn't live here full time worked hard on.

I turned off the engine once I made it to the parking spot at the edge of the trail and hopped out of the truck. I took a deep breath of that mountain air and told myself I needed to get out of my head. It had been eight years since my world had shifted and I hated the idea that my brain couldn't help but focus on the two months of peace I'd had in between when life had been normal and when it had broken.

The math just didn't add up. I hadn't spent enough time with her to regret her and yet that was a damn lie.

I turned the corner, eager to sit on the cliff's edge and breathe, when the scream echoed through the forest. I took off at a run, hoping to hell I wasn't about to end up on the wrong side of a bear's claws—or worse.

Then I realized the edge of the cliffside where locals didn't stand since the ground turned to shit once the rain hit had shifted. Meaning part of the place I liked to sit and think was now gone.

Another scream.

I ran toward the side, chest heaving, and finally knelt to get a good look at the situation, hoping to hell I wasn't too late. I held back a curse as I realized a woman clung to the side of the mud and rockface, her limbs shaking, and dirt covering her body and clothes.

Then she looked up.

It was as if someone had kicked me in the chest.

She might not have been able to see me clearly with the angle—but I could see every inch of her face. Reality froze in time as my world crashed. Because I knew that face. That voice. I knew the fear in those eyes. Those eyes I'd fallen in love with when I'd been too damn young to understand what love was.

Isabella Cage Dixon.

The ghost I thought I'd excised long ago.

Another rock fell from beneath my grip, and I cursed, pushing out thoughts from the past because there wasn't time for that. There never had been. Bella was one moment from falling to her death and I'd be damned if I failed her again.

"Reach for my hand, damn it!"

Bile coated my tongue as I clung to the side of the

rockface, my hand outstretched. My voice came out as more of a growl, but I didn't give a fuck right then.

"Come on. I don't have a firm grip and we're both going to fall off this fucking mountain if you don't *move!*"

Scrambling, her fingers bleeding, she reached out, trying to grip my hands. Her fingers brushed mine before she fell down another inch, and a scream ripped from her throat.

"I can't reach!"

"I've got you. I've got you." I kept repeating the words as she tried to climb, tried to save herself.

My world narrowed to that pinprick of time. *My Bella.* The woman I hated because of what she represented, the woman I used to love because she'd been mine, would *not* fall.

I refused to even allow the idea to come to fruition. So I moved farther down the side, knowing if I leaned too far, we'd both fall and there would be no coming back from that. And I'd leave behind the ones I'd broken everything for.

Then my hand was on hers and we were both shouting, muscles straining. Somehow, she lay beside me on the edge of the hillside, both of us breathing heavily, my chest heaving.

As my mind struggled to process what had just

happened, I sat up and looked down at the woman who had once claimed my heart. The woman who had every right to push me down that cliff and never look back.

"You. It had to be you."

Bella finally got a good look at me, her eyes widening, and I knew she'd clocked on who I was. We both looked different than we had all those years ago, but not *that* different. My beard was longer, my hair similarly so. I had more ink down my arms, and even more where she couldn't see.

Bella though?

Somehow, she'd become even more gorgeous and I thought I could resent her for it. She'd cut her hair a bit shorter than I'd last seen her, but the chestnut of it still called to my hands. I'd once loved running my fingers through it, then tugging slightly as I crushed my mouth to hers. Or I'd hold on tight so I could slide my cock between those pouty lips of hers. She had the same curves—her handful-sized breasts that pushed at her torn T-shirt, her hips that had been perfect grips for me, her sweet thighs that had clamped around my shoulders when she'd sat on my face.

"*You.*"

The vitriol in her voice didn't surprise me. The need to growl right back did. Because it wasn't her fault she hated me. I deserved it. But as I'd just saved her life, maybe she could have waited five fucking minutes before doing what Bella did best—tear me a new one with that passion that had always turned me on.

"Yes. *Me.* What the hell are you doing here, Isabella?"

She flinched at the sound of her name and I tried not to let it cut. Because Bella was the girl I left behind, not the woman with blood on her hands and jeans in front of me. I needed to use the name that wasn't *her*.

"Shit. You're hurt." I was a fucking asshole and needed to think of her for once and not my own pent-up feelings.

"I'm fine," she bit out. Yet as she tried to roll over and stand up, she let out a hiss when her cut-up hands touched the ground.

"You're not fine. You're going to get those cuts infected if you don't fucking take care of them."

She blinked at me, her dirt-covered face pale. "Don't yell at me! How are you here? Of all people. It's been *years,* Weston. How are you in this tiny town in the mountains?"

"Let me help you up," I said in way of answer. It's not like I had any real answers for her. Nothing made sense right now and I didn't know why she was here in *my* town. The town I'd been forced to cage myself in over time in order to protect my family. To protect the kids. Because nothing else would have worked.

"Please don't touch me."

I froze in the action of reaching out, her words a slice to the soul. "Isabella."

Once again, she flinched but forced herself to stand on her own. "How are you here, Weston? Was Cage Lake your hometown this whole time? The little mountain town that you always said suffocated you. The place that you swore you'd never go back to? *This* town?"

Considering where we were, there was no point in lying. Not when I now stood with Bella so close to me, I could feel the heat of her through my flannel.

"This is home." Simple words for a not so simple truth.

She swallowed hard, her chin rising. "Home." Before she could add anything to that whisper, she swayed on her feet and I reached out to steady her, cursing.

"You need to see a doctor. Come on, Doc Henry should still be in his office. That man was pretty much here when the Cages up and built the town all those years ago."

"I didn't know this was your town, Weston," she said after a moment, her eyes pleading. "Just…just let me go."

Like you did once before.

At least that was the subtext I let myself hear.

"The way I hear it, it's your town too." I could have kicked myself for mentioning it. For letting her know that *I* knew about her connection to the Cages. But now there was no going back. Not when I was the fucking idiot who'd put us here.

She took a step back and I reached out without thinking to steady her. "Don't touch me."

I didn't let my hand fall. "For fuck's sake, Bella. You're three steps from falling off the damn cliff again. So no, I'm not going to let you keep going because this is awkward. Now let's get you to the damn doctor so I can make sure you're okay."

She pulled away from me in that moment and I only let her because I realized my mistake.

Bella.

I'd called her Bella.

Fuck.

"I'm here visiting my friend. I needed a damn moment to breathe and I didn't realize that this town is cursed just like everything else around me. I don't need a doctor. I just need to go home. To my city. Away from..." She shook her head. "Thank you for saving my life. I know that sounds trite. But thank you. However, I didn't know this was your town. That you'd be here. And frankly...I can't care anymore. I can't look at you. I don't have time in my life for more blasts from the past. I've had enough of that lately with dear old Dad and my brand-new family."

"I'm sorry." I cursed. "About your dad. I'm sorry."

"It's not your concern. Though the news seems to think it's everyone's concern. I'm going to go now. Maybe you should tell whoever is in charge of this town that it's a death trap."

"I can do that," I said after a moment, an odd chuckle escaping my lips. That was Isabella. The woman who always had something to say when people were doing something wrong. Not because she judged, but because she wanted to help—to make sure no one got hurt.

And yet I was the one who hurt her...just like her father apparently.

"Okay then." A pause. "Weston, I—" But she cut herself off as tears filled her eyes. Then she practically ran toward the small parking area off to the side of my truck. I hadn't seen what must be her SUV there when I'd pulled in thanks to the angle, but now I saw what I'd missed before.

Like always—a little too late.

Without a word, she drove off and I watched her go, hoping to hell her friend in town—whoever that was—kept her safe.

Because once again, I sure hadn't. The only woman I'd ever loved drove away, leaving me dirty and covered in cuts and blood. And I had no words for that since this time it wasn't metaphorical.

My phone buzzed and I looked down at the read out, answering when I saw it was Sam. "Little sister. I thought you were studying."

"I am. But I was wondering when you were coming home. It's your turn to cook, you know."

I cursed and I heard her and her twin's laughter. "I'll be there soon. But it might be takeout night."

"You know our favorites. Be safe, big brother."

And with that, she hung up, leaving me staring at the place Bella had been, letting the memories of what once was wash over me. After all, that phone call was my reality. The reason for so many things.

And Isabella Cage Dixon was not the woman for me or this town. I would do well to remember that, even when the boundaries of the town itself closed in.

A reminder of what was lost.

And the dreams I'd crushed along the way.

Chapter Two

ISABELLA

I LOVED MY FAMILY. I TRULY DID. I KNEW THAT through the worst of what life threw at us, my siblings would stand by my side. Then again, when I proclaimed that sentiment to myself the first time all those years ago, I hadn't had *quite* as many siblings.

Family dinner now had a whole new spin to it—one that either came with stress, drama, or absolute loathing. It surprised me, however, because the latter turned out to not be with the other Cages. The seven brothers who were still strangers though we were slowly becoming friendly. Perhaps even family. No, the anxiety and anger occurred with the family I had grown up with.

Or at least, the woman who raised me.

"Mom. You have to stop. There is literally nothing I

can do," I repeated for what felt like the fifteenth time during this dinner alone.

It didn't seem like she was listening to me. Instead she continued to rant about *that* woman.

The other wife.

My mother was of average height and had the same chestnut-brown hair that I did. While I had cut my hair to my shoulders, she had cut it short enough to show the nape of her neck and she shined with it. She'd had long hair for as long as I could remember. It had been down to the middle of her back, and she would braid it at night so it wouldn't be too tangled in the morning. I'd always loved brushing it as a little girl, and then my sister Sophia would add ribbons and other pretty things to the braids when we had been growing up. Sophia, a future principal ballet dancer, always had lace and random satin ribbons on hand.

When Dad died, Mom had kept her hair long for the funeral—and for that fateful day at the lawyer's office. But after our first required family dinner, we had come by her home afterward to visit and been shocked at her new appearance. I didn't know if it was grief, anger, or finally wanting to do something that our dad hadn't let her, but either way, it was still a bit of a jolt to see.

Mom's voice brought me out of my reverie. "There

has to be something you can do. I don't understand why you have to spend a single evening with *those* people."

I winced at her tone, because it was so unlike Constance Cage Dixon for her to speak about people like that. In fact, the other woman, a.k.a. my father's real and first wife, was usually the one who spoke in those icy tones whenever Mother would defend us for even existing. Melanie Cage ruled with an iron fist and my brothers had been forced to deal with her their entire lives. I knew most of them—if not all of them—had cut her out of their lives, but she was always there…waiting.

And yet every time I looked at my own mother, I was reminded that she lied.

She had lied my entire life. And knowing that, it was hard to even speak with her anymore. This had been the first dinner I'd come to in a few weeks and perhaps my last. While I knew my younger sister, Emily, was doing her best to keep the peace, the rest of us were at a fragile state of not knowing what to do. Kyler had left town to go on tour. Sophia and Pheobe were each in love and spending more time with their significant others and their families. And that left me—alone and honestly too angry and confused to sit for too long with this woman I didn't recognize anymore.

It was no wonder the panic attacks had settled in and getting a full night's sleep hadn't been in the cards for me for longer than I could count. I wasn't sure if it was because of family, my mother...or *him*.

And not the him that haunted my dreams.

But the one who haunted my nightmares.

"Please stop talking about our family as if they're vermin," Sophia said, her voice smooth, if a little forceful. She squeezed her boyfriend Cale's hand, and he gave the two of us a sympathetic look. I liked the man for her. He treated her well and dealt with the insanity and antics that was the Cage family. The fact he stood up for Sophia when needed but also stood back so she could fight for herself spoke volumes.

"That's not what I'm doing at all," my mother backstepped. "But with all of those lawyers on that side of the family they take everything from us. With how smart you are, Isabella, why must you eat dinner with them once a month? Surely you can use those brains of yours that you always boast about to do something for good."

The pointed slap felt almost physical at this point. Growing up, we had our roles—even if we didn't agree with the labels. Pheobe, the youngest, the bright and sunny. Then Emily, the earnest and hopeful. Kyler, the only boy—at the time—and the most athletic and talented. Sophia, the graceful and willowy dancer.

And me. Isabella. The brain. And apparently the boastful brain.

"The will stated if we didn't have dinner with our siblings once a month, the company will dissolve. Their inheritance, as well as ours, will go away," I answered for what felt like the one hundredth time.

It wasn't as simple as all that, but getting into the legal jargon with my mother was an endless loop of exhaustion. One other thing that made my chest tighten.

"You've never needed that money. Why do you need it now?" Mom stared at me as if I had all the answers and refused to give them to her out of spite. Who was this woman and where had the kind and flighty mother I'd grown up with gone? Had that been a mirage the same as our father who hadn't been within our grasp in the first place?

I met Kyler's gaze from across the living room, and he just shook his head, bringing his beer to his lips. He had it dangling between two fingers, one leg sprawled over the recliner as if he hadn't a care in the world.

We both knew that wasn't true.

I help up my hand. "I really don't want to get into the fact that we could have had a little bit of a cushion when we were growing up." I'd had to take out loans for college, the same as Emily and Pheobe, not to mention classes for Kyler and Sophia. The interest alone killed us. However the other Cages had wiped that debt clean. Not because of charity, but because no Cage would be in debt because of our father. It was our new oath. I shook my head and continued. "But we can't go back. We can't go back to the vacations and colleges that we didn't even look at because we were afraid of spending too much money with so many siblings."

Kyler snorted. "And it turns out dear old Dad was completely loaded. In more ways than one."

I glared at my brother, as my mom put her hand to her chest, looking askance at the crude joke. And it wasn't even a *good* joke.

"I don't want to argue right now," Phoebe put in as she squeezed her fiancé's thigh. Kane had his arm around her shoulders and brought her closer. Between Sophia and Phoebe, the two of them had found their partners. The people that clicked for them. And so in this moment they had someone to lean on when it felt like all was lost.

Our other sibling, Emily, hadn't been able to make it to dinner tonight, and for that I was grateful. What once had been joyous, albeit a little noisy, occasions was now rife with stress and accusations. Nothing like the required meetings we had with the other Cages. Those were far more…fun now. Mostly because we leaned into the farce of it all. And I didn't have to be the most organized and strongest in the room anymore. It was a bit... unsettling.

"We aren't fighting. I just want to make sure that my children aren't forced into anything."

I sipped the last of my wine and set my glass on the table. "A little odd that you worry about us now considering you knew about Dad's other family the entire time."

"Isabella. I don't want to fight about this anymore."

She always said that when she was on the defense. As if she hadn't been the one to bring up the topic of the Cage family in the first place. I held up my hand as my sisters tried to speak, but I noticed Kyler didn't even bother. He was angrier than I was. In this moment it didn't matter that I actually liked my new brothers. No, it was the fact that my mother *lied*.

While we had thought our father was out on business trips, or dealing with his many responsibilities, he was living with his other family. In any other situation, I wouldn't have thought it would have worked for the thirty or so years it had.

But the sole reason it had was that the wives had been in on it.

Our father's first wife, Melanie, was his legal wife. She was ice cold, and honestly a little scary. While people thought I was scary because I lifted my chin and stood up for myself, Melanie was cruel.

I saw the way she acted with my seven other brothers. And while they had lived in a much higher economic status and a different purview, they hadn't had the comfort and love that we had.

Sometimes I needed to remind myself that although Dad hadn't been around much, Mom was. And she was warm, loving, and always there for us. She never missed a recital, game, or award ceremony. While we couldn't do every sport we wanted, because money had been an issue, we never felt without.

And she had been a liar the entire time.

That was what hurt. What felt as if I'd had the world stripped from me, leaving me bare to the elements where nothing was what it seemed. Once again there was a betrayer in my life. Would she leave just like the rest?

I wasn't sure I would ever forgive my father, but then again, I wasn't sure I cared enough to bother. That might make me a terrible person, but our father had turned into a controlling megalomaniac. Or perhaps he always had been, and I had been too lost in my own ways to notice.

When Dad had died, all his secrets had been unveiled. We had sat in that lawyer's office with a huge wooden table and learned our fate. Five siblings had to meet for dinner once a month. We had to photograph our evidence and send it to the lawyer. The time crunch on those dinners would end after three years, but that wouldn't be the end of it. There were always other tribulations when it came to that will and the company itself. There was also paperwork that needed to be done, and Aston and I usually took care of it.

I was the oldest sibling on one side, he was the eldest on the other. And while we had butted heads at first, he had turned into someone I could rely on. I couldn't take my anger out on the other Cages because they were in the same boat we were in.

Only they had a lot more to lose.

If we didn't have dinner where three siblings from one side and two siblings from the other met up, not only would the company be dissolved, and inheritances would be an issue, but a small town in the mountains of Colorado outside Denver would lose everything.

Because of course the Cages owned a town.

Cage Lake was situated a couple of hours outside Denver, and the Cage family as well as the company itself owned a majority of it. They had founded it, and expanded just enough to have that small town feel without losing all its amenities. Apparently, Dad had wanted his children to get to know each other at the expense of thousands of people's livelihoods.

That wasn't outrageous at all.

"Isabella. Are you listening to me?" Mom asked, and I looked up to see her eyes filled with tears.

I wasn't sure why my mother had agreed to go along with this soap opera of a relationship. Why she was okay with being the other woman. But I hated to see my mother cry.

"Okay. I won't talk about them anymore. But you can't change the court's decision. And they are our brothers." My mother flinched. I ignored it. I had to. "They aren't too bad once you get to know them."

"They are the best," Phoebe corrected, grinning at me. "It helps that I've known Ford for a while now."

"Considering I own a business with them, agreed," Kane put in as he leaned over to hug Phoebe. Kane and Ford were part of a security company they owned together and one of Ford's spouses was Kane's cousin.

There were so many connections, threads that tangled and wore over time. But I wasn't sure what to do. I didn't know how to get over this anger when it came to my mother.

Frankly I wasn't sure I could.

"Let's just have dinner then. You can tell me about your day," Mom said as she bustled to the kitchen.

Kyler finally sat up and rolled his neck. "I don't know why she's acting like this was a surprise. She might not have known every detail of the will, but she knew Melanie had our brothers."

It was still a jolt to hear 'our brothers' aloud even though I'd thought the words as well. Kyler had been my only brother for my entire life. I wanted to ask him what he felt about not being the only boy in such a large family, but Kyler was more closed off than I was when it came to the subject and I didn't want to hurt him any more than he already had been. He'd come to one of us when he was ready—I hoped.

"Maybe it's just hitting her now. Everything she could have had, everything that we're now faced with." I let out a breath, trying to let out the anger. Only it wasn't working.

"Hey, what's this?" Kyler asked as he lifted my chin before looking down at my wrist.

I winced and pulled away, doing my best not to be too suspicious. I had worn a long sleeve top and had been generous with my concealer, but since I had literally fallen off a cliff, I couldn't hide everything.

"I tripped and fell," I said, and it wasn't really a lie.

He narrowed his eyes. "You might be my big sister, but I'm bigger than you. Don't lie to me."

"I'm fine. Really. I promise." It didn't even hurt anymore. Weston had seen to that.

I needed to stop thinking of him. There was no way I could go back to Cage Lake now. And frankly, I had more pressing matters that had nothing to do with the man who I thought I'd once loved and the family that kept me on my toes. Something far darker.

"You would tell us if you weren't, right?" Sophia asked as she reached out and squeezed my hand.

I looked at my siblings and their men and beamed. "Of course I would. We keep secrets well, the Cages."

"Truth and lies, the Cage Dixon motto," Kyler muttered before he dropped his hands and we followed Sophia into the dining room for dinner.

I did my best not to bring up the other Cages because I didn't want to start a fight, but then my mother had to step in it. Because the hard truth was that our family and troubles were wrapped up in everything we did now.

"How is work, Isabella?" Mom asked as she nibbled on her green beans. I wasn't sure she remembered exactly where I worked now.

I met Sophia's gaze, and really wanted to lie at that moment. Instead, I told the truth. Because somebody had to in this family. "I really love it. I work with Flynn, James, and Aston often. And I can work remotely.

Which is great because I don't have to dress in a suit every day. But the company is brilliant. I can see why they want to preserve it. I'm really enjoying my job. Which is an odd feeling considering I hated the other one."

My mother dropped her fork before wiping her mouth with her napkin. "I had forgotten you moved companies. I still find it peculiar that they hired you out of the blue. I thought you were doing well and rising in the ranks of your other place of employment."

Kyler raised a brow, glancing at me as he sipped his beer. We hadn't mentioned my job change often, and for good reason. And yet here we were, in the same conversation.

Mom's eyes tightened.

"They treated Isabella like crap. They gave her way too many projects, little to no money, and made her work long hours. Plus there were no paths to higher positions because she's a woman." Sophia played with the stem of her wine glass. "At least our brothers treat her well and it's a real job they needed someone for. They really needed her."

My lips twitched, and I winked at my sister. "It's true. The person before me was decent at the job, but I'm better." Perhaps I was a bit boastful. But I never aspired to be humble in positions where a man could easily say something and not be looked down upon.

"I love when you're sure of your talents," Phoebe put in. "It makes me smile. And it's true. You are one of the best forensic accountants I know."

"I think I'm the only forensic accountant you know," I added dryly.

Mom was quiet for so long I was afraid another piece of my already shattered heart would erode into dust, but she surprised me with a tight smile. "I'm glad they were able to fit you into the company. You deserve the best, Isabella."

I knew my mom was trying, but I didn't understand her motivation. Was she showing her true colors underneath the woman we thought we'd known? Or perhaps she was hurting as much as we were—after all, she'd been Dad's mistress. Either way, I was just tired of this. Tired of so much.

And my family didn't even know the half of it.

We finished dinner with relative peace and afterward, we each helped with dishes. Kyler ended elbow deep in dishwater and later took out the trash, which I smiled at. The man was a freaking rockstar who had paparazzi and fans screaming for him and following him daily. If they only knew the real man behind Caged and Reckless.

I finally headed out to my car. I had more paperwork to deal with when I got home, and not because I was forced to, but because I wanted a second look. I hadn't lied to make my mother feel bad. I *liked* working with my brothers and wanted to make their company shine. I didn't consider it *my* company. I hadn't worked toward that and while it was a family company, I wasn't physically or emotionally ready for that talk.

"You want to tell me what really happened?" Kyler asked.

I whirled, not having realized he had been behind me. My heart raced, my hand shaking. I really should have been better at knowing my surroundings. Especially after everything that happened.

Kyler's eyes widened before he reached out and gripped my shoulders. "What's wrong, Isabella? Why the hell are you so jumpy?"

Bile rose in my throat, and I did my best to calm my breathing. I hadn't had a reaction like that for too long, and I didn't want to have it again.

"William is out," I blurted, hating that I said the words. Because William didn't even earn a place in my life. And yet, he was in my nightmares.

The reason that I couldn't breathe. The reason I woke up in a cold sweat nearly every night and had trouble focusing at work. The reason I had needed to visit my best friend Blakely in Cage Lake. The reason I had fallen. The reason I had seen Weston again.

Kyler's face went stony, his eyes narrowing, his jaw tightening. He gripped my shoulders even more and let out a harsh breath.

"Why the hell is he out?

I nearly let a tear fall but I held I back. "He got out early. He only served three years. I don't know why they let him out but he's on parole." I swallowed back bile, knowing the worst was coming. "And he sent a letter letting me know. He said he wouldn't visit but I don't trust him."

Kyler cursed, then began to pace. "I'm leaving on tour soon, damn it."

"I know you are. We are proud of you." Talking about him let me breathe. Honestly thinking of the immense talents of any of my siblings helped.

"You should stay with Aston. Or one of the other Cages that have those big houses that have high security. I don't like you alone."

I raised a brow at my little brother, a slight warmth sliding through the cold. "I have security at my place. I just freaked out for a moment because you startled me. William hasn't seen me in years. He probably isn't even thinking of me after that letter." *All lies.*

Kyler raised a single brow at my lie, and I let out a soft breath.

"I'm not going to spill all of my secrets to everyone. Nobody needs to know what happened."

"It's not your fault, Isabella."

"I know," I said quickly, too quickly. "Don't tell them okay? You're the only one who knows."

"I hate more secrets. Considering that you're angry with Mom about keeping them."

"That's completely different. This is about my past. Not about them."

"Maybe. But you know you can always lean on us."

"I know that. Just startled me is all. I'm going to go home and be safe. I promise."

"Text me when you're home."

"Okay."

"Think about telling the others, okay? And there's something else you aren't telling me, but I'll let you have it."

"There's something you're not telling me as well," I shot back.

"Well it seems that we are the Cages after all. Secrets and everything."

With a look of regret on his face, Kyler kissed the top of my head, hugged me tightly, and helped me into my car.

"Text me," he said again.

I nodded and headed home. It was only later that I realized I hadn't told him about Cage Lake. Or seeing Weston. My siblings knew of Weston, I hadn't been able to hold back my love for him. Kyler had even met him once. But that had been a long time ago and we were all different people now.

I was so tired. Of everything. Fighting with my mother, being worried about William and his letter. And I was tired because I hadn't slept well for the past three nights. Not since I had seen Weston. I couldn't believe he was in Cage Lake. After all of these years, that's where he had run off to.

I had loved him. He'd been every part of my soul.

And then he had left me with a note.

Yet seeing him reminded me exactly where I needed to be—safe, alone, and not dealing with the threads of my past that had worn beyond who I'd thought I could be. There was nothing left for me with Weston. That was something I had learned long ago, something I needed to grip on to if I wanted to make it through these weeks.

Even if it killed me to do so.

Chapter Three
WESTON

Spring in Colorado could mean anything in terms of weather and mood. A blizzard. A rainstorm. A scorching hot day. A pleasant day where all you need is a light jacket.

Or usually, all of the above within one twenty-four-hour period.

Today was a decent day. The sun was shining and there didn't seem to be a cloud in the sky as of yet. And though I could feel the sun on my skin, it was still crisp enough that I wore a long sleeve Henley and had already taken off my leather jacket. As I passed by other town residents, I figured each of us had decided a similar route. Layers upon layers, and hoping it didn't snow again. I was tired of snow. However, considering where I lived, and the elevation itself, I should be over it by now.

Cage Lake was situated right against Champagne Peak, a tall mountain within the Rocky Mountains themselves. A little past the foothills, and up the winding I70, the town had been here for a few generations. Of course, it hadn't always looked like its current incarnation, but progress happened everywhere it seemed.

I wasn't in the mood to deal with my town however, because with all small towns came a thousand questions about your day, your plans, or if you had 'heard the recent news'. I had no idea what the recent news was, but I had a feeling one of the locals or tourists would do something of note and the good intentioned whisper network would be at its peak. I honestly didn't care much about gossip unless it had to do with my family.

And didn't that make me sound like the grumpy asshole I was?

I woke up that morning with yet another hard on and I could only blame one person. It had been years since I had seen Isabella Cage Dixon, and yet with one encounter, she was once again the center of my dreams, the showcase in every temptation I wanted to ignore. Which of course, was a lie. She'd always been there. Just...not so present. Not so fresh.

The dreams had once only been of what we'd lost, what we couldn't have. I'd dream of the moments where we couldn't let go, then when I'd been forced to before we were ready. The dream last night, however? That had been all about the moments in between. The moments where it had been *good*.

The dream had started in a different place, however. A place where she'd been on the edge of a cliff once again but I hadn't been quick enough. Or I hadn't decided to walk down that path at that time.

I swallowed hard as I walked down Main Street toward the Rise and Cage bakery. Images of Bella's fingers losing their grip, rocks falling down over her, and those wide, beautiful blue eyes staring up at me in horror confounded into nightmare after nightmare.

Then it would turn back into the time we had together.

And me waking up with a hard on that I couldn't help but take care of myself. Rubbing one out in the shower thinking of an old girlfriend that I'd left behind in the cold really wasn't how I wanted to start my day. However, that was my lot in life.

I knew Bella had gone back home to Denver, or whatever suburb she now resided in, soon after the accident. And from the lack of news within Cage Lake, she hadn't told a single soul about the fall. Word would've spread like wildfire if a tourist had nearly fallen to her death within the Cage Lake limits.

I wasn't about to start those rumors though, because then I would have to deal with people talking to me. That was one of the worst things a person could do to a man who already had to deal with three younger siblings day in and day out.

I hoped to hell that Bella didn't visit again. And that was what I continued to tell myself. It was hard enough walking away from her the first time. I wasn't sure I would be able to do it again, even though I knew we were completely different people than we had been all those years ago. Life left scars and fucked you over when you least expected it. However, I knew that Isabella most likely owned part of this town now. I wasn't sure how the will had worked, but she was a Cage. Just like the rest of her family, she most likely owned a stake in nearly every business in town, and the land in which those businesses resided.

Hell, I might own Caldwell's, but I didn't own any of the land surrounding it. That was all Cage. And while they were good landlords, they rarely made an appearance other than for vacations. I had seen Aston recently, right when news had broken about the family's issues. He had brought along a woman who seemed nice enough and I'd been a complete grumpy asshole. I had been dealing with shitty news at the shop, countless college paperwork and essays, and my brother's life choices. I had barked at them as if I'd actually known them. Considering neither had really done anything to me, I should have just walked away. But it was easier to take my frustration out on a Cage, rather than myself.

The Cages were royalty here and owned nearly every scrap of land and had a piece of every establishment—including the resort and much of the property that would never be developed. Part of its charm was that it wasn't overdeveloped like many mountain resort towns. The guy who had run for mayor last time and lost had tried to run on the campaign of change and progress.

The man had wanted to bulldoze trees and landmarks in order to bring in townhomes and apartments for vacation rentals that his family happened to be in charge of. In other words, he wanted to increase taxes, take away what made Cage Lake beautiful, and try to take down the Cages.

The man hadn't stood a chance.

Cage Lake was home—royal family and all.

It amazed me to think about this place as my home for so long. I had tried to get out once. Had nearly made it, before everything had been taken from my family. Now I wasn't sure what I would do if I ever left. And that was a question haunting me more and more, considering the twins were about to graduate high school.

The chains that bound me were beginning to lessen and that worried me. Because while I liked my life, I couldn't help but wonder if there was something more.

I shook my head as I walked into the familiar bakery, the scent of bread, pastries, and various baked goods hitting my nose. My stomach rumbled, and I nodded over at Harper.

She smiled widely, those near violet eyes brightening. I had known Harper for all her life. She was younger than my brother, but older than the twins. She had been my backup babysitter when I wasn't able to get home in time after school before the twins had been old enough to take care of themselves. When Lance had been off in college and Sydney and Sam had needed someone to help with homework or get them to their various school activities.

The town might not be big, but there was elementary, middle, and high school. Just large enough that the classrooms were full, and we had some sports teams thanks to the surrounding areas feeding in.

"Hey there, Weston. Are you here to pick up your usual order?" Harper asked, nearly bouncing on her toes.

I had a feeling she was probably on espresso number three from the coffee shop next door, the Caged Bean. I nearly rolled my eyes at that name.

Even the Italian place had the name Cage in it. I knew in the last generation, the old man had required every business that they put money into to have the family name in it. However, that wasn't the case anymore. Considering one of the Cages was my best friend, I knew this set was a little more low key. Hudson wasn't about to throw his name around like that. If anything, I thought the man wanted to hide his connection.

The current generation was putting their money where their mouth was. Hence why twenty-two-year-old Harper was able to own and operate a bakery all on her own. Because the Cages owned the building and fronted her the money. They did everything they could to bring in business that would help the community, even if they took risks that a bank wouldn't.

The coffee shop next door didn't have the same baked goods that Harper did. And Harper didn't have the fancy coffees and latte flights that the Caged Bean had. In the end, they worked well together, and they weren't fighting for business. There were a few tourist shops that had a friendly competition, but most places had their own niche.

"Yes," I finally answered, shaking my head. I needed to get off this train of thought if I was going to get through my day. Because eventually I'd end up thinking of Bella. Again. Like now. Damn it. "It smells good in here."

Harper smiled as she packaged my pastries and doughnuts into a box. "That's always the goal. I'm trying to lure people in."

"I'm pretty sure you don't have to lure anyone in. You are doing pretty well for yourself," I said as I nodded toward the packed place.

"I'm going to have to hire someone to help in the mornings now. It's exciting."

"Is Joshua going to come and help?" I asked, speaking of her brother.

"He should be here soon actually. He's going to stay for a couple of weeks. He's bouncing around between businesses right now, helping out Dorian."

Dorian was yet another Cage, and Joshua's best friend. Joshua had grown up in Cage Lake and was also a few years younger than me. However, he was the same age as Dorian, who had stayed here more often than most of the Cages. I liked the man. Which was saying something.

"Let me know if you need help, and I can toss over one of the twins."

Harper rolled her eyes. "I would love for the girls to help, but between prom, graduation, all of those lists for college, and their final summer before everything changes, I don't know if they're going to have time for me and my bakery."

I shook my head. "Stop reminding me of things like that. Their to do lists are growing, therefore, my to do list is growing. Twice."

"It's really exciting though. You've done such amazing job with them."

I shrugged. "They pretty much did it on their own. I mean, they were already decently self-sufficient."

Harper met my gaze, and we both knew I was lying. The twins had been ten when our parents had died. Lance had been eighteen and ready for college.

Every life plan and goal Lance had before the accident hadn't turned out the way that we wanted, not until a couple of years later when the estate had finished going through probate, and we were able to get him off to college. I had walked out of the family business, ready to start over with my parents' permission and gentle nudging. Then in a blink, they were gone, and I'd come back, trying to figure out my own life, burying my grief. And the twins had been soft little zombies, trying to figure out how to grow up with two big brothers as their caregivers.

It was a wonder that both girls had gotten into college and were finishing their last semester of high school.

"Anyway, here you go. Everything is already on your tab, and I will just charge you when we hit the end of the month."

"Thank you, Harper. I'm sure the team down at the shop will come and bow at your feet later."

"That's really all I ask for in life. Praise and rent money." She winked at me and went back to help the next customer, a tourist from the looks of it. While I didn't know every single person in town, I knew enough of them to figure out that couple in particular wasn't from here. While truly old-timers didn't like all these tourists, I knew they were needed to keep the town afloat.

The Cage money helped, but they needed the cash-flow and tourists too. And the tourists' cars broke down all the time, which was great for my business as well.

Thankfully I didn't see the mayor's wife or anyone else who would stop me on my way, and I hopped into my truck and headed north toward my shop.

My family had been here for a couple of generations. Families that had done their best to strike gold in the mountains. And when that hadn't worked, they had done their best to find something worth living for. My grandfather had been forced to change his role in life when the quarry had dried up, and the town had turned to tourism, rather than mining. He tried a few odds and ends jobs, and eventually when my father had been old enough to help, they had started Caldwell's. It had nearly failed more than once, but eventually they found their footing.

I had grown up within the mechanic stalls, learning to hold a wrench before I could write. I was damn good at my job, and I liked doing it. But when I had been in my twenties, I had been antsy. I had done mostly online school for college, traveling back and forth to the city when needed to get my bachelor's in business so I could help the family. But after a while, the mountains had seemed to close in on me. Champagne Peak might look large enough to touch the sky, but I'd stood in its shadow for far too long.

That's when my dad had kicked me out of the house. Gently. My mom had joined him, the same soft smile on her face. They wanted me to figure out exactly what I wanted, and in the end, he decided to franchise the business. Me doing what I loved, working at Caldwell's, but not within the same town borders that I'd always lived within.

And I had a blessed two whole months before our worlds had collided into ash.

In those two months, I had fallen for Bella, nearly found my footing, then lost everything.

I headed into the shop and set the bakery box down

on the front table. My team scrambled toward it, and I just shook my head. There was nothing like a sugar rush in the morning when you were about to be covered in grease, and probably cut your knuckles more than once.

"Hey, the cute Cage is in your office," Allie said as she winked.

Allie was one of my best mechanics and could find the smallest issue in an engine quicker than anyone but me. She was also happily married to her wife of nine years.

For a moment, I thought she meant Bella. It felt like a kick to the chest, and I nearly dropped my coffee. But I realized there was no reason Bella should be here. She was long gone. I might have saved her life, a fact that would haunt me for the rest of my days, but she wouldn't be back to this town unless her family forced her.

"Should you really be hitting on Hudson?" I asked, knowing exactly who was in my office now that I was no longer thinking of Bella.

"Always, my friend. Always."

I shook my head before making my way back into the admin area. The building itself had grown over time, as we had added another bay and a car wash station in the back. I loved this place, even though sometimes it felt like the walls were hemming in. It wasn't my fault that I had been born and raised here. But it was my fault that sometimes I couldn't get over exactly where I was going and what I needed to do. But in the end, this was home. Even though all my birds were leaving their nest.

"What's with that look?" Hudson asked, and I glared at the man. He had on a thick flannel, worn jeans, and his work boots covered in dried paint. Work boots that were currently on my desk as he leaned back in my chair, sketchbook in hand.

The man hadn't shaved in a few months, his beard getting a little out of control, and he needed a haircut. But he had those Cage blue eyes. I knew when he shaved, he looked just like Aston and Dorian. They all looked alike. Though I knew Hudson had a twin—not that I really knew Flynn that well. It wasn't like I had been in the same room with all of the Cages. Not when there had been seven of them, and surely not when there were what, twelve?

"Get your boots off my desk."

"My boots are fine."

"Boots. Off. Who knows where they've been."

"I've been in the office all day."

"It's eight in the morning. Do you mean you worked all night?"

Hudson just shrugged, his pencil working over his sketchbook. Hudson was a brilliant painter, though I knew he hadn't always been. He had started in the army, did things I didn't want to think about, and things Hudson didn't want to talk about, and now painted for a living. He was also the only full-time Cage resident.

Each of the Cages owned a home around the lake. There were plenty of other homes from other residents, but the main land was all owned by Cages—not surprising. Hudson resided in his, and also took care of the other houses when the family wasn't in town. And because he was the only Cage around, that meant residents of Cage Lake constantly bugged him about the things they needed. It didn't matter that each one of them could contact Aston, Flynn, or James since they ran the main businesses. Or even Dorian, since he was the one who worked with different companies around the area to increase numbers and add revenue. No, they bothered Hudson because the man was in sight.

No wonder he was slowly becoming a hermit.

"So, to what do I owe your wonderous presence?" I asked after I shoved Hudson's boots off the desk.

He didn't seem to care as he set down his sketchbook.

"Just wanted to bug you. I've been up all night working, and figured I'd stop by here on my way into town for coffee."

I shook my head, lips twitching. "You do have coffee

at home, you know. Considering your studio is in your house right on the lake."

Hudson just shrugged. "I needed to get out. I have family dinner coming up."

I winced. "Which family dinner?" With Hudson, that could mean more than one thing, and that wasn't always a good thing.

"Just the brothers one. I can't really say the originals, because I tend to like the new Cages." Hudson stole my coffee from me and took a sip. I didn't bother growling at him. It was what the man did.

"So you're having it at Aston's house?" I guessed, considering the eldest Cage had the biggest place.

"This time. Blakely's cooking."

Blakely. That was her name. I felt bad I'd forgotten in my memory of our altercation. "Isn't that weird? Aston all settled down."

"Not really. We're getting of an age. And I like Blakely. Plus with her around, Isabella isn't as antsy. I mean, I like my new sister, but she is just as protective as Aston is, and I know that she's pissed off at her mom."

At the sound of Isabella's name, I stiffened.

"Oh?" I asked, trying to sound nonchalant.

With the way Hudson narrowed his eyes at me, I figured I hadn't done it well enough.

He shook his head and moved on. "Well, her mom

did keep the secret. And while I couldn't care less what my mother thinks because she's always been an icy bitch, I have a feeling that Isabella and her mom had a good relationship. Things are a little testy now, but us siblings are at least getting along. Which is weird. I have to have a flowchart in order to figure out everyone. And you know that's not my thing."

I remembered Isabella talking about her mother. The two *had* been good friends. They got along and relied on each other because her father was always working. It turned out that hadn't been the case. No wonder Isabella seemed to be having issues of her own—and why she had been on that lookout to begin with. She had a lot on her mind. And damn it, I didn't know why I wanted to be the one to reach out and see if she needed to talk. It wasn't like it was my place. I had burned that bridge long ago.

"You think you're ever going to have a family dinner in town?" I asked carefully.

"Maybe. We have the space. And I know a few of the siblings haven't been out here yet. Isabella was over here visiting when Blakely came to visit last. But the others not so much."

Again. Her name. There was no getting away from it. Or her. "I still find it weird that you have so many brothers and sisters."

"Tell me about it. Christmas is going to be big this year. At least, if we decide to celebrate as a family. That should be fun. How many Christmas trees should we get?" Hudson rolled his eyes before he got up from his chair. "First, I'm here to annoy you. But the real reason is, I wanted to say hi before I head out of town. I'll be back in a couple days."

"You need me to take care of your place?" I asked, a familiar refrain.

Hudson shook his head. "I checked all the houses on my way over here. We should be fine. But if there is a random snowstorm because it's spring in Colorado, let me know and check the house if there's an issue."

"You've got it. And I can always send Lance to do the work since he'll be home soon from school."

"Lance is the same brother who held a party in my place when I was out of town that one time?"

I winced. Because Hudson hadn't been out of town. He had been deployed. A very big difference. And Lance and his nineteen-year-old friends had nearly destroyed the place.

My brother had been working through his demons, and I had to put my foot down for the first time. It hadn't been pretty. Thankfully Hudson hadn't cared because we had cleaned it up. But if it had been anyone else? There probably would've been charges.

"Okay, I'll just send myself," I said after a moment.

Hudson grunted. "On that note, I'm heading out. Thanks for the coffee."

"I didn't get you coffee," I shouted to his back.

"I'll take a doughnut too."

I rolled my eyes and took my seat at my desk, knowing I had tons of paperwork today before I could get my hands dirty.

However, a thought couldn't quite leave my mind, so I picked up my phone and hoped I wasn't making a mistake.

ME:
> Just checking in. Did you rest up and go to the doctor?

I hit send and ignored the bile running up my throat. She had probably changed her number. There was no reason that she should even text back. This was lunacy.

Three little dots formed before they disappeared, and I let out a sigh, resigned to know that she wouldn't be texting back. Maybe if I saw her passing through town because her family was here, we would walk past one another like strangers. Maybe it would be better if we did that.

I had already hurt her once before and I wasn't sure I would ever be able to win her back.

My phone buzzed and I looked down, my heart in my throat.

> ISABELLA:
> I'm fine. I did rest. Thank you for checking in.

My lips curved into a smile, and I swallowed hard.

> ME:
> Just stay away from the edge of cliffs from now on.

> ISABELLA:
> I don't think I'm going to be standing on anything too high anytime soon.

> ISABELLA:
> How are you?

And with that, my heart shuddered. Because this was her reaching out.

I had messed up so many things in my life, Isabella being the main one.

A part of me couldn't help but text her back, an ache for what couldn't be. And maybe, what could.

Chapter Four
ISABELLA

A smile played on my face as I put my phone in my purse and headed into my new place of employment. I still couldn't quite believe that I had texted Weston back. Maybe it was just the shock of seeing his name on my phone to begin with. He hadn't texted me in all these years. Eight years of no contact, and one single fall from a cliff, and here we were, texting again.

I wanted to hate him, to hate what had happened, and maybe I still did. Yet part of me couldn't help but want answers to the questions that I was never able to ask.

It surprised me I could even smile with the headache brewing at the moment. I hadn't slept all that well the night before—constant dreams of what William had done echoing in my head. I had hoped the respite in

Cage Lake would help, but if anything, knowing I'd have to come back to the city where it all happened had made it worse. I had to push that all aside though because I needed to focus. I had to prove to myself and the other Cages that I deserved my new position.

If I visited Cage Lake again, which was a high probability, I would probably see *him*. It wasn't like the town was that big. There would be no hiding from him when I went with Blakely to the lake. *When*, not if. When had that changed in my mind? I wasn't even sure how today was going to go at work and here I was, wondering what could be.

That was so unlike me that I pushed it aside and made my way through the parking garage and to the main building. I walked inside Cage Enterprises, my shoulders rolled back, and smiled at the doorman in security.

"Hello, Ms. Cage. I hope you're having a wonderful day. Blue skies."

My name was Dixon, not Cage, but people tended to forget that—especially here. I smiled at the man and nodded. "Yes, Jeff. It does seem like a nice day. But of course now that I'm saying that I'm glad I brought my coat." I held it out and we both laughed before I made my way past reception toward the bank of elevators. A few people stopped me to say hello, and it was only slightly awkward this time

The Cages owned this building. *And* they owned a few buildings around it. Cage Enterprises worked in real estate, development, and countless other ventures that were split into three main areas. Aston, Flynn, and James handled those. I, on the other hand, wasn't really involved.

I might have just found out that we shared the same father, but I didn't have the same stake in this company as they did. And it wasn't as if I *wanted* it. Much. I didn't feel like I earned it just because one of my last names happened to be Cage. I had always found it odd that my mother had decided to put Cage as our middle names instead of making a second last name like our dad wanted. And now it made sense. Because we were related to these Cages.

I wasn't the boss here. I didn't own the company. If anything, I was a newbie trying to figure out exactly where I stood. If we went down the path the will laid out for us in the allotted time, and followed each of the steps that dear old Dad had filled out, I wasn't going to be a board member of Cage Enterprises. I would have a small stake in the company, which would be completely different than what I was used to. But I was never going to rise to the ranks of CEO. That wasn't my lot in life, and not something that I was trained for.

Aston, Flynn, and James had taken this company to a new level after Dad had moved on. Yes, they had grown up in a different tax bracket than us, but they had increased their revenue and businesses exponentially in the time that they had come on. So even if Cage Enterprises was broken into countless pieces and dissolved like our father had stated in the will, they would still have their own nest eggs. And I was pretty sure the rest of the family was the same way.

Dorian, while not a member of the day-to-day Cage Enterprises, owned and operated one of the biggest nightclubs in Denver. It served high-class clientele, and he had his fingers in many other pots. Hudson was an award-winning painter, and I knew some of his pieces sold for way more than I could ever afford. I had looked it up when we first found out about this new family arrangement, and I had been in awe of his work. But it still felt odd to think that he was my half-brother.

Theo was a chef and owned multiple restaurants, and did very well for himself, while Ford owned a security company, and was probably the most blue-collar of the family. Not that you could call him blue-collar at all.

While on the other side of the family, we were slightly different.

Kyler was the one you could say was well off, and that was only because of a recent surge in his popularity. My brother was an amazing musician and singer, and now he was out on tour making it big as a rock star. It was still funny to even think that my baby brother had countless fans screaming for him as he toured in stadiums.

And I was an accountant. A forensic accountant, but still an accountant.

I paid rent, paid my bills, and counted pennies. However, most of that was due to the fact that I enjoyed it.

A far cry from those who shared my DNA.

I made my way out of the elevator and down the hall on the main floor of Cage Enterprises. Blakely's office was on the other side of the building, and I knew soon I would go over to say hello. She had been my best friend for years. The fact that she had fallen in love with my half-brother had been a little weird for me when it had all begun. But in the end, Aston was good for her. Just like she was good for him. If anything, I had a feeling that their relationship thawed the initial awkwardness of blending our two families.

While at first, I wanted to rail against anybody who would dare come near the siblings I had known all my life, now I would do anything to fight for these other Cages.

They were my brothers, and that meant I would be their protector.

They would just have to deal with it.

"Hey there, you're in early," Flynn said as he came forward. He reached out to hug me, and then thought better of it before squeezing my shoulder. We were still in that awkward stage, neither of us knowing what to do. Yes, we were at work, yes he was technically my boss, but we were still awkward siblings.

When we'd first met, I'd been standoffish and done my best to protect my family. I wasn't proud of how I'd acted. Now that I knew it was the twelve of us against the world, I was trying my best to reach out as much as they were. "Hey Flynn. If you're here, I can't be too early."

"You worked late last night, and you just came back from a three-day weekend where Blakely ratted you out."

I rolled my eyes. "I was only going over some paperwork. It wasn't really work. I was just studying."

"You know that's still work," he said dryly. Flynn was the vice president of the company. He was the one who worked with the site planners and was also the one who was usually out in Cage Lake to work with the small businesses. I knew Hudson lived there so he had a say in it, but Flynn was the one who helped with growth. I had to wonder if he was the one who kept adding the word Cage to all the names of the places. It was a little ridiculous when I thought about it.

"It's really not work if you're enjoying yourself."

He rolled his eyes, and we made our way to the break room to get coffee. What I loved about this building was their coffee. It was so different than my old place.

Just as this conversation was completely different.

And I wasn't sure I was ever going to get used to it.

"You don't have to work eighty-hour weeks anymore for low pay. And you're allowed to delegate." Flynn handed over the creamer, and I poured some into my cup and shook my head. "I don't think I know what that word is. And for what I've seen between the three of you, you guys don't know what delegating is either."

"Hey, we hired Blakely. That's called delegating."

"And she does organize you guys quite well."

"She's probably one of the best hires we've had recently. With you being there as well."

I snorted. "You don't need to suck up to me."

"You are a steal, you know. Your last company? I can't believe you stayed there for that long."

I grimaced before taking a sip of my coffee. "They paid the best, and I don't like change."

Flynn met my gaze, and we both understood exactly what that meant.

"Frankly, my former boss is just like Blakely's former boss. If I would've left, I wouldn't have gotten a recommendation. And considering I started working for them right out of college, and even had my internship with them, that meant my entire resume would just be one man who didn't appreciate me, and didn't like me."

"Lucky for you, you have family who needed you."

"It still feels like a handout."

"Maybe." Flynn shrugged as we walked toward the back offices. "I was lucky enough to know I would always have a place here when I was growing up. We didn't have to work for the company. But I liked it. I liked figuring out new ways to help small businesses, and I like to make money." He shrugged again.

I burst out laughing. "At least you're honest about it. And my job is to make sure that we're doing it all legally."

"I don't mind that. Because we don't do shady shit. And we're glad to have you. Are you planning on coming to dinner tonight?"

I set my coffee cup on my desk and frowned. "Isn't this just for you guys?"

"Should there really be an us versus them?" Flynn asked as he leaned against the door. "I mean, we should just have people who happen to be in town at dinner. I know that Kyler's out of town, and Hudson's coming in from Cage Lake. But if you're around, you should join."

"Is your mother going?" I asked dryly.

Flynn grimaced. "God no. Aston kicked her out, and I'm full on grateful."

I fiddled with my purse before taking a seat. "And she let that happen? She's not trying to get back in your life?"

"Maybe with her favorites, but I've never been her favorite," he said but didn't elaborate. "Are things okay with you and your mom?"

I wish I knew. "They're the same as always. And I don't really want to get into it at work."

He gave a tight nod and straightened. "Got it. I didn't mean to get so much into our feels. However, you're welcome for dinner tonight. Blakely will be there."

"Blakely will be where?" my best friend asked as she popped into my office. She had pulled her long blonde hair back, and grinned. She looked like a woman in love, happy, carefree. I wonder if I would've looked like that if Weston and I would've worked out.

Why the hell was I thinking about him? Maybe

because he had just texted and was checking in. I didn't like the fact that I had answered so quickly. Had lit up at the sight of his name. He was my past. Yes, he had been there when I needed him this weekend, but he wasn't my future. And I would do well to remember that.

"I was just inviting Isabella here for dinner."

"Oh, you should come." Blakely smiled at me. "I mean, if you don't have a date."

I snorted, nearly dropping my coffee. "No. Not happening." Of course, Weston's face filled my mind, and I immediately pushed that away. Just because he texted didn't mean anything was going to change. He had broken my heart after all. And we were far different people than we had been eight years ago.

Blakely jumped into the silence. "What's that look? You're thinking of someone."

"I don't even know you that well and I saw that look too," Flynn put in.

"I don't appreciate getting ganged up on. And there was no look. Come on. We have work to do. We may not be at my old place with taskmasters, but I should still probably get in a full eight hours."

"Bossy," Flynn said. "But that seems to be a family trait."

"Tell me about it," Blakely said with a blush.

I winced. "I really don't need to think about things like that."

"Yes. Please don't put *bossy* and *my brother* in the same universe with whatever that look was, thank you," Flynn added.

"I didn't even mention Aston. But sure, he can be bossy if he wants." Blakely winked, that gleam in her eyes new and lovely considering all she'd had to deal with recently.

I threw a piece of paper at her, and she ducked. Thankfully Flynn caught it before it went outside of my office, and he just clucked his tongue at me before the two of them left. Immediately my phone dinged, and I looked at the screen, my heart racing. It wouldn't be Weston. It couldn't be Weston. I didn't want it to be Weston.

> **FLYNN:**
> Don't throw things. We are in a workplace after all.

I rolled my eyes and set down my phone. Working here was odd. People trusted me because I was good at my job, and maybe because I was a Cage. Yes, there was weariness, mostly on my end, but I felt like I could do good work here. And I wasn't slowly gaining an ulcer. I could even work from home if I wanted. They had given me the option, but I really wasn't a remote worker. I needed the vibes of other people around me. After all, I had grown up in a big family, and apparently an even bigger one than I had known. I liked the noise, and the interruptions. I immediately went to work and opened up my main file.

I wasn't technically working on the Cage's finances. My job was to take an accounting of the businesses they were acquiring or working *with*. Including any partnerships that they had. My job was to report misconduct, financially or within the workplace by the employees, officers, or directors of the organization. I wasn't just an accountant, I had to use investigative techniques in order to discover those financial crimes. It didn't always make me the most popular accountant out there. Not that many accountants were popular.

Once a year I would do a surprise audit of the Cage finances just to ensure that the company didn't have any weasels finding their way in. I liked the fact that the Cages were on top of that. Taking care of their own, while ensuring, as they helped others, they didn't get screwed in the process.

So far, I hadn't found anything out of the ordinary, but it could happen. Even a slip-up could lead to something worse.

My phone buzzed right before lunch, and I looked

at the screen without thinking, my mind in a million directions.

> **WESTON:**
> Are you planning on heading back up to town at any point? Maybe looking at a Cage house of your own on a lake?

My heart fluttered, and I had to wonder exactly why he was texting. It made no sense. I didn't know this man. Or why he had left. Or why I wanted him to continue to text me. But he was the one reaching out after all this time and I'd promised myself I'd stop being the icy princess others claimed I was.

> **ME:**
> I have a decent place of my own.

That was a lie. I had a small apartment that I didn't quite like. I could afford something better, but I was saving for a dream house. I hated spending money.

> **WESTON:**
> I'm sure one of your brothers would let you stay in one of their houses. They stay empty more often than not. They're not the type to rent it out to strangers.

> **ME:**
> Why do you want me to come up to Cage Lake?

> **WESTON:**
> It's your family's town. You should see it.

Disappointment set in over my shoulders, but I had to wonder why I would be disappointed at all. I didn't want him to want me. That would just complicate things.

> **ME:**
> The town was beautiful when I visited. But I'm really a city girl.

> **WESTON:**
> I remember.

Sadness twisted with the disappointment, because that was a problem. He had been a small-town boy, me a city girl. *Cue the rock song.* But he was supposed to have stayed. A summer fling was supposed to be more in the end between us. And it hadn't been.

And then things had changed. And not just because Weston had left.

WESTON:
I have to get back to work. I'm working on a Chevy that wants to explode on me.

ME:
I still don't know how to change my own oil.

WESTON:
I told you. You never have to.

I didn't know if that meant he would take care of it, or I could just hire someone. And I didn't want to know. I wasn't sure why we were even texting in the first place.

ME:
Enjoy your work. I should get back to mine.

WESTON:
Have a good day, Bella.

Tears pricked my eyes as I set down my phone. I didn't want to think about the past. Because when I thought about Weston, I thought about my heart breaking in a thousand pieces, and then I thought about William.

I shuddered at the memory, telling myself that I was safe.

William might be out of jail, but he wasn't

anywhere near me. Kyler knew about it at least, but Kyler wasn't even in the state. I didn't want to worry the rest of my family, and it wasn't like the other Cage brothers knew about what had happened.

Bile crawled up my throat as my palms went damp, and I immediately made my way to the bathroom. I splashed cold water on my face and let out a deep breath.

"He's not going to find me. He doesn't want to find me."

"Everything okay?" a woman asked, and I nodded.

"Yes, Ruby, right?" I asked, remembering this woman was on Blakely's team.

Ruby smiled. "That's right. It's nice to see you, Isabella. But are you sure you're okay?"

I put on a fake smile, hoping it at least reached my eyes. "Yes. I guess I'm just hungry. I skipped breakfast but had too much coffee."

"That will do you. You should take your lunch. In fact, we're ordering from that salad place. You know, the one that has tons of protein and veggies and fats on it so it will taste like something rather than rabbit food."

I laughed at that and washed my hands. "That does sound nice. Sure, let me think of my order."

"Come on, and we'll get it done."

I pushed all thoughts of William and Weston out of my mind and followed Ruby to her desk.

I was slowly making friends, slowly weaving my way into the company. I might not be the Cage of Cage Enterprises, but I still worked here. I still had a place.

I was safe.

By the end of the day I was tired, but still a little full of pep. Maybe I would go to dinner at Aston's. Or try to see if Sophia and Emily were around. Phoebe was out of town with her boyfriend, the two of them finally taking a break after everything that had happened. So maybe it was time just to have a night with my family. I didn't have many friends outside of Blakley, and I hadn't noticed the lack until now.

I walked to the parking garage and pulled out my phone, ready to text the group chat, when someone put their hand around my mouth. I tried to scream, but nothing came out. Instead, I kicked out, my purse falling. My phone clattered to the floor, and warm breath flew against my neck.

"Stay still."

I froze, my body stiffening. I didn't know that voice. It wasn't William's. Right? But maybe I couldn't remember. Who else could it be? All of my self-defense training went out the window, and I couldn't do a thing.

My chest tightened and my vision began to gray.

Bile pooled in my mouth and suddenly I couldn't think, couldn't breathe. Everything from my nightmares was coming true again. But this time William wouldn't stop. He'd finally take what he wanted and kill me when he couldn't before. Because I hadn't wanted to date him and he'd beaten me to make his case known. Then he threated so much worse.

He was back.

And I knew I was going to die.

"Hey. What the hell?" a voice called out, and then the man let me go, his gloved hand falling from my lips, and I fell to the ground, my knees bruising at the impact.

My fingers dug into the cement, my breath coming in ragged pants.

"Isabella? What the fuck?"

Aston was there, his hand reaching out to touch my shoulder. I flinched away from him, and his eyes widened.

"Isabella. Are you okay?"

I nodded as tears slid down my cheeks, and I realized that no, I wasn't okay.

And I wasn't going to be okay anytime soon.

Chapter Five
ISABELLA

Palms damp, chest aching, I pulled away from my brother, not quite sure which one was holding me at the moment. My head whirled, and I sucked in deep breaths far too quickly. My vision grayed again, and someone kept talking to me. Telling me to breathe at a different rhythm. To calm. But all I could do was feel the hand on my chest, tearing out my heart. Couldn't they hear that siren? Feel the pressure on their chest like I did?

"Isabella. Are you hurt? Talk to me."

I blinked, finally hearing the bite in Aston's tone. I had never heard him speak that way. Yes, I knew he could. After all, he dealt with a multi-billion-dollar business every day and had to worry about people trying to take over and take advantage of him. I knew he had probably spoken to our father's lawyer in that same tone after we had left, as well as his own mother. And maybe countless others.

But never so icy toward me. Even though I knew it had nothing to do with me, I still flinched.

Aston immediately took a step back and looked me over. "Talk to me. What did the police say?"

We were in one of the many various empty offices they had on the eighth floor of the main building. This is where people who wanted to work remotely, and didn't want a full office, or anyone working for a short period of time, or just visiting would work. It was empty for now, and the best place according to the others for us to regroup.

The police had come and gone, as had the paramedics. I hadn't needed them, thankfully. But my heart rate was still racing. I hadn't even realized that Aston had been the one holding me as I shook in his arms. The only reason my best friend wasn't here was because Blakely was out on a call. I had a feeling that nobody had told her or she would have broken through the police tape to get to me. I knew that Aston hadn't told her because he was worried that whoever had attacked me was still in the area.

He was protecting Blakely, and for that I was thankful. Because I wouldn't be able to forgive myself if Blakely got hurt because of me.

Because it could have been me. All of this could be my fault. Right?

"They don't know the guy, but they have him in custody. He just wanted to get my purse." I swallowed hard, my throat dry. Aston immediately handed over a bottle of water, and I was appreciative. I sank down on the couch, wondering why we needed such a large office for guests. Then again, I was grateful for it.

"You didn't know him?" Flynn asked before shaking his head. "Of course you don't. I'm so fucking sorry, Isabella. I'm just glad we caught the guy. But, sister mine? You're pale as a ghost. You should have let the paramedics take a look at you." My brother had held on to me for a moment when we had been in the parking garage, before he had run after whoever had attacked me. I wasn't sure I was ever going to be able to get past the sight of my brother in an expensive suit and shoes running down a darkened parking garage and right into danger. And I knew Aston would have been right along with him if he hadn't stayed with me.

I had grown up with Kyler. But he was my baby brother. He always tried to protect me now, but I had never had a group of men so overprotective and growly, it was a little disconcerting. And if I was in my true element, not stressing out, I would probably resent it. But part of me was so confused about this odd nature, that I was letting it happen.

"I'm fine," I lied, and when my brothers looked at each other and then at me, I realized that I wasn't lying very well.

"You've had a panic attack, Isabella," Aston whispered. "And while it was understandable, you didn't let the medics take a look at you, and from the dark circles under your eyes, your sleeping hasn't gotten any better since you went to Cage Lake to get fresh air."

I ran my hands over my face and knew I should tell them what I had already told the cops. "Did Blakely tell you?" I asked, uneasy. Blakely and Aston told each other everything. I knew that. But I wasn't sure how I felt about my best friend telling Aston something so personal. So traumatic.

He shook his head, and relief filled me. "No." Then he let out a breath and continued. "But before I met all of you truly and got to know you, I did a background check."

I stood up quickly, wobbly on my heels. "Are you serious?"

"Yes. I'm serious."

"Aston," Flynn muttered.

Aston didn't look the least chagrined, but did hold

my shoulders as my heart threatened to beat out of its chest again. "And as you can tell, I didn't share with everyone else. I'm the only one who saw anything. And I didn't go beyond public records. But for all I knew, you were vicious harpies like my mother. Rather than the people that I've come to know. All of that information is burned by the way. Nobody else can find it. And I don't know the details, Isabella. I only know from the initial report."

I sank back into the couch, chugging my water. Flynn's shoulders dropped as Aston just stood there, ready for me to yell at him. I looked at Flynn, knowing he was confused. "A few years ago I was attacked by a man named William."

"Isabella, I'm so sorry. You don't have to tell us details."

I held up my hand, noticed it shook, and set it down. "Aston, I don't blame you for the background check. Your family comes with a lot of strings. A lot of money."

"It's your family now too," Aston corrected.

I froze, wondering if I was ever going to get used to this new dynamic. There were so many people in my family now. It was hard to keep up with everything. I had eleven brothers and sisters. Eleven people who were now part of my life, and even though I felt alone most days, we were still finding our way.

I had no idea what the hell my father had been thinking keeping us from each other, and now forcing us together. I wasn't even sure the fact that we were somewhat getting along was what dear old Dad wanted. But he was dead and there was no asking him. He had taken his secrets to the grave, and I still didn't understand why my mother had gone along with it all.

"You don't have to talk about it if you don't want to," Aston continued. "If the police are already aware, then that's enough."

"You're right. I don't need to know. No one needs to know." Flynn paused. "Though it might be good if Ford knew. Considering he owns a security company and deals with protection services. In case of stalkers, or things like that."

"The others know. At least the Cage Dixons," I clarified. It was hard to call my initial group of siblings just my brother and sisters considering I had a whole new slew of brothers, and I wasn't sure how to qualify them without making someone feel left out. It wasn't as if there was a manual on what to do when your dad had a secret family. Maybe I should write one. And now my thoughts were spiraling again.

"I was attacked a couple of years ago. I was walking through the parking lot at night after working far too many hours, and this guy pressed me up against the car, put his arms around my neck, and I blacked out. He dragged me to the bushes and beat me in order to wake me up. He didn't get to do anything else though, because a random stranger was jogging at night, and he got the guy to run away. He didn't chase after him though, instead stayed with me until the ambulance came." I shuddered, bile rising in my throat. "I don't want to talk about it anymore though. About what could have happened."

"Shit, Isabella. I'm sorry. So damn sorry." Flynn met my gaze, and I knew he didn't have any more words.

Then again, neither did I. Not the ones that would help erase the memories at least. "He didn't, he wasn't able to do anything else. But he was able to do far worse to the next girl." I shook my head. "But because he left DNA evidence, he was caught. And he was supposed to be in jail for a long time. Because it's a class four felony. At least that's what he was in for. Two to eight years in prison. And he got one. One year because it took so long to get through the system, and he got out for good behavior."

Those were the letters that William had sent. Taunting me that he was out.

"Are you fucking kidding me?" Aston snapped. "They just let him out like that. You were alerted?"

"Yes. And he sent a letter."

Flynn began to pace, running his hands through his hair. "Does anyone else know about the fact that he's out or the letter?" he asked, his shoulders tense.

"I told Kyler, and according to the police, William is still in Wyoming with his parole officer in Cheyenne," I said, my voice soft. "So while this mugging wasn't connected as it's not him, it brought it all back and that's why I've been having panic attacks."

"Fuck," Aston muttered. "So it wasn't him."

"No. But I thought it was at first. So it was some other lunatic out trying to harm women. And between that and William sending letters, I'm just tired."

"Isabella!" Blakely called as she pushed through the door, past my brothers, and pulled me into her arms.

I didn't cry. I was the eldest sister. The strong one. I was the one that my sisters and Kyler needed to lean on. But as soon as Blakely wrapped her arms around me, I burst into tears. The pressures of the week, of waiting for the next shoe to drop, hit me, and I just let Blakely hold me.

"I've got you. It's okay. I've got you."

"It wasn't him," I muttered.

My best friend's hold tightened. "They caught the guy and he's going to go to jail. He's just lucky I didn't get to him first or I'd kick the crap out of him."

"Blakely, it seems William is out of jail," Aston

murmured, and my chest felt as if it were gripped in a vise. I knew he had to tell her because I couldn't, but everything felt as if it were falling out of my hands and control, and I couldn't focus or deal.

"I just don't want to be a burden." I leaned back and wiped my face.

"Isabella Cage. You are not a burden. Do not call yourself that."

"I'm going to let her yell at you for that," Flynn added dryly.

"I just, I don't know what to think. It just brought it all back, and I'm tired. Maybe I'll just go home and breathe. And the police will find everything by the next day."

The guys met each other's gazes as Blakely ran her hand up and down my back.

"Maybe you should take some time off," Flynn put in.

I narrowed my gaze. "I'm not weak. I just need to pull it together. I don't need to take time off. I'm fine."

"I realize that technically we're your bosses, but this is a tricky situation where I don't want to have to tell my sister what to do," Aston said as diplomatically as he could.

"He says that because it gets tricky when he's my boss as well."

"James is your boss," Aston corrected.

"How about you go to Cage Lake?" Flynn blurted.

I froze and stared at him. "How is me going to a small mountain town going to help anything? I'm fine."

"Isabella," Blakely whispered, and I knew that I wasn't fine. I was still shaking.

"You can still work remotely, take some time off, and frankly, there's a few paperwork things that we need to do for the businesses, and I am running a little behind."

I glared at Flynn, not sure he was telling the truth or not.

He held up both hands. "I'm not lying. We have that huge acquisition coming up, and I don't like putting things on Hudson's shoulders. Hell, he doesn't like doing it at all and will refrain. But we are landlords, and there is paperwork and other things to approve. So why don't you go out to Cage Lake."

"And you'll be able to get fresh air like before but have it be a little more long term," Blakely added, studying my face. "I want my best friend to be healthy. And you had a scare tonight."

"I'm already talking to my therapist," I stated, not caring if my brothers knew. I truly didn't want my panic attacks to be their burden.

"And they told you what last time?" Blakely asked as my brothers listened in.

"That I should rest," I mumbled.

Blakely cleared her throat. "That's settled then. You can breathe, work because I know you can't stop, and get to know Cage Lake."

Flynn stepped in. "It's a small town, where everybody knows everybody. It's hard to do anything without people knowing what you're doing. Especially if you're living there and not just at the resort. Hudson will be around, and frankly, it'll be good for everyone."

"So you're just trying to get me out of the city?" I asked, feeling so confused.

If I went to Cage Lake, Weston would be there. The man I was trying to avoid. And yet the man I was still texting. I swallowed hard, then remembered the hand over my mouth, and how it felt like that hand over my throat. Even though it was two different people.

"Okay. But not for too long. Because you need help with paperwork," I qualified.

I looked at my family, at Blakely, and realized that maybe I did need a break. Because I could feel that touch. Hear his voice.

But it wasn't William's voice.

It was someone else's.

Chapter Six
ISABELLA

I hadn't meant to visit this town so quickly after fleeing the first time. I still had a bruise on my arm, a few cuts and scrapes from my fall, and here I was, back in the mountains, Cage Lake in front of me.

It really was a beautiful town and a beautiful lake. But it didn't feel like home. I was used to seeing the mountains in the distance, always knowing where west was because of the city's placement. Now, however, I was surrounded by mountains. I had no idea where north was, no idea about the inner workings of a small town that was not my own. And again, I had a feeling no matter where I was, I was going to be off kilter. Because now I didn't know if the new bruise on my arm was from running into the wall when I had gotten ready that morning, from the fall, or from the attack. Maybe the others were right, and I did need this time just to breathe.

"So, are you unpacked?"

I jumped at the sound of that deep voice and turned to see my brother Hudson standing there, hands in his jean pockets.

I studied him, the brother I probably knew the least. Of course, I couldn't really say that I knew the core seven Cages as well as I should. It had only been a few months after all. And we had up to three years of those dinner dates, getting to know one another. And I only knew Aston as well as I did because he was with Blakely.

Hudson lived in Cage Lake full-time. He had been in the army, though I didn't know his rank, or what he had done there, and when he got out, he had moved here. He'd apparently gone through the G.I. Bill to get his bachelor's degree while on active duty. And then had taken a few business classes so he could help out the family. At least that's what Flynn had mentioned. Then he dropped it all to paint. I had seen some of his paintings at Aston's place, and online through his website, and I couldn't quite believe that somebody with that kind of talent for art shared half of my genetics.

I wanted to ask him when he had decided to paint, to change his career more than once. I wanted to know if he had taken art classes or had spent time learning how to do these things when he was younger. But for some reason the way that he glared at me even though I knew it was just his resting face, I knew he wasn't going to be open to answers. And frankly, I had always been so on the go, even during my one and only visit before recently, that I hadn't been able to ask. I had been so busy protecting the siblings I had grown up with, I hadn't taken time to figure out the others. But I was getting better. At least I hoped.

Maybe this forced work-from-home, or at least any home that wasn't my own, would help me get to know Hudson.

I studied his bearded face, the fact that he had pulled his long hair back in some form of a small ponytail or bun thing. I knew he had tattoos running up and down his arms, and an eyebrow ring, and looked so different from the rest of the Cages, that it was a wonder he was one. However, he was Flynn's actual identical twin, so it wasn't as if he didn't share their genetics. He just didn't bother with the suits that the others did.

"Isabella?" he asked, and I pulled myself out of studying this brother that I didn't know.

"I'm unpacked. I didn't bring much."

"I figured you'd stay for a little longer than a weekend. There are some clothes free to get down on Main

Street, but most of the things that you are probably used to aren't going to be there. Most people shop online these days or go to the city. Not much up here for a city girl."

I raised my brow at the tone. "City girl? I'm a suburb girl, thank you very much." Even though he'd called me a city girl before...

"You worked at the big building. That's downtown."

"And it's still not a huge metropolis like New York or Philly. But I do like suburbs. With a coffee shop close by. And sometimes fast foods. Like a salad-to-go place."

Hudson clucked his tongue. "You're not going to find that here. But you're going to find a bunch of places with our name stamped all over it. Good food, good coffee. And nosy-as-fuck people."

"Please, sell me more of this town," I said dryly.

He shrugged. "It's home. The others come and go, but I like it here. I get my privacy as long as I stay at the house rather than going downtown often."

"I like how you call it downtown."

"Fine. Down to the town." He rolled his eyes, his face brightening. Well then. Maybe he didn't smile, but maybe he wasn't just the asshole that people thought he was. There had to be a reason he was hiding up in Cage Lake. Then again, I was doing the same.

"It's still really nice that Aston is letting me borrow his place."

"He isn't using it right now. Most of them aren't. And I'm sure they'll set aside a parcel for you soon. You can build your own place."

I had just taken a drink of water from my water bottle and choked. "Excuse me?"

"What, each of us Cages has a house surrounding the lake, and we didn't allow others to build anything too crazy, or near us. We also made sure that we were still taking care of the environment around us. So, we have the space, and this is for family. When you're ready to build something, let us know. We are in the real estate business after all. And development. It's sort of what we do. At least, what they do."

My eyes widened even as I shook my head. "I do not understand this family sometimes. You're just going to what, give me a house?"

"Maybe. Or maybe give you the time to have it. We don't need all this space. Honestly, I'm pretty sure that Flynn and James decided to keep extra space just so Dad couldn't have it. And so other developers couldn't come in and build a shopping center or set of apartments that they would never keep up with."

"I guess that would ruin some of the beauty."

"Exactly. We're already taking up too much of it."

Hudson shrugged. "And I'm not even the biggest environmentalist of the family. Anyway, I'm not too far if you need me. The security system's is going at Aston's place, and we already went over it. And if there's ever anything you need, you got my number. And well, I know you're in Aston's place because you are friends with Blakely, but you also know the guy next door. I realize that you might think I bite, but I'm not that much of an asshole. At least to family that I like."

"So you like me?" I asked, letting out a hollow laugh.

"I don't actively hate you. I don't know you. But I guess you're here, so I suppose I'm going to have to get to know you."

He said it so dryly that I realized that this was his form of humor. "I have a feeling I'm actually going to like you."

Hudson barked out a laugh and gestured toward my car. "Do you have good tires on that?" he asked, and I looked over at my SUV.

"I do. I think. I mean, they got me up here."

"It's spring in the mountains, so we might get snow. You should head over to Caldwell's and have them check it out just in case. Don't want you to run off the road. We get enough accidents out here. And we've lost some good people."

89

I froze at that and shook my head. "I'm fine. I don't need to go to Caldwell's."

"Okay. But Weston will hook you up. He somehow got me to be his best friend, and I don't know how that happened."

Hudson kept speaking, and it was like I was seeing this through a new dimension. How small was this world that my ex-boyfriend was best friends with my brother? Just like my best friend was dating my brother. How the hell had this happened? My life didn't use to be this complicated. At least I didn't think it did.

"Anyway, just be careful. Especially on the bridges." He paused, his face darkening. "Weston lost his parents a few years back on that bridge. I guess, what, eight years now? Came back to raise his twin sisters and his brother. Then we've had a couple of tourists have accidents on the bridge across town. The mayor and the rest of the town does its best to keep everything going, to keep it safe. But accidents happen. So check your tires. Or give me your keys and I'll go over to Weston's. You can take my truck."

A dull ringing echoed in my ears as Hudson continued to speak, and bile rose in my throat.

Eight years ago. Eight years and he left a note. A note saying that he needed to go. And that he had had fun.

And this was why. Why he had come back to town. It was all making a sick sort of sense. And it was all I could do not to throw up right there.

"Isabella? What's wrong?"

I swallowed hard and forced myself to put a pleasant expression on my face. Hudson didn't know the connection, so I wasn't about to let him in on the fact that my entire worldview had been utterly shattered for the second time in my life.

"Nothing's wrong. My tires are fine. But I will stop by Caldwell's if I feel like I need to."

"Okay. Are you sure you're okay?" He sighed. "Of course you're not. You're here in Cage Lake doing remote work and checking in on the businesses for Flynn because of some asshole down in Wyoming. And apparently in Denver too. So if you need me, you call. I know you are just as independent as I am, and I hate people, but I don't want you to get hurt. And if you need to talk about whatever is troubling you...hell, I can send you over to the resort to talk to someone there. She never shuts up."

I had no idea who he was talking about, but I wanted to reach out and hug him, or tell him I was fine, but I wasn't. Because my world had just been once again rocked on its axis, and I couldn't keep up.

So many secrets, so many lies, and yet, it felt as if

this one truth had changed everything once more and it didn't make any sense to me. "Thank you. I'm just going to go drive downtown a bit. Walk downtown, I guess. The little shops. Walk around. The brothers won't let me work today."

"That sounds like them. Seriously though. I know you're good at faking it for others, but if you need to scream into the void or some shit, call me."

"I'll be fine. I promise," I lied.

And then I said my goodbyes and left the lake behind me before I got into my SUV. I assumed my tires were fine, so maybe Hudson or someone should check them out. But my hands shook as I drove down the winding road around the lake toward the main town area. It wasn't really downtown. It was just farther south and a lower elevation. The place was adorable, with its similar facade on each building. As if there was a building code that somebody paid attention to and was very strict about. But there was still a little bit of individuality in each thing.

And there really were way too many Cage names on this place. Cage Italiano had to be the worst culprit. They didn't even try with that one. At least the so-called dive bar I had driven past on the way here didn't have Cage in the name— they had just gone with Lake Bar.

The main street had many of the tourist businesses

and eateries of town. Cage Street was the main road that got you into the town and toward the lake before you turned onto Main Street. Because of course the Cages would name their own road that. I didn't know if it was Dad or someone else who had gone with the naming, but I knew Flynn and the others probably wouldn't stamp their face all over everything. At least I hoped they didn't.

I parked in an easy spot near the market, and put my crossbody bag on, and tried not to hold my pepper spray too tight. Blakely had even given me bear spray to add on to that, and while I would always choose the bear over the man, I didn't like the fact that I had spray to ward off both of them.

"You must be Isabella," an average-height woman with richly dark hair pulled into a bun on the top of her head said. She wore a wool vest over outdoor pants and hiking shoes and had on a scarf as well that looked fancy. Somehow, she mixed rugged and ladies-who-lunch together, and I wasn't sure how she did it.

"Excuse me?" I asked, a little scared that this woman had recognized me, and I had no idea who she was.

"Oh I'm sorry. I'm Ms. Patty. Aston sent a note over saying that you were coming to stay at his place. It's so good to meet one of his sisters. The town cannot wait to get to know all of you. I'm the mayor's wife, and well I suppose the welcoming committee." She laughed, and it didn't sound condescending or rude. Instead she sounded welcoming. It was not what I was used to. "Anyway. If you need anything, you just let us know. He said you would be working remotely up here, and also you have the power of attorney to sign a few pieces of paperwork. Which I know my husband will very much be wanting to talk to you about." She winked. "You Cages sure take care of us. You should head up to the resort as well. The resort manager, Scarlett, really knows what she's doing. And she doesn't really need Cage oversight, which I'm sure you all appreciate. Your resort is in great hands with that one. Anyway, you should try the Caged Bean, they have a lovely coffee flight. Although as you can tell, I've had a little too much espresso for the day." She laughed again, and my lips couldn't help but form into a smile, even as I struggled to keep up. "Anyway, Aston told me to let everyone know that you'd be in town, and to keep an eye on you. Just so you didn't get lost or if you needed anything. So don't worry, we'll be around for you." She reached out, squeezed my hand, and left before I could even get a word in.

Well, apparently the town would indeed be watching out for me while I went on this forced sabbatical. He let the mayor's wife know I was in town, as well as everyone else. So I was going to get the true small-town welcome. Where people kept waving at me, as if I was supposed to know who they were. Maybe he was right, I wasn't going to truly be alone in this place, even though I only somewhat knew Hudson. I swallowed hard. And Weston.

Countless people introduced themselves, and I tried to keep up, said hello, and then told me that they'd be keeping an eye on me, making sure I didn't find my way down a dark alley—not that Cage Lake had those. In other words, my brothers had found a way to keep me in a bubble without clipping my wings. I didn't know how the hell they had done that when they didn't even know me that well, but they sure had. Maybe it was Blakely, and that did sound like her as well. Or maybe I was figuring out exactly who these Cages were.

I turned the corner, heading toward the Caged Bean when I ran into a hard wall. Strong arms reached out and gripped me by my shoulders, and I flinched, that memory hitting hard before I looked up. I stared into those familiar eyes, my mouth going dry.

"Bella," he muttered, and I tried to pull back, only it was a lost cause. Because there he was, the man I told myself not to think about. Only he was the only person I could think about.

"Why didn't you tell me?" I blurted.

His eyes widened. "I was about to ask you the same damn question. What the hell are you doing here when some stalker is out to get you?"

I hissed under my breath at that, annoyed that Hudson must have told him. Because apparently, they were best friends.

"Just yell it for the whole town to hear why don't you."

He cursed under his breath and pulled me toward what I thought was an alley.

"Don't you dare," I bit out, but he was so much stronger than me, I couldn't fight back. Panic began to fill my lungs, memories assaulting me, but then we weren't in an alley. Instead we were in a small park between two buildings.

"Breathe. Fuck. Did I scare you? I just wanted to get you out of the eyes of everyone else. You know how they are. Fuck. Are you okay?"

"I'm fine," I lied. I wiped the sweat off my brow, once again annoyed that here I was, stressed out and sweaty over a man. I rubbed my hand over my chest and glared at the man. He had the sleeves of his Henley pushed up to his elbows, so his tatted forearms showed, and he brushed his hair back from his face so his eyes brightened even as he glared at me.

"Bella. Did I hurt you? Fuck. I just wanted to talk to you, I didn't mean to scare you."

"You didn't scare me." *A total untruth.* Then I swallowed hard and shook my head. "Okay, maybe. Did Hudson tell you?"

"Of course Hudson told me. He's my best friend."

"I wasn't aware you two were best friends until like twenty minutes ago."

"Well, there's a lot of things we're not aware of. It's been eight years, Bella."

"I really wish you would stop calling me that. I'm Isabella. Nobody calls me Bella anymore." Not since you left me.

"It's hard for me to call you anything else." He ran his hands through his hair, the muscles in his biceps bulging. "I'll try, but I'm not good at it."

"I can't handle this right now."

"You should have texted. Called. I'm sorry you went through that. Everything. Are you okay?"

"Did he tell you everything?" I asked, my voice low. The entire family knew about the attack now. Both of them. They had needed to, and frankly, they deserved to know. Secrets weren't good for us anyway. Though, then again, my mom didn't know yet. Because I didn't want to talk to her. I couldn't.

"He told me about William." I flinched at the name,

and he sighed. "I'm sorry. I don't know if he was supposed to tell me all of that, but he and the rest of your brothers wanted me to keep an eye out for you. He didn't know. That I knew you. About everything."

"They don't know that this world is so infinitesimally small I can't get away from people connected to the brothers I never knew about? How are you here? How are you Hudson's best friend?"

"He would visit, the same with the rest of your brothers, and we just got along. Then he moved back to stay after he got out of the military, and things just happened. He's just as much of an asshole as I am, so we get along," he said dryly.

I studied his face, trying to see the man I used to know and thought I loved. He had been twenty-seven, I had been twenty-one. A baby now that I thought about it. But he had been everything to me. A flash, heat, a spark so quickly ignited that it had been everything. Yet it hadn't been a fling. I knew that. Only...

"Why didn't you tell me about your family."

He stiffened, his face paling. "Hudson told you that too. Seems like he's talking a lot more than he usually does."

I raised my chin, not letting him get out of this so easily. "He doesn't know that we know each other. So he didn't realize that he changed everything. Why? Why didn't you tell me that your parents died, Weston? And you had to come back here and raise your sisters and brother. I know you told me about them. And I remember their names, but I don't know anything else about them. There wasn't time back then. I thought we would have more time. Why didn't you tell me?"

Anger shocked me, and my hands shook. I moved forward and put my palms on his chest. His heartbeat vibrated against my hands, and I let out a breath. "You just left. A single note by my pillow. And you didn't answer my calls. You did nothing. I don't understand. Why couldn't you tell me?"

He was silent for so long I was afraid he wasn't going to say anything. I was ready to take a step back, to walk away once again, but then he lowered his head and put his hands on my wrists. Over the bruises settling there.

"I didn't know how. I really wasn't thinking."

"And after?"

"After there wasn't time. I couldn't come into the city and start my own business or work for someone else. I couldn't expand Caldwell's. I couldn't do anything that we planned. Because I had to be the one to step up and watch two ten-year-old girls who were shell-shocked and scared. I had to figure out how to keep my brother in college because he was ready to drop out. To try to figure out how to help out with money. Because life insurance only goes so far, and I had no idea how to raise three kids. So I didn't think. I wrote a note, wondering if I was going to figure out how to come back, and I just left. I left you sleeping in your bed, and I had to somehow be a dad. So yes, I'm sorry. I'm sorry for being an asshole."

Emotions clawed for purchase within me as I tried to come to terms with his revelations. I wanted to reach out and hold him, tell him that I was sorry. But I wanted to scream and shout because nothing made sense, and I felt as if I were three steps behind. I needed to sound sure. Sophisticated. Not as if I were still broken remnants of the woman I'd once been. "You had a good reason to leave. I get that. But I don't understand."

"There's not much to understand."

My breaths came in ragged pants, matching his.

He had lied when he'd said forever, he had hurt me, and I hated the fact that the man that I hated, that I resented, wasn't that man anymore. Now there was a glimmer of reason. Of the why of it all.

And I couldn't think.

"Bella. That man hurt you. I don't know what I would do if you got hurt again. Please, stay safe here. Let us help you."

"Weston," I whispered.

"Just for once let us keep you safe."

"Don't get angry with me," I snapped back. "I'm trying. I'm letting people take care of me. And you know how much I hate that. The man who attacked me is in jail and I'm fine." Another lie. "But you keep changing the subject to me when I want to know *why*."

"I don't have a reason. But there's still this." And then he crushed his mouth to mine, and I groaned into him, flashes of memory of before slamming into me. Of his taste, of his need. He kept his hands on my wrists, my palms on his chest. But his tongue lashed along mine, deepening the kiss. My body tensed, needing him as his rough kiss sent shivers down my spine. And when I pulled away, gasping for breath, he let my hands fall.

"That's why I needed to leave. And that's why I can't stop thinking about you."

And I just stared at the man who I thought I had known, wondering what the hell I was doing in Cage Lake.

Chapter Seven

WESTON

"I told you, it's right there."

"I don't think so. If it was right there, I'd be able to see it. And I can't. Therefore it's not there."

"That logic doesn't work because I'm literally pointing to it right now."

"Whatever. You are totally wrong. And we're going to be late. How could you do that to me?"

I pinched the bridge of my nose, telling myself that this was almost over. I only had a few more months of twin sisters sniping at each other over something that was probably so ridiculous it didn't make any sense.

I pushed my hair from my face, annoyed because I had been on my way to take a shower. I needed to wipe off my workout, get the sweat away, and then try to pour the coffee directly into my veins so I could make it to work without damaging something. Mainly myself and my sanity.

"Sam. Sydney. Are you too serious right now? It's seven in the morning." I looked at the clock over the stove. "Correction, it's not even seven in the morning. I thought you two had some form of practice."

"I don't know why you're saying that as if you don't have our schedules permanently engraved into your head." Sam grinned at me. "Plus, we already figured it out. Her notebook was just under those papers. Right where I said they would be."

"No, you said they would be on the table. This is the side table. Totally different thing."

Then the two little miscreants winked at each other, hugged one another, and proceeded to babble on about some form of gossip that I really didn't want anything to do with. However, because my life was only about these two twin girls and my other brother, I sadly knew way too much about this information.

"And Candace is seriously stressing. Because Haylee and Kaylee were supposed to go to prom together, but instead they're going to ask different dates. So now instead of a group of three friends, two of them have dates and one doesn't."

I paused in the act of pouring coffee. "I thought Haylee was dating Jason. When did they break up?"

Sydney rolled her eyes. "They broke up ages ago. Seriously. They decided that they were going to go to different colleges so why bother dating now? Plus neither one of them wanted to have sex, since getting pregnant or getting an STD is so last century." She rolled her eyes and continued her conversation as if I hadn't interrupted with my pesky question. It's not like I really wanted to know the answer, but as I had been raising my twin sisters for eight years everything that had to do with the two of them was my life. Whether I liked the information or not.

Then her words caught up with me. "Wait, they're not having sex?" I asked and then took a very large gulp of my too hot coffee. "I don't actually want to know these things, but really. Does that mean you two aren't having sex with your boyfriends?"

Raising teenage girls had already given me my first gray hair. At least, I thought it was a gray hair. I was thirty-five years old and had a single silver hair right at my temple. The girls loved it and thought it made me distinguished. And they thought maybe I would finally catch a wife. Their words, not mine. I blamed them for everything.

Because I loved the two little miscreants.

"We've had the sex talk before. I don't know why you're harping on it now," Sydney said, while she put her attention back to her phone. Her fingers moved like the wind, and I wasn't even sure how she could type that quickly.

"And it was a very descriptive talk. Full of support. You did great." Sam held up both thumbs, as if I wasn't ready to scream into the void.

"Do I really want to know what this conversation's about?" Lance asked as he came down the stairs and shoved me out of the way to get to the coffee.

While the girls were eighteen, Lance was now twenty-six and starting business school. He wanted his MBA, and there was no stopping him. I had been able to get him through college, but the MBA was all on him. Thankfully his internships and scholarships were making it so he wasn't starting his life off in complete debt. But I hated the fact that I was a mechanic. I might own my own business, but this was a small mountain town. I serviced the cars and trucks and vehicles for five to eight different small towns in the area. Not to mention every tourist that came by and needed help. That didn't mean I had the type of money to send three kids to colleges of their choice, or grad school and beyond. Mom and Dad had left behind enough of their provisions and life insurance to get us by, but it wasn't enough to do everything.

"You're getting that look on your face again. What do you blame yourself for now?" Lance asked, and I flipped him off before draining my coffee and going to pour another one.

"I have a shit ton to do and stop making fun of my face."

"But it's such an easy thing," Lance said as he wrapped his arm around Sam's shoulder. "I mean, you make it pretty easy, big brother."

"He's right about that. And don't worry, I am not having sex." Sam beamed, and I choked on my coffee.

"Good to know."

"Seriously? You and Mason haven't..." Lance asked, his voice trailing off.

Sam blushed, shaking her head. "No. We like things the way they are. And Weston always told us that sex changes things. Maybe when we're in college, but no. That's not our thing."

An odd sense of relief slid through me at that, and I told myself that all three of my kids knew what the fuck they were doing. They had strong heads on their shoulders, and I didn't have to worry too much.

And then Sydney opened her mouth.

"Steve and I have tons of sex. I mean everywhere."

I glared at my baby sister, the bane of my existence. "You better be joking."

"I thought you said that it was my body, my choice. As long as I am adult enough to vote, and to make my own decisions, I should be able to have sex with somebody that I love and am in a committed relationship with. Or, I could have sex with anybody I wanted as long as it was safe. Consensual. And we aren't doing anything that hurts someone. Because there is no such thing as being a slut. Only someone who is irresponsible with theirs and other's safety and heart."

Lance just blinked at me over his coffee, as if telling me that this was my ball in my court.

I missed my parents every damn day.

But in this moment, I missed them more than usual.

"You know what. I don't care if you're fucking with me or not. You know the rules, just don't lie to me. And be safe."

"Of course I'm being safe. And I am just messing with you." She winked at me, and I didn't know if she was messing with me because she hadn't had sex with her long-time boyfriend or hadn't had sex everywhere. Sydney was a handful, and I loved her to death. And she had a nearly full-wide scholarship to her college. All thanks to field hockey and academics. Sam had similar scholarships, but for soccer and academics. Thank God my kids were smart, talented, and gave me gray hairs. Or rather, gray *hair*.

"And on this note, I need to go shower and not deal with any of this."

"So you need to go get ready so you can meet Isabella," Sydney said, fluttering her eyelashes.

I froze on my way upstairs, and turned slightly, glaring. "Excuse me?"

"Mrs. Hanford saw you and Isabella totally making out behind The Pantry."

"And Miss Stacey said that the two of you seemed to know each other. And that Isabella is one of the Cages. That means she's Dorian's sister." Sam nearly swooned as she said Dorian's name, and I rubbed the spot between my eyebrows.

"I'm not going to justify an answer to anything you just said." Mostly because for a man who had lived in a small town his entire life, I had fucking forgotten the way small towns worked. Of course even though I had tried to hide my kiss with Isabella, or the fact that I was even speaking to her, everybody had seen. Or at least, one person had seen, and now everybody knew. There was no hiding in this town. Hence why Isabella was here in the first place. And at that damning thought, bile rose in my throat, so I swallowed it down and glared. "And stop thinking about Dorian that way. He's too old for you."

"Older men are hot," Sydney said as she and Sam bumped fists.

"You really are going to have to beat up your best friend's brother, aren't you?" Lance asked sweetly, and I flipped him off.

"Thank God Dorian has a head on his shoulders and is used to dealing with women throwing themselves at him," I mumbled.

"We wouldn't throw ourselves at him. Plus, he's old. Like you," Sam said before the twins got their bags and ran out of the house giggling.

Lance blinked slowly. "Somehow they're confusing me more now than they did when they were pre-teens and screaming for some boy band with funky hair."

I made a gesture toward Lance's hair, and the fact that his bangs were nearly past his forehead. "Are you one to talk right now?"

"It's a look."

"And you were screaming for that boy band right alongside them. I have recordings," I teased.

"If you're going to bring that up, I'm going to ask about Isabella. Because I remember that name."

I froze and turned to look at my brother. "What?" I asked, my voice coming out sharper than I intended.

"I might have blocked out most of that time for good reason, but I remember Isabella. I remember that name."

"Don't, Lance. Just don't." My free hand fisted at my side, and my grip on my coffee cup tightened.

"I'm not going to make fun of you for it. Not with that look on your face. But the girls remember that name too. They weren't as young as you think they were."

And yet they'd been so tiny when I'd rocked them to sleep because there had been no one else. "I can't talk about it. Okay? She's just a friend."

"If that's what you say. But you know, this whole fate thing seems pretty cool."

"What fate thing?" I didn't even know why I was asking. Nothing good could come from that question.

"I mean, it seems like it's a small world that the one girl you had a serious relationship with in all of your life happens to not only be your best friend's sister but is now in your small town. Hell, her family owns this town. Interesting, don't you think?"

"She is a new Cage. It's not the same thing."

"That wasn't even an answer to my statement. Or maybe it was an answer in itself." With that, Lance shuffled off to the living room, and I made my way upstairs.

I was so damn tired already. I didn't know what the hell I was going to do with Isabella. I had been so angry that someone would want to hurt her, that I hadn't even thought about what I was going to do until my hands were on her.

I needed to keep her safe.

With that one kiss, I had been shoved back into my past, shoved back into who we had been.

We weren't those people anymore. Far from it.

She had been through so much since that moment. Since I had walked out.

And as I got into the shower, imagining that face of hers, I couldn't help but blame myself. Because if I had been with her, if I hadn't left, maybe she wouldn't have that look of fear on her face.

Or maybe I was truly so self-centered that I could think that.

I quickly showered but couldn't get the thought of Isabella out of my mind, or the taste of her off my tongue. The kiss had been rougher, more demanding than it had been prior. We had always liked rough sex, always liked the touch of each other. But we weren't those same people, I reminded myself.

Without thinking, I slid my hand down over my cock and squeezed at the base.

I was going to hell for this. But I couldn't help it. I was already hard just thinking about her. I slid my fist over my length, letting my thumb slide over the slit. A drop of pre-come slid out, and I used it to roll over the tip, before sliding my fist back and squeezing the base once more. I moved one hand to cup my balls, needing that moment, before dropping that hand and pushing it against the shower wall, bracing myself.

I moved my hand up and down, imagining her mouth. The way that she would hollow her cheeks, letting her tongue flick against the vein running underneath. She used to tease the barbell there, letting it run over her tongue. I'd always loved fucking her bare, knowing that my piercing would be rubbing against her inner walls, sending her over the edge. My grip tightened, as I sped up, needing that release.

I imagined her on her knees, legs spread. She would have one hand on her pussy, sliding her fingers in and out of herself as I told her to. She'd flick her thumb over her clit, and she would moan around my cock. Then she'd use one hand to grip at my thighs, keeping her steady. And I'd have one of my hands wrapped in her hair, holding her still as I her fucked her face, my cock going deep down her throat as she swallowed hard, gagging. And I'd use my other hand to pluck at her nipples, pinching and squeezing as she moaned into me, needing that pinprick of pain.

I'd keep going even as she came, even as she bobbed her head in time with my thrusts.

With that moment, I came, spurting over the wall as

I swallowed hard, draining myself dry as the water grew cold.

I was such a fucking asshole that I was over here jerking myself off thinking about the woman I had left behind.

She wasn't far away anymore. No, she was here. In town.

My town.

The town that just happened to be hers in name and truth after all.

I shook my head, feeling slightly disgusted, as I finished washing up, and got ready for the day.

Lance had already left since he was working a part-time job for the next couple of weeks before he headed back to Denver to finish his scholarship and start his semester. He was on an off-semester now that wasn't with the full school schedule, so it was helpful that he could be here as often as he was to help with the girls. Between graduation, prom, and their countless sporting activities, I needed the help.

I was grateful that the town had helped along the way as well. Well-meaning individuals who had tried to step in too far, and others who had just been there with a kind word and warm meal when we'd been behind and lost. And that was why I had needed to leave Isabelle. Why I had made that choice for us both.

I'd made my way to work, nodding at my team as I went through paperwork. I needed to get under the hood of an engine soon, but being the boss and owner meant that I had paperwork galore. I knew that Hudson needed to come over and get me a few more things to sign because of course the Cages owned the property all around us, and we had business to deal with, but I didn't know when the man would show up. He would be there for you if you needed him, but any other time? You never knew when he'd arrive. And I didn't mind it. Hudson had his own demons after all.

"Hey, Weston. There's someone here for you." I looked up at Allie and frowned.

"You okay?"

She paused, a grimace covering her face. "It's Drew."

"Fuck," I growled.

"My thoughts exactly."

Deirdre had already come and picked up her car, and I had done my best to keep the costs at a minimum. I hadn't even charged for my own labor. She worked too many hours and gave too much of her money to that asshole Drew, but there was no way I was going to be able to fix everything. Just the tires themselves.

Drew paced in the front bay, anger radiating off him. A few of the other crew members looked up at me, questions in their gaze, but I waved them off. I could handle this. There was nothing else that they could do without causing even more of a scene. As it was, a couple of the clients in the waiting room could see the action, so no matter what happened today it would be around town by this evening.

"Hey Drew, what can I do for you?" I asked, keeping my voice as pleasant as possible.

It wasn't going to matter though.

Drew whirled on me. "I want you to stop fucking my wife."

I paused, blinking as one of the clients nearby gasped. "I don't know what you think is happening between me and Dee, but it's nothing. She needed help with her car and I provided that service."

"That's not all you're providing. You fucking asshole. Don't you dare call her Dee. That's my wife. She's mine. She does what I tell her to do. So you forcing her to come in so you can act like the big man with a big cock? No. I had it handled. You don't need to come into my marriage and try to fuck things up."

I could barely follow his line of reasoning, and I could scent the whiskey on his breath.

No wonder Dee barely had any money. Drew drank it.

"Let me go get you some coffee, and we can talk this

out. But your wife came in with an issue with the car and I fixed it. I know you're busy, so I was just doing you guys a favor."

"I don't need fucking favors from this small-pricked asshole."

Drew moved forward, fist outstretched. I ducked the first blow but let the second blow hit. I wasn't going to demean the man completely. Though I wanted to, his kids didn't deserve the shame.

"No. We're not going to fucking do this. Not in my place of business."

"Fuck you. You're just like the Cages. You think you own everything and you think you're better than anyone else. You're going to regret coming on to my wife."

"Your wife is a friend. And needed help. And so do you, Drew. Come on. Let me get you some coffee."

Drew threw out his fist, so I ducked, except I ducked the wrong way because Drew slipped. So his fist slammed into my jaw. I blinked, stars dawning between my eyes as I tasted blood. I bit the inside of my damn cheek.

"That's it. I'm fucking done." I pinned Drew to the ground as my team ran over, eyes wide.

Allie lowered to her knee. "You want me to call the cops?"

"No, fuck. I don't know." I pinched the bridge of my nose as my team helped keep Drew down.

"Weston, are you okay?"

At the sound of that voice, I was damn glad that the others were holding Drew because I staggered back to see Isabella there, eyes bright.

I swallowed the last taste of blood and waved off some of the guys who came looking for me.

"I'm fine. Just dealing with something."

She looked so damn pale, and I had to wonder exactly what that asshole had done to her.

"Come on, let's get you out of here."

She frowned at me. "I'm fine. You're the one who was bleeding. Are you sure you don't need to call the authorities?"

"He isn't getting a choice, I already called the sheriff," Allie said, and I sighed.

"Okay then. Apparently, we're already dealing with the sheriff."

"Good. Because that asshole punched you, and I'm pretty sure you only let that happen by accident."

I snorted, shaking my head. "Lucky hit."

"Come on, is your office back here? Do you have ice?"

And without thinking, I let her lead me to the back,

as I ignored the knowing looks from my team. Oh, they were going to have questions soon.

And it would be all over town.

Damn it.

And yet maybe that was okay.

Because Isabella had her hand on mine.

And even with blood in my mouth, and my life as chaotic as it was, something finally felt right for the first time in way too fucking long.

Chapter Eight
ISABELLA

Heart in my throat and palms damp I pulled Weston back toward where I thought an office would be. It wasn't as if I knew this place. After all, I had never been here before. This is where he had been for most of his life. Including those eight years where we had known each other and yet he had been gone. Nothing was the same. Everything I thought had been true had been slightly off and I felt rocked to my core. Still.

And yet none of that mattered because Weston was bleeding.

Bleeding just like he was when he had pulled me from the cliff. He had saved my life and it still hadn't truly hit me.

I could have died that day. And yet he had been the

one to be there. Out of every single soul on this earth he had been the one.

"I'm okay, Bella," Weston whispered, and I froze at the sound of his voice.

How could he do that to me? So quietly, so quickly, and I stood there, shaking.

"Does that happen often?" I asked, turning toward him. I let my hand fall, the contact no longer there. I ignored the fact that I missed it already.

"Fighting with Drew? Sadly yes." He held out his hand when I opened my mouth to speak. "I didn't sleep with his wife."

"I may not have known you the way that I thought I did, I may not know you now, but I know that much."

His lips twitched as if he wanted to smile, but he shook his head. "Deidre, Dee? She used to babysit me. She went by Dee with everybody. In fact, my mom used to babysit her when she went by Dee. Then she married Drew, and the guy didn't like her going by that, so she changed her name. Sometimes I forget. And possibly sometimes I'm a fucking asshole who doesn't like the idea that Drew is a controlling, neurotic, narcissistic piece of shit."

My eyes widened even as I went over to his small fridge and was grateful when I saw a tiny ice pack in the freezer section.

"Come on, let's put this on your jaw."

"I'm fine, Bella," he whispered.

I ignored him and put it on his jaw anyway. He flinched at the touch, but I put my hand on his chest, and he immediately calmed.

I didn't want to think about what that exactly meant.

I swallowed hard as I stared into those light eyes of his. Every time I was near him, it's as if my body wasn't my own. It had a mind of its own and did what it wanted. So I clenched my thighs together, even as the hurt and pain and confusion of everything that occurred warred within me.

I was always a mess when it came to Weston Caldwell. And here I was, in his family shop, in *his* shop, confused as ever.

"I know you didn't sleep with her," I whispered again.

"He knows it too. He just hates the fact that people in this town take care of each other. It's why you're here after all," he added with gritted teeth. But before I could say anything else he continued. "She got in a car wreck on the same fucking bridge my parents died on. The one coming into this town. And the asshole didn't get the car checked out. Instead he said he would take care of it himself, and he made it worse.

She's lucky she didn't wreck, hurt herself, the kids, or God forbid someone else. So I fixed it. I only charged her for parts, and even then, I nearly didn't. The only reason I did was because I knew she wouldn't take it as some form of charity. And Drew can't help but be the jerk that he is. If he isn't finding ways to be a truly big asshole, he's at Lake Bar, drinking his way under the table."

Someone cleared his throat and I turned to see a man in a sheriff's uniform. He looked to be about the same age as a few of my brothers, but I still couldn't quite think. The man nodded at me, then raised a brow at Weston. "I'm just glad that you're okay. Are you going to have him arrested?" He gave me a look. "I'm Macon, by the way. I used to go to school with this guy over here and sadly, this isn't the first time I've been called here. So, Weston, charges?"

Weston let out a breath. "No, because it just ends up being more paperwork for you. And it's going to hurt Deidre."

Macon sighed. "I knew you were going to say that. I keep thinking that maybe if I keep him behind bars then he's not going to reach out again. But he never learns." He gave me a small smile, though I read the exhaustion in his gaze. "By the way, welcome to Cage Lake, Miss Cage."

"It's Dixon actually. Cage is my middle name. And hello. Nice to meet you. I guess."

"I'm Sheriff Brothers. If you need anything, let me know." The sheriff gave me a knowing look and I held back a curse. Of course.

"I take it one of my many brothers contacted you?" I asked, the ice seeping into my tone.

"Yes. He found it especially important because there is a man out there on parole, who seems to be threatening you. Or there's someone else trying to threaten you. We're keeping an eye out. I promise we're not going to hem you in." He looked at Weston then. "Let me know if you need anything. We will go make sure Drew takes a walk. Get him sober."

Weston cursed. "I just don't want him to go home and hurt Deidre."

Macon's jaw tightened. "That's not going to fucking happen."

And with that, the sheriff walked out, leaving me alone with Weston. Again.

"I'm glad that it seems that he's trying to help," I said.

He nodded, turning toward me. "This town is good for something sometimes. Though there are no secrets. Considering somebody saw us kissing, and the twins had questions about it this morning."

My brows rose. "What?"

"That's small towns for you. I'd say I'm sorry. But I'm not."

"I...I don't know what to think right now. I was just here to drop off paperwork because James needed it, and he couldn't get ahold of Hudson. Plus, it's part of my whole work remotely thing. Get me out of the city, into this town where everything is so complicated, and so here I am. Working." I pulled a stack of papers from my bag, ignoring the shake in my hand.

"You were here for work," Weston said, and I could have sworn I heard the disappointment in his tone.

"Yes...I mean... no. I just... I couldn't stop thinking about our conversation. And I'm so damn confused. So when you have a moment, I figured we should talk. The one thing that we never really did."

"Bella," he said after moment, and then I shook my head. "Yeah. We should talk. Though I don't know what you want me to say."

"Good, because I don't either."

"I have a few things to finish up here, and to make sure that the clients and my staff aren't freaking the fuck out about what happened."

"And I bet since it's a small town they're going to have questions about why I'm here," I said dryly.

Weston threw his head back and laughed. "Oh, dear Bella. Just you fucking wait."

"I don't know what to think about that. But I'll be at the house. Um, I'm staying at Aston's place."

"I know," he said calmly, though I sensed something beneath his tone. "Hudson mentioned it."

"I'm sure he did. You think the town is small, this world is damn tiny when it comes to Cages. They pop out of anywhere."

"Don't I know it," Weston added dryly. "Give me a couple hours? I have to be back at the house and make sure homework and dinner's good, plus, the prom's tomorrow."

"Prom? Already?" They'd grown so much. So much time had passed and it continued to dawn on me that he'd raised an entire family since I'd seen him.

"Yeah. Senior prom. I don't know how it happened, but the kids are now adults."

I opened my mouth to say something, but instead shook my head. "They're lucky to have you." I paused. "I should go."

He nodded, his gaze searching mine, and I turned away, knowing I was making a choice that could change anything.

I could feel him watching me walk away, but I kept going. I'd truly gone there only to hand off paperwork—

lie. Fine, I'd gone with the intention of dealing with Hudson's paperwork, but I'd known the moment I saw him things would be different. That I wouldn't be able to not think about him.

And we truly needed to figure things out.

I didn't know what that meant, but there was no going back now.

By the time I got back to Aston and Blakely's I didn't bother getting into comfier clothing like I normally would while working remotely—not when I knew Weston would be here soon. I ignored my heartbeat going far too quickly in that moment and got to work. Maybe if I focused on numbers and reports, I wouldn't be thinking about the fact I would once again be alone with Weston.

My thoughts were more confused than ever.

Because he had left for a reason.

To protect and raise his family. And while I would do *anything* for my family and was continuing to do so day by day even though I didn't trust my parents—either of them. And that was the crux of it.

Trust.

I had trusted Weston with my heart, and he'd broken that trust.

Before I could spiral more in my own thoughts, the

doorbell rang and then Weston was there, and my heart was racing.

I stood in my open doorway, wondering what the hell I was supposed to do. I knew it was that damn outfit again. He had on jeans, old work boots, a Henley with his sleeves rolled up, and leaned against the doorframe.

It should be illegal for a man to do that.

Forearm porn.

Doorway porn.

Henley porn.

Damn that man.

"Are you going to invite me in, Bella? Or did I make a mistake in thinking you actually wanted me here? I'll go. I'll walk away. Because I already took your choice away once."

And damn that man once again.

"Oh. Come in. Though it's weird to say that about a house I don't even own, and you've probably been in more than me."

He shook his head as he straightened and walked across the threshold. "I don't know Aston. He doesn't come up like the others do. So no, I've never been here."

I closed the door behind him and stood there, feeling awkward as hell. I didn't understand this. I wasn't the awkward one. I was the one who dealt with things. Even as I stressed and tried to make things work, I was always on top of what needed to be done.

Pheobe and Sophia were the awkward ones. Kyler the one who ignored the world. And Emily was the one who went face first into every interaction and tried to see the bright side.

I was the bitch who got things done and was called the ice queen along the way. A title I'd never resented until faced with my new brothers and their intimidating ways. It had been a miracle we hadn't fought until the end of the earth at first. But now I knew they'd fight alongside me, rather than with me.

A novel concept. But none of that mattered in the face of Weston.

"I don't know what to say, Bella."

His words brought me out of my thoughts once again and I stared at the man I'd once thought I'd loved. No, that was a cop out. He was the man I'd loved and the man I'd locked away because it hurt too much to think of.

And now here he was, flesh and blood.

"I don't know either. Because none of this seems real. From the moment you saved me on that cliff, it seems as though we've been living in a damn dream that I can't wake up from and I don't know what I'm supposed to do about it."

"What do you want to do about it?"

I scowled before I began to pace, needing the distance from him. "I'm so angry that you did what you did, even if I can understand it. But being near you? I don't know what to do, Weston."

In answer, he reached out and gripped my elbow, freezing me. My heart beat in my throat and I stared into those gray eyes. "I've thought about you every damn day for eight years. Even when I told myself it would be better to move on and try to figure out how to live without you. I couldn't, Bella. Even when I told myself that you'd moved on with someone who could treat you right. It was all I could do to not rage against that imaginary person. And now there's a *real* flesh and blood person after you and I want to rip them limb from limb. Bella, I...I want you. I know it's fucking stupid and complicated and we'll both probably end up broken in the end, but I can't stop thinking about you."

My breath came in pants as he spoke, and my hands shook. It was all I wanted him to say, and I needed him to take back the words. "I spent my life trying to be what everyone needs. And I let you become the one person I could lean on until you weren't there."

"And I'll hate myself until the end of time for how I treated you."

I wanted to believe him.

I wanted *him*.

And I couldn't trust myself.

"How can I trust you? Trust these feelings every time I see you." And I didn't even know what those feelings were. Because I wasn't in a place to even want this... connection. But here we were, my heart racing while standing in front of the man who broke me but who I never feared. "You've always been the obstacle. The one I always compared everyone to. And yet in the end, I realize that you left. With a note. I called. Texted. And you never responded. All you did was leave me in the cold. And now I know it's because you were breaking. So now, every feeling of heartache and fear and anger that I had for years twisted into this guilt. Because you were dying inside, and I couldn't be there because you didn't trust me to be there."

His eyes darkened and he reached out, but I took a step back, needing space. The devastation on his face nearly broke me but I needed to say the words. Because everything was different now and I didn't know how to move forward.

"Bella."

"Please let me finish because I'm trying to figure things out, Weston. Okay? Your family needed you. I above all people know that. But I loved you. And I would've helped in any way I could."

Weston moved then, not giving me time to step away. He cupped my face, and I let out a shaky breath, everything that had slammed into me in the past few days finally colliding. "And you didn't deserve that. I had to drop everything. My entire future changed. I was suddenly a single dad. The responsibilities on my lap were insane. And I...I couldn't think."

My heart broke for him. For how he had to drop everything to raise Sam, Sydney, and Lance. All while grieving parents who loved him with every ounce of their souls. "Why didn't you tell me? I could have...I could have been there, Weston."

"Because how was I supposed to tell a woman I loved that our entire future would change. Because you would have to give up everything right alongside me."

"You don't—"

"I do. I know what you would have done because even in those short months, you were *everything*. And you did everything for your family. I stayed here to give these kids some form of normalcy. Consistency. And you would've had to give up everything. And I didn't know how to love you and the future we could've had and tear myself into a thousand jagged pieces in order to be the man that my family needed."

Tears blurred my eyes even as his words hit home.

"You didn't give me a choice. You couldn't let me decide. And maybe that's selfish, but you took my choice away."

"I didn't want you to have to make it in the first place."

"Then what is this? What are you expecting now?"

"Bella, baby."

"Maybe there aren't any answers. We can't turn back time. We can't go to the moment where you could have said a single word. Even if you had to leave me. Even if we weren't right for each other in that moment, you were *breaking*. And you didn't think I was strong enough to be by your side. And even beyond that, you had no one to lean on. And I hate that my friend, the man that I loved, had no one. That kills me. I can't hate you anymore. I hate that. Because I understand it."

He looked at me then, his eyes dark. He looked so much like the Weston I knew, but he was so different. Changed. Then again, I'd been irrevocably changed by every scar I held. "What if I still hate myself?"

This was the moment. The moment I could walk away and forget. Yet I knew I couldn't. Not when the darkness lurked behind me. And Weston had never been that darkness. He'd only been the light—even through the pain. "Don't. The shadow of the man that I loved, the people we used to be—they're gone. I can't compare you to anyone else because you aren't anyone else. Everything is so monumentally complicated."

He turned his head to kiss my palm, and I swallowed hard. "It always was."

"But we're older, and I don't know what that means. I don't know what I want. But the girl that was your friend who turned into the woman before you wants to be friends with the man you've become."

"Only friends?"

"I don't know. I have scars too, Weston. Scars I can't change."

"Your scars are safe with me, Bella."

My hands shook as he spoke, and I stared into those gray eyes. "Weston...I...I'm so scared. All the time. And yet with you? I'm scared for so many other reasons."

I hated being vulnerable and yet he changed everything like he always did. I couldn't hide behind who I needed to be when it came to Weston Caldwell.

"Let me show you what we could have, Bella. Just for now."

I pressed my lips together, leaning into his touch, and I let out a breath, knowing I could be making a mistake, or leaping into the unexpected.

"Okay."

And then his lips were on mine, and I was his.

Chapter Nine
WESTON

I wrenched away, breath coming in pants. I still had my hand around the back of Bella's neck, the other on her hip. I forced myself to step away, wondering where the hell my sanity had gone. Or perhaps it was exactly where it needed to be. Nowhere near here.

"I'm sorry. Here we are, trying to have a fucking conversation and I can't keep my hands off you." I ran my hands through my hair, grateful for some distance. My cock pressed hard against my zipper, and I knew it would probably leave a mark. But I didn't care in that moment because I could still taste Bella on my tongue.

None of this felt real. And yet in this moment it was far too set in reality.

"I didn't tell you to stop." I blinked at her, at the warmth in her tone, and wondered if I had misheard.

"What?" I said, my voice shaky. "What?" I repeated, knowing I was mumbling at this point.

"I don't know what's coming next, I don't know anything. And for someone who spends their life making sure that they adhere to the plans, it makes no sense. But I really want your mouth on me. I just want to forget. And I want to remember you. So kiss me. Please. I just need your touch."

I stalked toward her, sliding my hand through her hair before I tugged slightly. Her mouth parted, and I slid my thumb over her lower lip, tugging down marginally.

"If I kiss you right now, I'm not going to stop. I'm going to want to taste every single inch of you. I want to taste that cunt of yours, slide my tongue between your lips, letting that tart taste settle over my tongue. I want you to gag on my cock, taking me as deep as you can go. And then I want to shove into you, feeling exactly what I've been missing all these years. I'm not a nice man right now, Isabella. Outside this room, in any other moment I would do anything for you, for those I...care for." I had nearly said love, and I could have slapped myself. Because I didn't know this Isabella. But I sure as hell wanted to.

"So what do you say, Bella? Because if I kiss you, I'm not stopping until you tell me to."

Because I knew she had been through enough. I wasn't going to be the one she wanted. I had broken her heart, and then somebody had shattered her safety along the way. I wasn't the right choice for her, and I had known that all along.

But then Bella went to her tiptoes, my thumb sliding from her mouth, and she bit my jaw.

My eyes widened in surprise, and I tugged on her hair harder, loving the gasp that escaped. I slid my hand underneath her breast, cupping her. My thumb slid over her nipple. When it pebbled against my skin, I pinched it between my thumb and forefinger, harder than I would normally. She arched against me, and I swallowed hard. "I'm going to need the words. Say it out loud. I'm not going to guess. We both know I've never been good about reading your mind."

"And we both realized that I was never good at reading yours. But take me, Weston. I just want to forget."

"I need you to be sure. Because I can be a good guy. Out here. For my kids. For anyone. But in bed? I'm an asshole. Here and now? I'm not a good guy."

"You need to stop trying to scare me away. Because I remember exactly who you are. Now take me."

I wasn't sure I liked that answer. Because I didn't want her to forget this. But then again, with reality closing in, maybe it would be good to live in our own fantasy.

So I nodded tightly before crushing my mouth to hers.

I gripped her by the hips and lifted her up. She wrapped her legs around my waist, and I carried her to the bedroom. It was a short hallway, and I realized as soon as we walked in it wasn't even her room. I didn't care though, and I knew I was about to fuck a Cage in the Cage guest room. It wasn't exactly what I had planned for my night, but it was exactly what I needed.

"On your feet," I whispered, and she let her legs drop as I gently set her on the ground. With that, I went to my knees in front of her and looked up.

Her lips were swollen from my kisses, her chest rising and falling with each deep breath. I slid my hands up her tights, grateful she was wearing a dress.

"I want to rip these off you, so I can get closer to that pussy of yours."

"I don't have that many clothes here," she teased.

"Well, it looks like I'm going to have to buy you more."

I ripped her tights at her waist, and she let out a

shocked gasp. Somehow, I was able to rip them through the seam and pull them down over her boots.

"Weston!"

"I'm not done unwrapping my present."

I then leaned forward and pressed my face to her pussy, inhaling. "So fucking sweet." I could feel her blush all over her body as I used my nose to rub along her clit.

"Weston."

"This is my pussy. Do you get that?" I looked up at her as I slid my finger along her lower lips.

Her tongue darted out as she wetted her lips, but she nodded.

"Whose pussy is this?"

"It's yours." She swallowed hard. "For now."

In answer, I slapped her pussy over her panties, and her mouth parted.

"Weston!"

"You didn't answer correctly. And now you get to be punished." I slapped her pussy again, and then ripped the side of her panties.

In one movement, I shoved her down on the bed, then pulled off her boots, tights, and panties, and threw everything to the side.

She squirmed under my hold, but still on my knees, I wrapped her legs around my neck and feasted. With one long swipe of my tongue against her cunt, she shifted against me, so I reached back and slapped her swollen folds again.

"If you keep moving, I'm not going to let you come. I'm going to fuck this pussy, and your ass, and your mouth, and I won't let you come. You'll walk all day in just this dress, no panties, no tights, but your clit will be so swollen it'll ache. *But I won't let you come.* So are you going to listen to me?"

"You weren't like this before."

My lips tilted into a grin and I swallowed hard, my cock pressing against the seam of my jeans. "Well, we're both a little older, and I need a little more from you. What do you say?"

She looked like a fucking goddess above me. She leaned on both her elbows, looking down at me between her legs, and she finally nodded, her teeth biting into her lower lip.

"Good girl."

In answer, I leaned forward and licked at her slit again. She moaned, her pussy wet for me. I spread her, studying her pink flesh, the way that she swelled for me, and I continued to lick, suck.

"Eyes on me," I ordered, and she shifted to look down at me. With my gaze still on her, I spit, loving the way she gasped.

"Did you..." But she didn't have a chance to finish her question before I lowered my mouth to her pussy again and ate. She tasted sweet and tart and I couldn't get enough of her. I speared her with my tongue, loving the way that her hips rolled against my face. I shook my head, rubbing my nose against her clit as I used two fingers to spread her, before spearing her with three fingers with my other hand.

She nearly shot off the bed, but I didn't let her move. Instead I slid my fingers in and out of her in a hard and fast rhythm, one that I knew would send her over the edge soon. Wet sounds of flesh against flesh filled the room, and my palm dampened with her arousal. But I kept moving, alternating between fucking her hard with my fingers, and then eating her out with everything that I had. And when she came, her body arching off the bed, I continued to suck and lick, taking every ounce of her orgasm.

I pulled away as she rocked beneath me and tugged at her side so she sat up.

"Lick. Taste yourself," I ordered, and she nodded tightly, her eyes wide. I slid my fingers over her lips, and she grinned against me before taking them inside. She licked every drop of herself, and I just smirked, sliding my fingers along her jaw.

"I remember how beautiful you looked when you

came, at least I thought I did. You're even more beautiful now."

She rolled her eyes at me, her fingers playing along the edge of my jeans. "You say that, but I'm not some young twenty-something anymore."

I raised a brow. "Yes, because you being, what, twenty-nine now makes you such an old lady. Did you see the gray hair at my temple that the twins left? I'm the old man now."

"First, I did see the single gray hair, and oh my God, it just makes you look hotter. It's not fair with men. And my boobs aren't as high and tight as they used to be."

"We're just going to have to be the judge of that." I tugged on her dress, and we were both laughing, the tone shifting ever so slightly as we tossed her dress over her head, and I undid her bra with ease.

She lifted a brow at that, but I just shrugged before pulling my Henley off in one movement and staring down at her breasts.

"I think you need to look in the mirror more often." I leaned forward, cupping her breasts with both hands, running my thumb along her nipples. "I've dreamed about these for years. Do you see how they overfill my hands? You're so fucking beautiful, Bella. You haunt me."

She blinked up at me, her hands still on my hips. "You say the strangest and yet most beautiful things."

"I wasn't saying much with my mouth on your pussy just now."

Blushing, she shook her head. "You were always a dirty talker."

I slid my thumb between her lips, loving the way her eyes darkened. "And I always knew how to shut you up."

She rolled her eyes again, and I laughed before using my free hand to undo the button of my jeans. She immediately slid my zipper down, then reached into my boxer briefs.

Her small hand around my cock nearly sent me over the edge, and I groaned.

"I want those lips on my cock. Can you do that? Can you take me?"

She nodded hard, her throat working as she swallowed before she took me fully out of my boxer briefs and leaned forward.

"You kept the piercing," she whispered.

"You always liked it." Not all women that I had been with liked it. Some of them had actually been repulsed. They didn't matter. Nobody had mattered but Bella. But it wasn't like I could bring that up in this moment. Nobody needed to hear about the people they had been with in between. And fuck, now I was thinking about the people Bella had been with in those eight years, and I wanted to rip them limb from limb.

I had a fucking problem.

Before I could say anything stupid though, Bella's head lowered, and she swallowed the tip of my dick. I groaned, one hand on her hair, wrapping it around my fist, the other playing with her breast.

"That's it, Bella. Take me."

I moved my hips, going deeper, and she relaxed her throat, taking me.

Bella had always been good at blowjobs. It had been one of our favorite things. Lying on our sides, me having my breakfast the exact way that I needed, fingers in her pussy and her ass as I licked every ounce of her, with my cock buried deep in Bella's mouth as she took me.

I still dreamed about that, waking up with either a hard on or nearly ready to blow.

I had hated the fact that Bella could still do that to me from so far away when she was just a memory. But now she wasn't a memory anymore.

So I moved forward, taking her mouth as she looked up at me, eyes wide and tearing up. I moved my hand from her breast to wipe a single tear falling down her cheek. I froze my hips.

"Too much?"

She pulled away, and I let her. "No. I like it. I promise."

I tapped the tip of my cock and piercing against her lips, frowning. "Are you sure?" I asked.

In answer she took me again, and I just grinned as I fucked her mouth, slowly at first then harder. I leaned forward, going deeper as I used my hand to fuck her with two fingers again, spearing her hard and fast. When she scraped her teeth down my length, I pulled my fingers out and slapped her pussy hard. She pinkened, her whole body shivering, and I knew she had done it for that exact purpose. So I speared her with three fingers and kept moving. When she came again, clamping around my cock, I swallowed hard and pulled back, knowing I was close.

"Weston," she whispered, falling back onto the bed.

"I want to come inside you, not down that beautiful throat of yours." I crawled over her, my dick wet from her lips and leaving a trail on her stomach as I crushed my mouth to hers. She wrapped her body around me, holding me tight as I just explored her mouth, kissing her as if this was our last moment on earth.

I had missed this so much, this moment, her taste. And I couldn't help but take my time to explore her even though I was so on edge I was ready to rut on her and come in an instant.

While she writhed under me, I reached for my wallet and pulled out a condom.

"I have to have you."

"Then take me. I need you inside me." She cupped my face with her hand, and I moved my mouth to kiss her palm.

"I've got you," I whispered and then I sheathed myself in the condom before sliding deep into her in one stroke.

She let out a shocked gasp as I froze, trying not to come right then and there. She was so soft, and yet tight around me, the heat of her inner walls nearly sending me over the edge.

"Bella," I whispered.

"I need you to move. Move," she ordered.

I leaned down, bit her lip before kissing away the sting, and I moved. I slid in and out of her, slowly at first to watch the way her mouth parted, her cheeks pinking.

Then I looked between us and groaned. I shifted upward slightly, so I was hovering over her even as I fucked her.

"Look at us. Look at the way that your pussy is swallowing my cock. It's begging for me. It's missed me."

Her lips quirked into a smile as she lifted her head up to kiss me softly on the mouth. "I've missed you."

I knew that admission had taken so much from her, so I nodded slightly before taking her lips.

"I've missed you too," I muttered against her mouth, and then there was no more talking. I moved into her, thrust after thrust as she met me with each motion. And finally I rolled to my back, needing to watch her breasts bounce as she rode me. I squeezed one hip with my hand, her breast with my other, and we both moved in motion as if we had been doing this for thousands of years. As if there had been no gap in time.

And then there was no thinking at all, because she was coming again, my name on her lips as I followed her, filling her with everything that I had.

When she collapsed on me, I held her close, my cock still buried balls deep inside her, and I knew I never wanted to let her go.

Even if I probably should.

After, when we could finally breathe, I ran my hands up and down her back, and moved to clean her up and take care of the condom.

When I came back to the bed with a warm washcloth in hand, thankful it was in the bathroom since I didn't know this house, she sat at the edge, rolling her shoulders back. That's when I noticed the bruises on her hip, the red marks that I knew would remain for a few days.

I cursed under my breath. "Fuck. I was too rough. You were hurt and here I am, fucking you hard into the bed and leaving marks."

She frowned up at me before she stood up and wrapped her arms around my hips. "I wanted this. It's-it's what you and I were, but now? It's better. So don't make what just happened wrong."

I cursed, then kissed her hard on the mouth, needing her taste.

"Shh, just let me... You're going to be sore tomorrow." I slid the warm washcloth between her legs, and she gasped. But she was already swollen from my rough attentions, so I was gentle, not sending her near the edge where it would be too much.

"Let me take care of you," I whispered.

"You are, Weston. You are." I wasn't sure what I heard in that. Desire, need. Or weariness. Maybe everything.

Her panties and tights were long gone, but she slid the dress over her body, and I shoved my jeans back on. I hadn't even remembered fully taking them off, but with Isabella, I tended to lose my mind.

My phone buzzed, and I reached down to the ground to pick up his phone and read the screen. It had apparently fallen out of my pocket in our haste.

"Fuck."

"Is something wrong?" Isabella asked, worry in her tone.

"Just things for the prom. I need to pick up a few things that they forgot, and now they have 1,000 worries for this thing. I have no idea what I'm doing. Yes there was a formal and a junior prom, but they weren't like this. Both Sam and Sydney have boyfriends, and there's an argument with one of their friend groups, and I have no idea what I'm doing."

"I can't even imagine. Although, I did have to deal with some of it with Emily and Phoebe. There's not much of an age gap between us like there is with the twins and you, but there was enough of one especially with Dad not around."

I ran my hand up and down her back, knowing there were no words I could say to make that better. Her father, the eldest Cage, was a fucking asshole and there was no taking that back. No fixing it. But it seemed as if the siblings were trying to do that themselves now.

"So what's the emergency?" she asked, looking at my phone.

"Some flower thing. And a lip balm or gloss. I'm not sure."

Isabella snorted and leaned forward. "It's a lipstick and lip stain. And I know exactly where she needs to get that in town. I might be new, but I've already fallen in love with the cute shops."

"Come with me. Tomorrow and tonight. Help."

She blinked up at me, and I hadn't even realized I had said the words. "You want me to help you and the girls with prom?"

"Yes. I really have no idea what I'm doing. I've been playing pretend all these years. And the girls want to meet you."

It was a step. A step I hadn't known I wanted, but it was out there, and there was no taking it back.

"Okay. I mean, I was a teenage girl, and I helped raise my sisters. I can do this."

I swallowed hard. "Damn straight. Better than I can."

"I don't know about that. You're doing a pretty good job from what I hear."

I didn't have an answer to that, so I kissed her softly and was grateful when the phone buzzed again with another prom emergency.

"I guess you really do need my help."

That evening we collected everything we needed for the girls, and while I wanted her to sleep underneath my roof, or me sleep with her, that wasn't the time. The girls needed me, and frankly, I wasn't sure what the hell I was supposed to do. But the next afternoon Isabella showed up complete with snacks, sparkling cider, and a worried expression on her face.

"Okay, am I ready for this?" she asked, and I grinned.

"You're doing damn good. Come on, let's introduce you to the crew. It's just the twins here for now. Their friends will be here later."

"What about Lance?" she asked as I took everything from her. I leaned down and took her lips with mine. There was really no holding back. I moaned against her before she pulled away, her hands over her lips. "I have to look somewhat respectable," she teased.

"Well, I don't," I said with a laugh. "And Lance is down in Denver. He'll be up next weekend. He's on a weird schedule right now."

Nerves settled over her features and she nodded tightly. "Oh good. So it's not everyone at once."

"No it's not. I guess it helps that I've met some of your family. But not all forty."

"I do not have forty siblings. At least I don't think so. Oh my God. What if Dad has like four other secret families out there and I *do* have forty siblings?"

Before I could say anything to that ridiculous and yet could be true question, voices came from upstairs as the twins moved forward.

"You're here. You're here."

Sam and Sydney pushed me out of the way as if I hadn't raised them for the past eight years and threw their arms around Isabella. I was glad that I had taken the food and drinks from her hands, or we could have had an accident.

"Oh. Hi." Isabella met my gaze, and I shrugged, mouthing sorry.

"I'm so glad that you're here. I mean, we can do each other's hair and makeup, but Weston's just not very good at it. And we could have gone over to one of our friend's houses and had their mom's help, but we just wanted it to be family. And well, we're so glad you're here. I'm Sydney by the way, and this is Sam. Yes, we're identical, but we're totally different. I play field hockey, and she plays soccer. We want to hear all about Weston, and we can't wait to hear every juicy detail you have. He's very secretive, and we just need all the details."

"And sometimes she lets me speak too. It's very nice to meet you, Isabella," Sam put in.

"Okay, why don't we let her go, and then we'll figure out what the hell we're doing next."

"You're not supposed to curse," Sydney teased.

"You curse more than I do. So shut the fuck up," I said with a laugh, as Isabella just shook her head.

"It's nice to meet you both. And while I didn't play soccer, I did play field hockey. I hear you got a scholarship."

"Weston told us you played field hockey," Sam said with a smile. "It's okay that you picked Sydney's sport. I'll win you over in other ways."

They talked a mile a minute, taking Isabella away as if this had all been planned for months rather than a few hours.

And Isabella didn't even look behind her in fear or need. Instead she fell right in with the girls, and I followed them, running around the house for whatever they needed.

And by the time their friends and boyfriends showed up, things felt normal. As if we had done this countless times.

I had no idea what to call Isabella, no idea how long she would stay, but in this moment, it felt right. And that worried me. I saw the questioning looks from some of the other parents, and there would be those questions spoken aloud soon. This was a small town after all, and Weston Caldwell bringing a woman to any form of social function was unheard of.

Let alone a Cage.

Let alone the fact that I wanted this to happen again.

Isabella met my gaze before going back to take photos of the twins, and I knew I was well and truly fucked.

Chapter Ten
ISABELLA

A HAND SLID OVER MY MOUTH AND SQUEEZED. I thrashed, trying to get out of their hold. Another arm slid around my waist, locking me to them. I kicked, tried to bite, but it was no use.

"He says hello," a voice whispered but it wasn't a voice I knew. It wasn't William's. But I thought it had to be. Because who else would be there? Who else would be holding me? I kicked out, but it was no use.

And then I blinked, and we were no longer in the garage, but at the hilltop facing the lake. And this time I knew the voice was William's.

"You think you can get away? He never got away. I'll come back for you. I always said I would. Don't you like my letters? You've been waiting for them, haven't you?" he whispered, and I scratched my nails down his face.

But William only laughed, and then it shifted once again and I was holding on to the cliff side, screaming for help.

And familiar blue eyes blinked down at me, but he didn't hold out his arm.

"Dad! Daddy. I need you. Help me!"

"Why would I? You know I have to leave. I always leave." And then he wasn't my father anymore, but Weston. Staring down at me, before he got up off his knees and walked away without a second glance.

My fingers slipped, blood on my skin, a scream ripped from my throat, and then I sat up in bed, sweat soaked and shaking.

I ran my hands over my face, annoyed with myself. "Well, I don't need to go too far into the symbolism of that, do I?" I asked myself before I swung my legs over the side of the bed and forced myself to get up for the day. I glared at the alarm clock since it wasn't even six a.m., but I didn't care. I turned off my alarm on my phone and set out to get ready. I had a few more places to visit today. While Hudson usually got it done for James if James couldn't visit the town, now I was the one in charge. It felt odd to have that part of my family position on top of everything else, and yet it felt right.

Years ago when the town had been founded, it had been by a few families who needed a refuge. There were dozens of small mountain towns within the area. Some that had been for coal mining, others for gold. Cage Lake had been for a few different reasons. Yes minerals, but it also had a large water source that came from the natural tributaries from the mountain peaks. So it was one of the coveted land spots for travelers. The Cages had been one of the founding families, and then it had turned from a small grouping of families into an actual town itself complete with a sheriff, firehouse, and all of the municipalities that a small town could need. It didn't have everything, and some things were shared with other towns, but it was one of the larger ones. Yet still a small town.

So very different from the city. Even though I was a suburb girl, and my job was in downtown Denver, I was still used to highways. Hell, my old job used to be in Centennial, and those high rises were trying to rival Denver, just like Parker was. The area was growing so much that the I25 corridor was all one giant grouping of homes and businesses and city. Cage Lake was different.

And because the Cages owned so many of the properties, they did their best to make sure that they weren't the overbearing landlords who took and didn't give.

From what I was gathering from the town residents, that hadn't always been the case. Dear old Dad had left behind so many broken promises, and not just within our family.

I quickly got in the shower and washed my hair, trying to also wash away that dream.

I still didn't know who that voice was at the beginning. The man who had attacked me. The authorities didn't know, and while I could go back home and try my best to act normal, I wasn't sure what normal was anymore. Yes, I was afraid he was still out there, and frankly I didn't know if it was connected to William at all. William was still situated in Wyoming, far closer to the woman he had attacked brutally. It was odd to think I had gotten off easy, and it made me ill to even say those words. But I had in the end. So I wasn't sure if I was ready to go home. And it didn't have everything to do with William.

No, I had given into temptation. I had taken Weston into my bed, or rather, the guest bed, and I hadn't wanted to let him go.

It had been rough and erotic and everything that had been missing in my life.

And I had no idea what it meant. Because not only had we slept together, but I had also ended up at his house, helping the girls get ready for prom. We had fallen into a situation that others would call a relationship so quickly, and yet, it didn't make any sense.

Because we hadn't spoken. Not really. And now I wasn't sure what the timeline was. Because my time here was finite. I did not live in Cage Lake. I didn't have one of the many homes the Cages owned. I didn't work at any of the businesses that I was speaking to today. My life wasn't here.

And Weston's, once again, was.

I finished showering, and then got out, drying myself with my fluffy towel. Aston only liked the best things, and for that I was grateful. I knew I had to work today, to visit the actual town, but that wasn't all. The other Cages would be joining me today, because tonight was the infamous Cage family dinner. I didn't know exactly who would be showing up, but it was on the spreadsheet, and there would be enough of us. We weren't going to let dear old Dad win. Yes, maybe following his will seemed like he was winning, but in the end that wasn't it. We were not going to let this town down.

I finished getting ready and made my way to Main Street. It wasn't a far drive, but because of the chill in the air and the rocky landscape, I hadn't walked. Some people could easily walk to Main Street and Cage Street, and it was such an interesting concept to me. The town itself called to me in a way I didn't understand. Each block had flower beds and topiaries that were made of native plants that alternated depending on the season. The front facing buildings had an old mountain town feel but were crisp and cream. Each building had its own unique feel, but there was a theme to it all—including art pieces by certain local residents and other artists the Cages brought in. I knew they'd built and decorated the resort on the outside of town to be the same. It was a small town yet inviting for tourists so they could keep the place running.

The first thing I did was walk into Caged Bean and got myself a coffee. The owner grinned at me, and I also went over a few paperwork things with them. There were items that they needed for the building itself, and while that wasn't underneath my authority at all, it felt good to know that they trusted my family to at least look at it. Because I knew that hadn't always been the case with Dad.

Next, I went into Rise and Cage and grinned at two familiar faces. There was an older woman named Melody, and a woman a little younger than me who was the owner and manager of the place.

"Hi Isabella," Harper said, a bright smile on her face. "I see you went to the Caged Bean for coffee, what'd you get?"

I looked down at my latte and felt a little odd. "Am I okay bringing other businesses in here? I realize you guys sell coffee as well." I didn't know if there were any business rivalries or competitiveness going on. This was something I was going to have to learn, even if I didn't plan on living here for long. I didn't want to hurt anyone's feelings.

Melody had gone to the back to work, so Harper just grinned at me. "Oh no. We don't mind. We actually work together. They do more of the lattes and the fun drinks. They even have a flight of flavored themes."

A smile spread over my face. "Blakely was telling me about that."

"I love Blakely. She and Aston are so adorable together."

"It's so odd to think that you guys know everybody so well." I shook my head. "That's not what I'm used to."

"We don't know everybody that well, but I try. Plus, Aston did help me set up the business along with James. And Dorian of course," she added quickly, a blush staining her cheeks.

I didn't question that, and I wasn't sure exactly what was going on there. Though I knew Harper was a few years younger than Dorian. And Dorian was in a serious relationship. Or maybe I was reading too much into it.

"Anyway, it's a caramel brûlée latte with oat milk and some vanilla drizzle thing. But it's as sugar-free as they could possibly make it for me."

"That sounds amazing. I'm going to have to try it.

We do have coffee here, because some people don't need all the fixings, but we are mostly here for the baked goods. That's why it helps that we try to be sister businesses."

"I love it. You guys really know what you're doing."

"Honestly it was James's idea, I think. Or one of the Cages. Once their dad died, they had more freedom to do things like that." Her face paled, leaching of all color, and she put her hand over her mouth. "I'm so sorry."

I smiled and reached across the pastry case, gripping her hand softly. "It's okay. Yes, he was my dad as well. But it's been a while now, and complicated emotions doesn't even begin to describe what I'm feeling. It's okay. I promise."

"I still feel terrible even mentioning it so casually."

"You don't have to. I promise. Now, I have something for you to sign from James. And while most of it could be done electronically, we needed a notary for this."

"Oh, do we need to go to municipal hall to make that happen?" she asked.

I shook my head. "No, like James, I'm a notary. So, we can get things done quickly. And, that cheese Danish with apple filling looks to die for."

"I've got you. Don't worry." We set up our paperwork in one of the corner tables as people walked in and out, and Harper didn't stop moving. She was constantly talking to customers and coming back to sign whatever she could. I didn't mind because I sipped my latte, did a few of my other jobs that I could do in public, and ate the best pastry I'd ever had in my life.

"Did you bake this?" I asked, as I nearly licked the crumbs off the plate.

Harper beamed. "I did. I love baking. And my brother Joshua is the one who really pushed me to do it. He's the best. And that means he and Dorian can have all the food that they want."

The second time she brought up Dorian. Interesting.

"Dorian is my brother's best friend. He is always there to get free baked goods." She rolled her eyes. "I keep trying to get Hudson in more often, but he only shows up to check on me usually."

I laughed softly at that. "Hudson is one of the new brothers that I don't know as well. He seems kind of quiet."

"He is." Something crossed her eyes that I wanted to ask about, but I didn't think it was my place yet. "But you're here now. Do you have any idea how long you're going to stay?" she asked.

It was such an innocent question, but also a kick to the gut. "I'm not sure."

Harper reached out and squeezed my hand. "With the whole small-town thing, we know a little of why you're here. So I know we're keeping an eye out for you, but there are a few rumors about you and Weston."

I grimaced, even as I patted her hand before I let go. "I'm really not used to all of the attention." I gestured toward the rest of the customers who were trying not to stare. They weren't doing a very good job about it.

"We gossip. Sometimes there's only that to do for the day. However, it's out of love. Okay, the watching you because of a jerk is out of love. The whole Weston thing? We have so many questions. But I will be good and not ask them."

"I'm not going to be good, I need to know. How did you get the stoic and quiet Weston to finally fall?" an unfamiliar voice said.

"Tracy, shush," Harper said with a laugh before looking at me. "Ignore her. Seriously, we're just glad you're here." She paused. "And glad that Weston showed up earlier with a smile on his face. A big smile."

I could practically feel the heat radiating off my skin. "And on that note, I should probably get back to work."

"Please don't leave because I'm nosy."

"I'm nosier," Tracy called, and I laughed.

"You guys are adorable. And I am getting used to

this whole small-town thing. Maybe. I do have to get to work though. Plus, my best friend's coming tonight, and I want to make sure her house looks nice."

"Oh, Cage family dinner tonight. Tell Blakely I said hi in case she doesn't have time to come by."

"You guys really do know everything," I grumbled.

And everybody eavesdropping laughed.

I headed back to my car, drove to a few more businesses, and before I made my way back to the house, feeling slightly overwhelmed with all the curious questions and looks, I looked down at my phone and smiled.

> **WESTON:**
> I hear you are making the rounds today. Are they staring at you as much as they're staring at me?

I ignored that little clutch at my belly.

I had no idea what we were to each other, but there was no forgetting our moment. No forgetting everything that had happened. No forgetting him.

> **ME:**
> It is a bit weird. Mostly because I'm not used to it.

And I didn't have any answers.

> **WESTON:**
> I can growl at them if you want.

That brought a smile to my face.

> **ME:**
> Maybe. But I think I like your growls just for me.

> **WESTON:**
> Well, on that note, I now have a hard on at work, and I want to know if your panties are wet.

I squeezed my thighs together, grateful for the tinted windows in my car.

> **ME:**
> I guess you're just going to have to find out later.

> **WESTON:**
> After your damn family dinner.

> **ME:**
> I can hear the grumble in your text. But yes, after the damn family dinner.

I paused, wondering what I was supposed to do now. I wasn't good at this. Though, I'd never truly had a real relationship. I had dated, but Weston had been the closest to anything real. And here we were, in a completely different situation and yet the feelings were complicated around that familiar tension.

> ME:
> I'd say you can come visit for the end of it, but that's a lot of Cages.

> WESTON:
> I know most of them. I might drop by just to get you out of the dragon's den. Depends on the twins.

My heart warmed, and I pressed my lips together, wondering what the hell I was doing. This couldn't last. We weren't in the same place in our lives or geographically. He might not be a father, but he was sure acting like one. The twin girls were in a huge transition part of their lives, so was Lance. And I had no idea what I was doing. I had started a new job and yet I wasn't even there. I was doing so many new things, and I didn't have an anchor.

> WESTON:
> I can hear your mind whirling from here. I'll stop by later.

> ME:
> You need to stop reading my mind so well.

> **WESTON:**
> If I could read your mind, I'd own the universe.
>
> **WESTON:**
> But I'm trying anyway.

We said our goodbyes, and I knew I would always make sure to end a conversation. Because we hadn't before. What an odd thing to be worried about. Because it was true. We hadn't ended our conversation the correct way before. And now it completely changed every interaction I had with him and others in my life.

And now I was being way too philosophical this morning. I made my way back to Aston and Blakely's place, and quickly made myself some lunch, and got back to work.

By the time I was done for the day, I was tired, a little cranky, and nervous.

This wasn't my house, so it wasn't as if I were the one who was playing hostess, and yet, I was here for a reason that still wore on my mind.

The door opened as I was working on dinner, and I grinned at the sound of my best friend's voice.

"Isabella! Where have you been!"

I rolled my eyes at the familiar line from one of our favorite movies and laughed.

"I'm in the kitchen cooking."

"Do we need to be worried about poison?" Dorian asked, and I flipped him off as he walked into the kitchen.

"Nice. Go grab an apron and get to work. I didn't know you were coming."

Dorian practically bounced on his toes as he came over and placed a surprising kiss on my cheek. "I'm here to annoy the hell out of you. Of course. And Joshua needs me to check on Harper. You know, big brother things. Which, I can do to all of you. I enjoy this whole big brother thing."

I blinked at him and tried to do math. Without the family tree in front of me, it took a moment. "But you're not that much older than me."

"A year counts. I'm still the fourth in line."

"And I'm still the old man," Aston said as he came over and wrapped a single arm around my shoulder. It was odd because he had never done it before, but maybe Blakely was wearing on him. Or from the worried look in his eyes, it had everything to do with why I was here in the first place. "You doing okay?"

I shrugged and gestured toward the half-done dinner. "I'm fine. I could use some help in here."

"Oh my God, I cannot believe you just used those words," Blakely said, hand on her chest. "You just asked for help. Maybe Cage Lake does work miracles."

"If we're going to be all happy and chipper in here, I'm going to need a drink," Hudson said as he stomped into the butler's pantry where Aspen had it set up as a bar.

"I counted everybody and realized we had three from one side, and only me from the other."

"I know Sophia's coming, and Tyler's in town, or at least in the state. So hopefully they get here soon so you can get the legal part out of the way."

"From your mouth to the lawyer's ears," Dorian said as he handed me a glass of wine.

"You like Brut, right? Dry?"

I grinned. "I do. Sparkling's my favorite."

"Which always surprised me because I was the one who bounced around like I was on bubbles," Blakely said with a laugh.

The doorbell rang, and Aston frowned.

"I told every single sibling that they can just walk in tonight."

I shook my head. "If it's Sophia or even Kyler, they're not going to do that. We don't just walk into each other's houses."

"You walked into mine before," Blakley added.

I snorted. "Because you were trapped in your closet, and then that one time in that jacket."

"You promised you were never going to talk about that," she said quickly.

Aston gave us a curious look. "I'm going to need all the details. But let me get the door."

"I've got it," Hudson growled as he prowled toward the front of the house.

"I know Hudson has humor and smiles, but is he okay?" I asked softly.

Dorian shrugged. "Not sure. I'm going to come back and visit in a couple of weeks to annoy him. Plus I have a few business opportunities I need to deal with."

"Should I be worried about those business opportunities?" Aston asked dryly.

"Yes. I've decided to work with the mob. The Cages need to be their own Family."

Dorian twirled his invisible mustache, and I rolled my eyes as Kyler, Sophia, and Cale walked into the large open space kitchen.

I dropped what I was doing and ran over to Sophia, hugging her tightly. "I've missed you."

"And I suppose you've missed me too?" Kyler asked with a roll of his eyes.

"She didn't even move for us," Blakley said, shaking her head.

"I'm just her favorite." Sophia fluttered her

eyelashes, before squeezing my hand and lifting them up between us.

Light glanced off something on her ring finger, and I let out a squeal. "Oh my God!"

"What?" Hudson asked as he whirled, and everyone stared at us.

Cale cleared his throat. "I know in some families you're supposed to ask the patriarch, or the eldest, but I am frankly a little confused as to the pecking order of the Cages. And, well, I love Sophia so much I couldn't wait."

"Oh my God, my baby sister's getting married?" I asked and promptly burst into tears. As Sophia hugged me, and everybody looked a little worried, I waved them off. "Stressful day, but I'm really so happy for you. But wow. Wow."

As I met Blakely's gaze, I knew she was thinking what I thought.

That's fast.

Is it too fast?

Probably not. Sophia is finally allowing someone in.

Well, hopefully Aston pops the question soon.

Blakely rolled her eyes, and I just held Sophia's hands. "I'm so happy for you."

"Same," Blakely said as she wrapped her arms around Sophia.

The Cage brothers moved around to say their congratulations, slapping Cale on the back, and I finally found myself in front of my future brother-in-law, and hugged him tightly.

"Are you sure you're ready for us?"

Cale just laughed. "No. But I'm ready for Sophia. I know that it's fast. And some people might question it, but I love Sophia. She is everything that I could ever want. She makes me a better person. And I love seeing her happy. I want to start a life with her. And I don't want to wait."

I was fully crying now as the others spoke, saying that Cale should start writing his vows now. And as conversation turned into wedding planning, and I knew I needed to add my own thoughts, I couldn't help but blindly reach out for my glass of champagne as Dorian filled glasses for everyone else in a toast.

Everybody was growing up and moving on.

And I couldn't help but think what would've happened if I would've known why Weston had left. Would I have gone with him? I wasn't sure of the answer. Because I had been there helping with my family. Starting my career. And I hated to think that Weston might've done the right thing.

"To Sophia and Cale," Aston said softly, breaking

through my thoughts. "And to a man who dares to enter into the world of the Cages."

"I think I can handle you all," Cale said and then paused. "Well, Sophia can help me handle you all."

I grinned, and as I took my sip of champagne, the bubbles playing on my tongue, the doorbell rang again.

"I'll get it," Kyler said as he moved to answer.

"Should we have him answer in case it's a fan girl?" Dorian asked, tilting his head.

"You know, that's actually a good question," Sophia put in, worry etched on her face.

When Hudson whistled through his teeth though, and the hairs on the back of my neck stood on end, I turned, knowing exactly who was there.

Weston Caldwell smiled at me and didn't look the least worried or nervous about standing with so many members of my family.

And I just blinked into those gray eyes, knowing that everything had changed once again. And I didn't have a path.

Chapter Eleven

WESTON

I blamed the twins for my current predicament. There really was no other option. I wasn't sure exactly how I had ended up in this space, in this moment, but there was no escaping it.

The Cage family, not in all its glory as I knew there was more than double to come, stared at me.

I met Hudson's gaze as he whistled through his teeth, and I barely resisted the urge to roll my eyes.

"Weston, bro. You're here." Dorian came forward and hugged me hard, slapping me on the back.

I blinked at him, grateful for cutting the tension. "Sorry to intrude, but I told Bella here that I would come and annoy her."

I winked at her, and she rolled her eyes before coming over to me. She pinched my side, but didn't kiss my cheek or touch me more than that single brush of her fingertips. As I didn't know what we were to each other, nor had we shown any true affection in front of my family, I didn't blame her.

"I thought you meant later. Not while we were making dinner," she said drily.

"The twins kicked me out."

"Twins?" Blakely asked, her voice high-pitched.

We had met before, but only in passing at the coffee house. I had been sort of an ass to Aston then, so I had a feeling Bella was going to have more than a few questions after this dinner. I nearly mouthed the word sorry to her, but frankly, I was going full steam ahead with this. After all, I had brought her over for a large family event at my place, it was only right for me to be on the chopping block here.

Because with the twins and all the other teenagers asking Isabella a thousand questions while their parents looked on in curiosity, it had changed things. Even more so than finally having the woman I'd dreamt of for too long. We'd acted as if it were natural. Yet we hadn't spoken of what it meant.

Not that I wanted to be a man of words.

"My sisters. Sam and Sydney. They just had prom and were appreciative that Bella helped out, so they kicked me out of the house to say thank you."

Bella cleared her throat. "Weston and I knew each other from before. Well, a while ago. It just so happens that he happened to live here. And I just said happened like eight times in that sentence. So ignore me."

Blakely just grinned as Sophia clapped her hands silently, and all of the men glared at me. Okay, maybe it wasn't a glare precisely. But they were studying me as if they had never seen me before. And considering I was best friends with one of them, more than an acquaintance with the other, and had met a third, that was saying something.

"Well I'm glad that Bella here has tons of food. The more the merrier." Dorian squeezed my shoulder, and I glared at him.

"Really?"

"What, does she only go by Bella with you? Oh, I have so many questions. I really should have brought Amy here. I mean, if we're all for bringing dates, oh and fiancés."

A man with light hair and broad shoulders gave me a small wave. "Hi. I'm said fiancé. Of Sophia. It's nice to meet you. And don't worry, my first dinner was even more chaotic."

"He's not wrong." Sophia skipped over to me and beamed. "I know we didn't meet, but I remember you. I have so many questions, and thankfully we have an agenda first for our dinner, and then I can ask them all." She squeezed my hand, and I just looked at Bella.

A man who looked like a harsher version of Hudson with longer hair and a beard raised a brow at me. I knew this man and not just because I had every single one of his albums and the twins had his poster on their wall.

"Kyler."

"Weston."

"I forgot you two had met," Bella said as she shook her head. "I'm not doing this right. Let me introduce you to everyone. Belatedly."

I ran my hand down her back, reassuring her. The act wasn't missed by a single damn person in the room. "It's good to meet you all. Or see you again." I looked over at Aston. "Sorry I was an asshole. I was having a long day."

"That could be said about many days," Hudson said with a grunt.

Dorian staggered back comically. "Did Hudson just joke? Okay, we're going to have to have Weston here at all times. I mean, look what he just did to big brother over here."

"So Hudson's older?" I asked, not knowing why I was wading into the family tree.

"Yes, he and Flynn are twins, and then came me, the

apple of their eyes." Dorian wrapped his arm around Hudson's neck and squeezed.

"More like the apple that fell from the tree and got bruised and a little dented," Hudson mumbled.

Bella's lips twitched, and without thinking I wrapped my arm around her waist.

The motion was not lost on anyone, but Bella persevered. If I was going to be here, I was going to be here. And hopefully not fuck everything up.

"Let's go finish making dinner, I have appetizers ready, but I don't want to burn anything else."

"We've got this. And we can grill Weston so that way Cale gets a break. I mean, Cale's marrying into the family now so you're going to have to be all blissful."

I looked down at the ring on Sophia's finger and smiled. "That's new, right?"

The woman who looked so much like Bella smiled brightly. "Yes. Yesterday. And I'm just so happy."

"Congratulations, man," I said as I held out my hand to Cale. I'd already said something to the like, but I hadn't realized the engagement was so new.

"Thanks. I'm really glad that you're here because I was sweating about this dinner."

"We haven't forgotten about you. She might be my new little sister, but I am ready to grill both of you. We can make it like a game show." Dorian rubbed his hands together, and I narrowed my gaze.

"You forget I've known you longer than some of your newest siblings. I know where the skeletons are."

Dorian waved his hand at me. "I don't have any skeletons."

Aston choked on the rest of his champagne. "Oh, you're not going to say that in this family, are you?"

"I want to know some skeletons. But only the good ones. The happy glowy skeletons," Blakely said, and then she set down her drink. "Apparently one glass of champagne has already gotten to my head."

Bella pulled me into the kitchen with the others, pointedly not looking at me. Did she not want me here? Or was she just nervous. But when she squeezed my hand, I realized that it had to be the latter. Well, I had been just as nervous before the prom, and it wasn't even our prom. We were just going to have to figure this out. Whatever this was.

"I have appetizers ready, but first, family photo for the damn lawyer."

"Can't we photoshop this?" Cale asked.

"We don't ask questions, plus, they can do a surprise visit." Bella rolled her eyes. "We have to tell them when and where the dinners are. It's ridiculous."

"To Dad being an asshole," Dorian said as he held up his drink.

"To the asshole," the others chimed in, and for some reason I was in the photo.

"Are they going to think you're a Cage brother so that way we can just add people on?" Sophia asked, tapping her chin with her finger.

"No, I'm pretty sure they have our photos on some form of murder board in their office, complete with red strings so they know who's who and what we do," Bella said with a roll of her eyes. "Seriously. Eat. And I need help."

I blinked down at her. "Did you just say you need help? Are you really not doing okay?" I reached to touch her forehead, and Blakely burst out into laughter.

"Oh, he really has your number."

"I bet that's not all he has," Hudson mumbled.

I raised a brow at him. "Really, you're sounding more and more like Flynn and Dorian right now."

"This is all just so interesting," Sophia said as she leaned on the breakfast bar, her chin on her fist. "You know them more than we do. I really do want to know all the stories. Did you grow up here?"

I looked at Bella as she handed me a small plate with appetizers on it and nodded. "Yeah. Born and raised. I had a little while down in Denver, and I went to college down there too, but this is where my family is from."

Everybody looked between us, and Bella cleared her throat. "Okay, let's just get it out of the way. Wes and I dated for a little while eight years ago. Then he had to move back for personal reasons, and we're just figuring things out. Please stop asking about future things."

"We were just asking about the past," Aston said pointedly. "But don't worry, I'm not going to be the one that pries. Considering everybody pried into mine and Blakely's relationship." Blakely leaned into Aston and grinned. "And they were relentless. I promise I will be good. Until we're in private, and then I'm going to need all the tea."

"I would like to be there too. Complete with wedding planning." Sophia beamed. "Oh, you have to come to the wedding." She set down her drink. "I mean, if you know you're around, I mean, in town. I'm really going to stop drinking now. But I still would like you to come to the wedding. The more the merrier. We need people on my side of the family because the other Cages outnumber us. Not that it should be other. I love you guys."

"How much did you have to drink, love of my life?" Cale asked as he handed over a water.

"One silly glass, but I'm a lightweight. All those years of dancing."

Everyone began to talk at once, and I leaned over to whisper in Bella's ear. "I'm sorry for getting here so early. But I wanted to be here. After all, you were there for mine."

"It's okay. Seriously. We're a lot to deal with. You should get used to it." She met my gaze, raising a brow.

"I want to get used to it. Even if we're pointedly not talking about the future."

Aston cleared his throat. "You own Caldwell's, right? The auto shop?" he asked, thankfully breaking the tension between Bella and me. We needed to have that talk, but maybe not in front of her entire family.

"I do. My grandfather started it, thanks to the land that they owned. Though we do lease it from you now," I said with a laugh.

"Well, if my father was too much of an asshole for you, I'm sure you could talk to James or Bella here. For any of your needs."

"Really, Aston?" Isabella said with a laugh.

"What? I've never had a younger sister before. And now I have four. This is fun. I get to be the overprotective older brother, and lead with innuendo. It's not just Dorian."

"You really have lightened him up, Blakely," Dorian said with a laugh.

"I do my best. Between my best friend being Isabella and my boyfriend being Aston, it is a lot to handle."

"Hey," they both said at the same time, and I grinned into the beer that Hudson had given me.

"So you're a mechanic," Dorian said.

I blinked at him. "You know this. Why are you acting like you're just getting to know me? You've known me as long as Hudson. Hell, we played summer league soccer together when we were kids."

"I'm just trying to make sure everybody here knows. We don't have a note card on you."

I blinked. "Do you have note cards on everyone else?"

Dorian blushed. "What? Isabella wrote some notes down for me so I would know a few details. I like flashcards."

"And that's how I know he's my brother. Because flashcards are how we get through life," Bella put in, a smile on her face.

"And that part I don't understand," Sophia said with a sigh. "I might own my own business, but I'll never be the color-coded sticky-note person like you."

"You own your own business?" I asked, trying to get the spotlight off me.

Sophia smiled. "I do. I own a dance studio. I used to be a professional dancer, and now I get to teach young minds."

"She's not bragging enough about herself," Cale put in as he played with the ends of her hair. The man looked so far gone in love, it was a little startling. Because I wasn't sure if I looked like that. Or maybe I was afraid I already did. "She was a principal dancer for the Denver Ballet, and decided to retire early so she could work with kids."

"I didn't want to keep breaking my body like other girls. I got to the highest point that I wanted, and when it wasn't as fun as it needed to be anymore, I changed positions."

"You know, we could use a dance studio here," Aston said, a thoughtful expression on his face.

I raised a brow. "In the place behind the flower shop? That could work. There's already enough plumbing to have two small restrooms and dressing areas. Though I don't know what goes into it." Everyone stared at me. "What? When I wasn't working on cars, I was helping with construction in the summers to pay for school. And then my brother did later as well. I forgot what the place used to be, as it keeps changing hands, but if you're looking for a studio, it could work."

"Oh, I'm not sure I'm ready for franchising yet," Sophia said with a laugh.

"We can work numbers," Cale said, and I looked over at him.

"What do you do?"

"I'm boring, and in marketing, but in the end, I think it might be cool to have another Cage business here. I mean, I think you only have what, fifteen, sixteen?"

"We don't count, the Cages are everywhere," I said drily.

"And you love us," Dorian said, and then popped an appetizer in his mouth when everyone stared at him. Because they were purposely not looking at Isabella.

"Anyway, you have a brother, right? And then the twin sisters?" Blakely asked as she looked between us.

I cleared my throat, not sure what everybody else knew. "My parents died around eight years ago. Wet road, deer, bridge." Such a trivial statement for the worst moment in my life. "So I came back to raise the kids here. We could have moved down to Denver, but it was cheaper here, and we had the community. Small towns know how to circle back and ensure everybody has what they need. Lance is working on his MBA now, and the girls go to college in the fall. I have no idea how they're technically adults now. It's scary."

"I'm really sorry about your parents," Sophia said softly.

"Thanks." I wasn't sure what to say, but Bella had her arm around my waist, patting my hip softly. And just like that, I was okay. Because she was touching me in front of her family, just a soft touch, telling me she was there.

I might not know where we were going with this, and it felt like we were going the speed of a bullet train at this point, but I didn't care. It was Isabella Cage Dixon.

A woman I had thought I had left behind.

By the time we finished dinner and worked on desserts, I felt as if I knew the Cages on a different level. Sure I was friends with Hudson and Dorian, but I didn't get to sit with a group of them like this. Sophia was all bright and joy and I knew that some of it was her personality but a lot of it came from the man who looked adoringly at her. He was quieter than the rest of us, even quieter than Hudson sometimes. However, everything he said had meaning. And I liked him. And I didn't often like people right away. However, while Sophia might be Isabella's sister, Blakely was the sister of Bella's heart. You could tell from the way they looked at each other. It was as if they were having a full-on conversation when nobody was looking. Or maybe, while everybody was looking.

It was nice to see that she had had a support system when I had been gone. I didn't know exactly what she had told her best friend after I had left. I had been expecting to face pure hatred, especially from Kyler, but instead, Blakely welcomed me with open arms because I was at Bella's side.

Kyler on the other hand brooded more than Hudson. He had been the quietest of everyone. In fact I'd only heard him say a few words. I knew he was out on tour, so I was surprised to see him here. However, knowing exactly why Bella was in Cage Lake to begin with, it just reminded me that Kyler was trying to be the big brother.

And I didn't blame him. He might be younger, but he was just as protective as the rest of the Cages.

We began to clean up, and I knew it was getting late. I wanted to invite Bella back to my house, considering Blakely and Aston would be sleeping here tonight. I wasn't sure how that would go, but Bella froze as she looked down at her phone.

Alarmed, I moved forward. "What is it?"

She swallowed hard, her hand shaking. "I... I need... I think I need to forward this to someone." She kept stuttering over her words, and I took the phone from her and cursed.

"What the fuck?" Kyler snapped as he looked over my shoulder.

> **UNKNOWN NUMBER:**
> You think you can hide. But I'll find you.
>
> **UNKNOWN NUMBER:**
> You shouldn't have done what you did.
>
> **UNKNOWN NUMBER:**
> Do you miss me?
>
> **UNKNOWN NUMBER:**
> Or did you miss him?
>
> **UNKNOWN NUMBER:**
> You're not looking in the right place. You never were.

"Fuck," I said as Aston took the phone from me.

"I'm going to call her contact with the authorities."

"No, I can do it," Isabella said, rolling her shoulders back. "This is my problem. And I'll handle it."

"Like hell it's your problem," Blakely said before I could. "We're all family in here. And I'm sorry, you don't get to do this alone. So you drink the water that Hudson is now handing you." Hudson was in fact handing her a glass of water. He had moved so quietly, I hadn't noticed. "And then you're going to stay with us, and we're going to take care of you."

"She's coming home with me," I growled, and everyone stared. "I have a state-of-the-art security system thanks to Ford and Hudson over there, and I'm not letting her out of my sight."

"She's safe here too," Aston put in.

"She is standing right here and can handle herself." She looked at me then. "The twins are under your roof too."

"He doesn't know where you are. But I need to know where you are. Okay? Can you do that for me?" I cupped her face, ignoring the looks from others. "I can't find the bastard to end him. To keep you safe. So let me at least keep you protected at my side."

"Smooth," Dorian said before he let out an oof when Kyler elbowed him in the gut.

"I'll be checking your security," Aston put in.

"So will I. And if it's not good enough, I'll get to use the money that I don't need to make it even better. Because nobody hurts my family." Kyler raised a brow. "Except for maybe my family."

Bella snorted then moved forward to wrap her arms around my waist.

She had to be fucking scared if she was showing such vulnerability in front of her family. Or in front of anyone. I ran my hand down her hair and looked at her family, wondering what the hell was I going to do.

Somebody was scaring my woman. And they were going to have to pay for that.

Chapter Twelve
ISABELLA

There hadn't been a single call, text, or letter since the series of texts I'd received while at Aston and Blakely's. I wanted to believe it was behind me. William would stop contacting me and I'd be far away from everything that haunted me. That it had just been a mugger that hadn't stolen anything from me because they hadn't had time. William was still in Wyoming, on parole, and from what his parole officer could tell, hadn't been contacting me. While I didn't want to believe that, maybe it was just all over now.

And even if I let that complicated and not quite real thought slide through me, I didn't know what to believe, but I had other things to focus on.

Namely, the fact I was now waking up in Weston's arms.

In his home.

It had been two weeks since the family dinner that Weston had barged into even though technically, we had each invited him. And things felt completely different.

I didn't spend the night at his house often, in fact this was only the second time. He did spend the night at my house though—though technically it was Aston's home. That wasn't something I wanted to think too hard about at the moment, however. We walked around town together, I worked in his office sometimes, and he even worked on my car in the driveway.

But in the end, I still hadn't returned to Denver. And I wasn't sure when I would.

Emily and Phoebe were taking care of my home and the sad plants I had left there, but it wasn't as if I had left a large group of friends or pets behind.

We weren't that far from the city itself, and I saw Blakely and my family—sans my mother—every week.

But I hadn't returned home.

Aston and Blakely didn't seem to mind that I was still here. If anything, my big brother was acting very much like a big brother, enjoying the fact that he could at least offer me something.

And while the unknown of William and the attack still wore on me, that wasn't the real reason I was here.

No, it was currently the man with his hand on my breast as I lay down, my eyes still closed.

As if Weston had been in my mind, he moaned a bit, pressing his rock-hard erection toward my backside. He was wearing his boxer briefs, and I had on his T-shirt and my own panties, but his hand was underneath that shirt.

He nuzzled his face into my neck, and I held back a giggle, slightly ticklish.

"Weston. The alarm's going to go off any second."

"I bet that we could be pretty quick."

I rolled my eyes even as one hand slid in between my thighs.

"Not that quick," I moaned as my alarm did indeed go off.

Weston groaned, patted my pussy slightly, as if saying goodbye for now, and slid his fingers out from underneath my panties. And because he was Weston, he licked his fingers before rolling onto his back.

I turned to look down at him and winced at the way his erection tented the blankets.

"Don't look at him. He's going to be angry. I knew I should have set an earlier alarm."

I shook my head and turned off my alarm. "You have to get everyone ready for school, and I have a few meetings. Which I'm very grateful that I can do online."

Something crossed his face, and I had to wonder if it was the same thing on mine. How long would this last? This temporary moment before things went back to the way they were. When we weren't in each other's orbits and I had to go back to the place I rented, and the work I had been hired for. Yes, I could do so much of it from here, in fact I could do pretty much all of it, but I didn't live here, and it wasn't as if people were offering me a choice. I rented my place down in Denver, and I had to figure out exactly what that lease would look like next year.

And yet at this moment I was putting the cart before the horse, so I licked my lips and slid my legs over the other side of the bed.

"I'm going to get ready and head out. Do you think I can tiptoe out before the girls wake up?"

He rolled his eyes. "They know you stay here. And I'm pretty sure they're already up."

A door slammed before I could say anything, and I winced. "It's not that I'm trying to hide this, because we can't. But I also don't want to be a poor example."

"You are not a poor example. If anything, you're a woman with a job, a career, and a family you take care of. Sounds like a decent role model to me." He smacked a kiss to my lips as he walked by, then grabbed his things. He headed to the guest bathroom, so I could get ready in his.

He did it without even saying anything. As if taking care of others was just what he did. Yet that was what I did usually. The person who made sure everybody was taken care of. And I felt like I was falling down on my job.

We still had so much to do for Sophia's wedding that was coming up within the month. Because the two hadn't wanted to wait, and their perfect venue that usually had a one-to-two-year wait had a cancellation. So now, we were rolling everything into the small wedding at once. However, because the Cages were showing up in force, it wasn't exactly a small wedding.

Emily was finishing up her master's degree, and working on an internship with another company, so she and I were constantly texting to make sure that she found the company she wanted to work for. I knew that if she asked and applied, she could get any job she wanted with our brothers and myself, and yet, that idea just felt odd. It had felt odd for me even taking the job. But I couldn't be the one to tell my baby sister exactly what to do.

I had a feeling Phoebe would be getting engaged at any moment, and that would be yet another wedding to plan. Not to mention Blakely and Aston. That was only a matter of time.

I quickly showered, getting ready for the day as I thought about all the changes that had happened. My family was growing up, and doing things on their own, all without our mother. And I wanted to feel sad about that, but instead I just felt an emptiness.

At least when it came to her.

I had no idea what I was doing, but for once in my life, maybe giving in was okay. Because Weston was the only man I had ever loved. And I didn't want to go away yet.

I used the blow-dryer one of the girls had let me borrow to finish getting ready before I grabbed my small bag and headed downstairs. Weston hadn't returned, so I assumed he got ready in the bedroom while I was putting on the rest of my makeup because I had an on-screen meeting. The scent of bacon and eggs however, surprised me. I walked downstairs and nearly tripped over my feet as the four Caldwell siblings stood around the kitchen island, each of them getting ready for the day.

I was grateful I hadn't come down in Weston's shirt, but it still felt awkward.

"Oh. Hi. Good morning," I babbled, my cheeks pinkening.

Sydney smiled. "Hi there. Weston told us how you like your coffee, so it's all set for you. We're just finishing up cutting up fruit, and since Lance wanted French toast, he gets to be the one that makes it."

"And I added the almond extract," Sam put in. "It's my favorite touch." She beamed as she said it, and I couldn't help but remember when Emily had done the same thing.

"My sister Emily also adds almond extract. In fact, she loves almond creamer in her coffee, and oat milk. She slowly converted me."

"Good thing I have oat milk then," Weston said softly. He padded toward me in bare feet and pressed a soft kiss to my lips.

I stood there frozen, surprised he was doing this in front of his siblings. He hadn't before. Yes, everyone knew we were sleeping together, and we didn't really have a label for what this was, but he hadn't kissed me like this in front of his family at his house in the morning before school and work.

"Oh. Good morning."

He smiled against my lips. "The bacon's going to burn, I need to get it out of the oven. But sit. You've got time before your meeting."

I stared at him as I looked at his wet hair, worn

jeans, and Caldwell's T-shirt, and shook my head. "You guys don't normally do such a big breakfast."

Sydney shrugged, and Lance didn't say a word, just focused on turning the French toast. "We have finals starting tomorrow, and all of us are really stressed out. So we are having a big breakfast today since we don't have morning period, and Lance doesn't have to be down in the city until later."

Lance finally looked up at me and grinned. He looked so much like Weston, but with slightly blonder hair like the twins.

Weston sighed. "Meaning I don't have to deal with the finals prep tonight or for the rest of the week. Thank God."

"We're still not as bad as you are," Sam put.

"Just wait until you're in college, you'll learn a whole new meaning to studying," Lance said.

I smiled. "I had to change how I went from studying in high school to college because it wasn't just memorizing anymore. I sort of had to teach myself how to study. It wasn't easy. But I kind of liked it."

The man I told myself I would be weary of loving again raised a brow. "You're a nerd, of course you did."

I scowled at him. "Excuse me, I vaguely remember you helping me with some of those flashcards when I was finishing up that night class."

In addition to my degree I had a few specialty classes that I had taken, one had been while I had been dating Weston the first time.

Weston didn't look ashamed to be caught in the least. "Color coding is fun. You should see my office."

"I have," I said, and blushed because the last time we had been in his office, he had bent me over and fucked me from behind. I could still feel him slowly sliding in and out of me, using my panties as a gag so I wouldn't scream too loudly as I came.

He met my gaze, and Lance coughed.

"Oh ew," Sydney said. "You know we could go into that office. Please tell me you haven't had sex anywhere around here either." The young woman held up her hands, and my face heated.

Sam leaned forward and handed me my coffee. "Ignore her. She's just sad because she's not getting any," she teased, and Sydney flipped her off.

"Excuse me, I'm not getting any for a reason. I don't want to date Steve forever. You and Mason though? You guys are totally going to make it."

"I don't want to put that much pressure on us. Neither one of us do," Sam said with the shrug. "But just remember safe sex. I'm not ready to be an auntie," Sam said solemnly, and I nearly choked on my coffee.

"Do you guys always talk so freely about this?" I

asked, then I paused, remembering our dinner conversations around the kitchen island when Mom and Dad hadn't been around. "You know what, never mind. My siblings are the exact same way."

"And now you have a million of them," Sydney put in.

"I do. Well, only eleven." I paused. "I cannot believe I just said *only* eleven."

We dished up our plates, and everything felt so homey, like a family. I wasn't quite sure what I was supposed to do with that, but here I was, feeling oddly comfortable.

I had no idea how that had happened. "What finals do you have this week? All of them?" I asked.

Sam and Sydney looked at each other in that twin way, and I had wondered if Hudson and Flynn had that. It was odd to think that there was a set of twins in my family that I hadn't watched grow up. In fact, I didn't really see those two interact often. They weren't usually at the same family dinners, and I had to wonder if there was a reason for that, or just distance.

I had so many questions about the family I hadn't grown up with, and perhaps moving back down to Denver would let that happen. Although I saw Hudson on a regular basis up here now, I was separated from the others. And I wasn't sure how I felt about that.

"Sadly all of them. Plus we already had to take our major testing for college and everything. It's just weird to take finals and really hope that you pass because you're already planning on going to a certain college," Sydney answered.

"Is there anything you're having trouble with?" I asked.

"A couple of things," Sam answered but my moan interrupted her next statement.

Weston raised a brow and didn't say anything, and I blushed. "Sorry. Lance. This is the best French toast I've ever had. And please don't tell my sister Emily that. Because she would probably hit me."

"I'll just have to give her the recipe when I meet her," he said with a wink, and I had to frown because I realized Lance was actually two years older than Emily.

My sister had still been in high school the first time Weston and I had dated. The twins, babies. Well, ten years old, but that was still so young. I met Weston's gaze, and he gave me a soft smile, still quietly eating as he watched his family talk about finals and upcoming projects and what they were going to do once they moved out.

"So are you still going to keep this big house, big brother?" Sydney asked, and I paused as Weston froze.

"Why wouldn't I? This is home."

"Yes, but you won't need it for all of us all the time now. Now you can go and do what you were going to do before. You're not stuck in Cage Lake if you don't want to be," Sydney blurted.

Then she pressed her lips together as Sam elbowed her in the side, and Lance cringed.

Could Weston move? But it wasn't as if he was on the same track he had been on before. So many years had passed. And he was right, he loved this town. It didn't matter that I was starting to love it too, my home was in Denver. In the city. But were the connections and ropes that had pulled him back here slowly leaving? And if so, would he stay?

"Oh, we have a question," Sam blurted.

I blinked out of my thoughts, wondering why my chest ached. "What is it? How can I help?"

"You're a math whiz, right?"

"I wouldn't call it that, but yes, I love math."

"Do you think you can come over tonight and help us study? Our first final is in Calc Three, and I'm a little worried."

"Sure. I can do that."

"Girls, Bella does have a life you know."

"So, Bella likes us," Sydney said as she preened in her seat. "Sorry, bro, she's with us tonight."

"Yeah, bro," Lance put in. "She's ours."

Lance caught the grape that Weston threw, and I just stared at this family that had pulled together in times of adversity and were closer than ever. And soon the girls and Lance would be fully out of this home, and Weston would be doddering around alone. Did he want that next step? Did he want that family he hadn't been able to have?

My thoughts whirled, and I tried not to think too hard about it.

Because this was just temporary. It had to be. We were once again on two different paths, and worrying about it wasn't going to help anything. Weston reached over and squeezed my knee and winked.

"Stop thinking so hard. You need to use that brain to help the girls pass math. I'm counting on you."

I let out the breath I hadn't realized I'd been holding and nodded.

"Fine. But I'm a stern taskmaster and I expect color-coded flashcards."

"We can do that. We love flashcards," Sam said with a grin.

I quickly ate my breakfast, wondering why I felt as if I was torn between two families. Just like Weston had been before.

And I had to wonder what choice I would make next.

"I TRULY HOPE THEY PASSED. THEY STUDIED SO hard," I said as I sat across the table from Weston. "I have all the faith in the world but you know that doubt monster in my brain can be loud."

"You're sounding more stressed than I am, and these are my little chicks. Though I really don't know what we would have done without you for Calc Three. That was way over my head."

Rachel, our waitress, set our meatloaf and mashed potatoes in front of us, and we nodded our thanks. "You two just let me know if you need anything. And seriously, you two are the cutest. I'm so glad that you're finally venturing out into the town more. We need to get looks at you. I mean, you know we wanted to walk up to Cage Lake to just say hello and be neighborly. But well, we were also trying to give you privacy." She winked as she left, and I just stared open-mouthed at Weston.

"Are they always so open about their gossip?" I asked, my voice low.

"Oh, that wasn't even that bad. You know how many people have come into my garage to check the air in their tires? Just to try to see a glimpse of you, or ask me what's going on between us?"

"You're kidding."

Weston shrugged. "It's home. It's what they do. I bet you if we were down in Denver, your family would be doing the same thing. They just have a little bit of a longer drive."

"That is true," I said as I dug into possibly the best meatloaf I'd ever had in my life.

It was still finals week for the girls, but they had wanted peace and quiet to get studying done. In answer, Weston had taken me out to Cage Free, the local diner that the Cages owned, but it was pretty much left to free rein for the older couple who had first created it. When they had gotten into financial trouble, Aston and the others had stepped in to buy it, but made sure that whatever needed updated was updated, and that if things needed to be organized, they were there. It was truly remarkable how much my brothers had put into this town while trying to erase the past deeds that our dad had done. It wasn't that he had tried to run the town into the ground, he had just tried to make it in his image. The only good thing he had ever done was ensure that certain companies and shady builders couldn't come in and destroy the environment.

And I wasn't sure if that was out of the goodness of his heart or the fact that he was waiting to do it himself later.

Either way, people were starting to treat me as if I

was a Cage, and I wasn't sure how I was supposed to deal with that. It wasn't as if I had built any form of this community. I hadn't even been to the resort. It wasn't that I didn't want to go, but Hudson and James had that place handled enough that I just hadn't been out there yet.

"So, how was your meeting today?" Weston asked.

I blinked up at him. "You knew about that?"

He raised a brow. "Yes. I remember that you had an important meeting today. You have an important meeting most days, but you were nervous today when I left the house."

"Oh. Well, it went well. It was with a company that the Cages are working with. I can't go into too much detail, but it was a lot of numbers."

"You're an accountant. I always assume there's a lot of numbers."

"Yes, but I'm not a tax accountant. You would be surprised how many people think I am in this town."

"Let me guess, people that you don't even know who happen to know who you are asked for tax advice?"

"Exactly," I said as I pointed with my fork. "I'd never met Mr. Ed before, and yet he came right up to me and asked if his boots were allowed to be tax deductible. First, I have no idea, second, why would he know who I am?"

"You're shiny and new in Cage Lake, and yet you've been here long enough now that you're not a tourist. And you're a Cage. People know who you are." He winked. "But I saw you first. Sorry."

"Claiming me, are you?"

He shrugged, taking a drink of his water. I watched his throat work as he swallowed, and the damn man winked at me as he set down his glass. Oh, he knew exactly what he was doing.

"Yes. I am claiming you. Sorry. However, if you think the tax stuff is bad? Think about how many people have asked me to diagnose their car as I'm just trying to have a beer. I mean, I was at Lake Bar a few weeks ago before you got here, and I couldn't even drink in privacy without people coming up and talking about every single little sound they've ever heard in their car."

I snorted. "Well, now that you say that, I think my steering's a little off."

"It's not. I fixed it."

I blinked. "What?"

"Of course I fixed your car. You're driving along these mountains. I'm not going to let you get in a wreck." All thoughts of humor fled from me as I reached out and squeezed his hand. "I'm sorry."

He shook himself, as if brushing it off. "I was just kidding. I did fix it, but it's because I want to."

"Still. I won't make light of it. Promise."

"I was just teasing. I wasn't thinking of my parents until that moment."

"I'm still so sorry. About everything."

"It was a long time ago, and while I miss them every single day, we're okay now. It sucks, but we're okay. One of the hardest parts of that whole thing was leaving you behind though. And well, you're here now. For however long."

We both sat in silence for far too long, the rest of our dinner growing cold. We were doing the one thing we had silently promised we would never do.

Talking about our relationship.

Instead we needed to just live in the moment because I didn't know when those moments would end.

"You know, I've never been to Lake Bar," I said, trying to change the subject.

He raised a brow. "Oh yeah?"

"Yes. Why don't you take me?"

He looked down at my jeans and double tank top with a sweater and shrugged. "You don't look too fancy. Which is good," he said as I glared at him. "You look too fancy, then you're a mark. But I'll take you. Show you the darker side of Cage Lake."

I blinked.

"Is there a darker side of Cage Lake?"

"You'll see."

We paid for our dinners and walked the two blocks down the street to the Lake Bar.

It really was a hole in the wall, a small building with wooden slats strategically placed over the windows. It wasn't fully caved in or downtrodden, in fact I had a feeling that the owners, possibly my brothers, made their best effort to make it look like a dive bar. We walked inside, the floor sticky underneath my boots, and I just smiled.

"This reminds me of that place we went in Arvada. Do you remember that?"

"Oh I do. Though, I'm really grateful that smoking isn't allowed anymore."

I shuddered. "Oh, thank God."

A few people turned our way, but then went back to their own beers, not really caring. There was a pool table and dartboard in the back, and a few people dancing to whatever music was playing. But the centerpiece of the business was a large wooden bar, shiny in some places, dented in others. And it just felt like a good dive bar. Somewhere I hadn't gone in far too long. After all, I was the prim and proper Isabella Cage Dixon. I had a family and siblings to take care of. I didn't do shots and beers at a bar.

"What will you have, Weston, and Ms. Cage?"

I didn't bother to correct him about my real last name, I just looked over at Weston and grinned. "How about a shot of whiskey and whatever local beer you have on tap that would go with it?"

"Well then," Weston said with a laugh. "Make it two. You know what I like."

The bartender whistled through his teeth before he went to pour.

"Whiskey and beer? You're asking for a hangover on a work night, Bella babe."

"Well if we're living in the moment, I'm going to pretend."

"I can do that." He put his hand around the back of my neck, tilted my face up, and crushed my mouth to his.

Somebody whistled beside us, as others clapped, and I just ignored them.

"Just making my claim," he said, though he wasn't looking at me.

I rolled my eyes and gestured toward the drinks the bartender had handed over.

"Thank you," I said with a grin.

"No problem, Ms. Cage. You keep this one on his toes. He needs it."

"That I can do."

I held up my shot. "Ready?"

"Oh, I think I can handle you."

I rolled my eyes, tapped the shot glass to the bar top, and tossed the whiskey back down my throat.

It burned, but it was a good burn, so I swallowed without coughing and licked my lips. Weston had done the same thing. As everybody shouted in cheers, I knew we had done the right thing.

"That was the hottest fucking thing I've ever seen," he said as he leaned forward, whispering in my ear. His warm breath on my neck sent shivers down my spine, and I reached for my beer, needing something to quench my parched throat.

"We'll just have to see about that."

We drank our beers as I laughed with a few of the regulars, getting to know another side of Cage Lake. Nobody here seemed to care that my family owned much of the town and I was still a newcomer. All they cared was that we bought our drinks, didn't make too much of a ruckus, and when Weston pulled me to the back room, I didn't think much of it. But when he closed the door behind us, and put my back to it, I frowned.

"What are you doing?" I asked, my voice low.

"What I've wanted to do since I first saw you tonight." And then he crushed his mouth to mine.

I shivered in his hold, a little drunk, a little warm

from the whiskey, and raked my hands through his hair, before sliding them down his back.

He was on his knees then, my breath coming out in pants as he undid my zipper quickly.

"Weston. We can't. Not here."

"Oh. But we can."

More aroused than I had been at any time in my life, I spread my legs and helped him wiggle my too-tight jeans over my ass. And when he shoved them down past my knees, I held on to the edges of the door.

"We have to be quiet. So quiet," he whispered, as he slid his finger over my panties.

"I don't know if I can be that quiet."

"You will be. If you want to come. Look at you, so swollen. I bet your clit is throbbing, just thinking of me."

"If you don't put your mouth on my pussy right now, I'm going to scream."

"We wouldn't want that, would we?" Then he shoved my panties to the side and feasted. His tongue flattened against my clit, and my knees shook. When he spread me, continuing to eat and lick, I rolled my hips, rubbing myself along his face. I put one hand over my mouth, keeping my moans in, knowing that anybody could walk in at any time. There was no lock on this door. But with Weston's mouth on my pussy, it was hard for me to think.

And when the orgasm came, my toes curled in my boots, and I couldn't breathe. The floor was sticky with old whiskey and beer. The place had old cigarette marks, and gouges from bar fights, and yet all I could think about was coming against Weston's face.

And when he finally stood up, holding me tight, he crushed my mouth to his and I could taste myself on him, tart and sweet.

"I don't have a condom," he growled.

"I'm on birth control and we're both clean," I muttered.

He froze. "I can have you bare?" he asked, his voice guttural.

"Please."

And with that, he kissed me again, and then whirled me to face away from him. Cheek against the door, he shoved my pants down even more, before I heard the sound of a zipper, and then he was inside me. One plunge, one thrust, and I was stretched to the limit.

He put his hand over my mouth, keeping me silenced, as he put his other hand on my hip.

"You feel so fucking good, Bella. I can't breathe."

I couldn't answer him, not with him keeping me silenced, so I rubbed my ass along him, needing him to move.

We both shuddered, and then he was sliding in and

out of me, hard and fast, and I knew anyone outside could hear us. We weren't keeping it quiet. The door banged, and finally his hand slipped, going down to cup my breast, playing with my nipples, and we were both moaning, and when he came, my knees shook, and I followed him, mumbling his name as he leaned against the door, pressing me tightly.

I could feel him warm inside me, seeping between my legs as he pulled out, and I couldn't help but want to keep him there, in all the ways that mattered.

And I knew right then and there, I was in so much fucking trouble.

Chapter Thirteen
WESTON

"Yes Ms. Patty. I promise. I'll make sure I pick that up."

"You do that. And then I want to make sure there's photos. And not just the photos that you're going to put on your social media. Because you know we follow you there."

I held back a groan because I hadn't realized Ms. Patty followed me on social media. Not that I posted anything. In fact, I wasn't sure the last time I had logged in.

"I also want you to make sure that you take good care of Ms. Isabella. Because we love her so much. I'm not going to ask how you feel." Ms. Patty stood there with her hands up, looking innocent as she waited for me to tell her exactly how I felt about Bella. That wasn't going to happen.

"I'll take good care of her." Even though I still didn't know why I was going down to Denver.

"Anyway, we would love her to stay. I know, I know, it's way too soon," Ms. Patty continued.

"Well I don't know about that, kids these days either move too quickly or not quickly enough," Ms. Janice, one of Ms. Patty's friends, said.

"And before you know it, the twins are going to be out and married before you even settle down," Ms. Faith added, and I had to wonder exactly how I had been cornered by these three older women on Main Street. It had been an innocent walk to begin with. I had just needed to pick up a few things at the market before we drove down to Denver for Sophia's wedding. Again, I didn't know how I had been invited, nor how Sydney, Sam, and Lance were also invited. It just snowballed into the fact that the girls had senior week, so instead of going on a random road trip with their friends for the entire time, they did a smaller trip, and now would be going to Bella's sister's wedding. Lance was still finishing up his internship but would join us as well. The entire Caldwell family would be there. Hell, even Joshua and Harper were coming because Dorian had somehow ended up with a plus three. He was bringing his girlfriend, his best friend, and his best friend's sister.

I had a feeling that Ms. Patty and the other women were kind of wondering why they didn't get an invite even though I wasn't even sure they had met Sophia. Yes, Sophia was a Cage just like Bella, but not everyone had been ingrained in the town yet.

I wasn't even sure that Bella was comfortable with the idea of being ingrained.

I pushed that thought away once again, because the more I thought about the future the more I wanted to punch something. Things were going well between Bella and I because we did our best not talking about it.

"Do you know what her plans are once they find that man? Because they will find that man," Ms. Patty asked, and my hands fisted at my sides.

"I don't know anything other than I have to head out and get ready for the wedding. If I'm late, I'm going to have to deal with Bella. And I will blame all of you."

I wasn't exactly lying with that pointed comment, and all three women tittered before Ms. Patty reached out and cupped my cheek. I froze, since the woman didn't tend to touch me.

"You are doing such a good job, Weston. I know we joke, and we prod, but we do adore you. Those girls of yours are bright and shiny, and just true pillars of this community. They are going to go off to college, start new lives, and thrive. And it's because you helped with that foundation. Your parents did so much, and you helped provide the comfort they needed. The same with Lance."

My throat tightened, not wanting this conversation especially when people we knew kept milling about, either listening in or nodding as they said their hellos.

"Ms. Patty's right," Ms. Faith added when Ms. Patty took a step back. "I know Lance had to take time off for a while, but we've loved watching all four of you grow up. And now you're here, going to a wedding with a woman we adore. She was so frightened of all of us when she first got here, and now we see her working at a little table in the café or coming into Cage Italiano just to get a tiramisu and talk with us. She doesn't shy away from us anymore. I hope she stays. Even if it's just to build or buy a home with the other Cages. She makes you smile, Weston."

"She truly does," Ms. Janice put in, and I wanted to be anywhere but here. "We'll stop pressuring you, but we are so proud of you, Weston."

Ms. Patty reached forward and squeezed my hand again, my fist finally relaxing. "We'd like to think of us three as your honorary aunties. Even though you wouldn't want to call us that."

"And we're far too young for that," Ms. Faith added, and my lips twitched.

"Far too young," I added, my voice gruff.

"When the children are off finding their new paths, I hope you know that while Cage Lake is your home and we never want you to leave, you're allowed to follow your heart too."

I stood stunned at Ms. Patty's words as they each said their goodbyes and left me.

Ms. Patty and her husband were pillars of Cage Lake. Her husband was the mayor, and one of the only people not a Cage who held strength and lineage to the community.

They had been there for us when our parents had died, and Ms. Patty had been at the forefront ensuring that I wasn't alone trying to figure out how to braid hair and get Lance off to school. They had always been there for me. Even when I had thought they were too much.

And I wasn't sure what I was supposed to do now.

Was I supposed to leave once the kids left?

That dream was far gone. I wasn't going to be opening up another shop or finding another job in the city. It wasn't eight years ago anymore. I was comfortable here.

But Isabella wasn't here.

I shoved that thought off, because no matter what

happened later, I had to focus on the now. Namely a road trip with my siblings, Bella, and a wedding I still didn't know how I was invited to.

"THIS HOUSE IS AMAZING," SYDNEY SAID AS SHE bounced on her toes before throwing herself at Blakely.

Blakely laughed, hugging Sydney tight before doing the same to Sam.

"I know right? I have to pinch myself every time I look at it. I don't know what Aston was thinking of living here alone. He obviously needed me here." She fluttered her eyelashes at Aston, and the other man just snorted.

"Yes. Because you've added so many decorations and flares to the house. Totally making it your own and adding your style," he replied dryly.

Blakely flushed. "Stop. I'm not that bad. I'll figure out if I want to touch anything and break it later."

Aston gave me a look as he tilted his beer toward me. "She refuses to add her personal touch to anything. As if it's going to hurt the Cage ambience."

"You have great style. I like the house as it is."

"And you should make it yours too."

The two continued on with what had to be a

familiar refrain, and I just stood back as Lance and Bella came back from the hallway.

"I see you guys didn't get lost," I said as Lance just beamed at me.

"No, but I tried to go into the wrong room, but thankfully I didn't use the coat closet instead of the bathroom."

"You should ask Dorian sometime about when he found my bottle of Gavilan, and almost did that exact thing," Aston put in.

"Dorian did that?" Sam asked, her voice far too soft.

I narrowed my gaze. "Hey, watch it."

Sam beamed. "I really just like putting more lovesick into my voice whenever you're around when I talk about Dorian. Because you get all growly."

"I'm going to have to beat that man up now." I sighed. "And he's my friend."

"Who are we beating up?" the man himself asked as he walked into the foyer. We were at Aston and Blakely's house before the wedding, where the twins and Lance would be staying since they had the space and Bella didn't.

In answer to Dorian's question everybody burst out laughing, and he blinked. "What? Is there something on my face?" When we only laughed harder, he waved us off. "Anyway, I'm glad that we could finally get you down into our little area rather than up in the mountains. Though I do love the mountains."

"Cage Lake is quite beautiful," Amy added, and then that's when I realized that Amy, Joshua, and Harper had joined them.

Harper immediately went to Blakely's and Isabella's sides, hugging them tightly. "Are you sure I'm supposed to be here?" Harper asked, looking around the large room.

"I keep asking myself that same question," I murmured.

"Sophia wants you all here. We have the rehearsal tomorrow and the wedding the day after," Bella added. "But she wanted people who made her smile there, and a lot of the dancers she used to dance with really didn't fit that."

"And I suppose she wanted people to outnumber the Cages at some point," I added dryly. Bella grinned at me and I felt like I'd finally done something right.

"Anyway, tonight is the stag party, as well as the bachelorette party, but I realize that it's not a huge event because Cale and Sophia wanted to go small," Aston put in.

"Why do you call it a stag party? We're not in Europe," Dorian said.

"Because I like to annoy you," Aston said with a grin.

Bella laughed at my side, and I wrapped my arm around her waist.

"Should I be worried?" I asked.

"Should I be worried that you're going out into the big city all alone," Sydney said with her eyes wide, making fun of me.

"And just for that, you're grounded," I said dryly.

"I'm an adult now. You can't ground me."

"Graduation isn't here yet."

"Seriously?" Sydney asked, and Sam burst out laughing.

"If you're grounded, then somebody has to stay back and make sure you stay that way."

"Oh, you two are with me this whole weekend." Blakely clapped your hands. "So if somebody's grounded, I'll make sure it happens. As in no extra sprinkles on their mocktail chocolate martini."

"There's sprinkles?" the girls said at the same time, and I shook my head.

"Are you sure you're going to be able to handle them?" I asked Blakely.

"Hey!" Sam exclaimed.

"We have the room here. In a house that I'm not decorating," she said, and Aston rolled his eyes.

"Seriously. The kids each have their own room, and you get privacy with Bella back at her apartment."

"My place is not this nice," Bella added, and I rubbed the small of her back.

"You'll remember that I'm a mechanic. I'd rather stay at your place than get oil somewhere here."

"Dorian is here, you'll be fine."

"Hey," Dorian said, and the twins and Lance burst out laughing.

Somehow everybody was getting along, and blending, and I wasn't sure how to feel about that.

This wasn't my place. Isabella was a Cage now. Would this be how she lived? Yes she had that apartment, but she was staying in that huge fucking house in Cage Lake. And she had the ability to build one of her own. At least that's how I thought the Cages worked.

I didn't know, and everything just felt odd.

Bella gave me a look. "Everything okay?"

"Yeah. It's fine. I was just trying to figure out the plans for the day."

"Well, you and Bella are going to go drop off your things, and then we'll come and pick you up for our guys' stag night thing."

"Okay. That doesn't sound ominous at all."

"I'm just excited I can go out with the adults. No more kid table," Lance said.

"Considering you're older than a sum of our siblings, I would hope not," Dorian said with a shake of his head. "Harper though, sorry hon, you're with the twins."

"Hey," Harper said, and Joshua put his arm around his little sister's shoulders. "See, I like that. Putting her in her place."

"Don't worry, I'll take care of you," Amy added, and I just stood back as everyone spoke at once, and suddenly I was in my car, driving toward Bella's place.

"How did that happen so quickly?" I asked.

"I have no idea. Usually I'm the one that organizes things like this, but Blakely and Aston had this down." She was on her phone, doing a thousand things at once, and I didn't know if it had to do with work, or the wedding that she was planning with Sophia. I didn't know how she could handle that and her job at the same time, and spend so much time with me, but I wasn't going to complain.

Because for some reason it felt like time was quickly running out, and I didn't want to think about that.

"We're here, baby," I whispered, and Bella looked up from her phone and blinked.

"Wow. That was quick."

"I didn't hit as much traffic as I thought."

"You probably will when you guys are doing your

thing tonight. We're heading to a hotel that has a lovely bridal section so we can get ready and have a good time tonight. But I know that you guys should have fun."

"You're talking pretty quickly, why are you nervous?" I asked as I turned off the car.

"This is the first time you're in my home. My real home."

I reached over and slid my thumb over her lips. She let out a deep breath, and I smiled. "I'm glad I'm here, but if we don't get inside your apartment right now, I'm going to fuck you in this car, and I have no idea what your neighbors are going to think."

She blushed, then looked down at her phone. "We don't have much time."

"We have long enough."

Laughing, we grabbed our bags and made our way into her apartment. It was a well-lit area, and I knew that her brothers had added security, as well as her family coming over to water the plants and just take care of it. I also knew that her lease was up soon.

What she was going to do after? I didn't know.

I barely had a chance to look around the inside before the door was closed behind us, and I had my mouth on hers.

I growled, needing her taste, her touch, and when

she slid her hands up my back underneath my shirt, I let out a deep breath.

"I've wanted you this entire fucking day. But our families are everywhere."

"That's what happens when you have big families."

"Well, I'm glad it's just the two of us right now then."

"Same."

I kissed her again and went to take a step, but when I did, something crinkled underneath my foot.

I froze as she looked down, her entire face paling.

"What the hell is that?" I asked as I leaned down and looked at the manila envelope.

"Don't touch it," Bella said, her voice high-pitched.

"What?" I asked, frozen in bending.

"I need—I need to call the cops."

"What the hell, Bella?" I asked, then I stood up, staring down at her.

"I know that handwriting. That's... That's William's."

I cursed under my breath and cupped her face. "I'm not going to let him hurt you."

"I know. I know."

But it didn't sound like she believed me.

"I don't know what the hell this man is thinking, but your brothers and I are going to deal with this."

"The cops can deal with it."

"Like they dealt with it by letting him out early? No fuck that. We're calling the cops, and we're calling your brothers."

"No. Don't tell them tonight. I'm not going to ruin this wedding."

"Are you fucking serious right now?"

"I'll be with people the whole time. I promise. But I can't ruin this wedding. Sophia's been through so much. She deserves this happiness."

"And you deserve to be safe."

"We'll deal with it. We'll tell Aston or someone. But not anyone else, okay? I can't be the center of this. I just need to be normal."

I pulled away, pacing. "I don't want to hide this from your brothers."

"And then what are they going to do?"

"They can keep an eye on you."

"You guys are going out tonight in a group. I'm staying at a hotel with the girls until we both come back here. And tomorrow night I'll be at the hotel for the full night. I won't be alone. We'll call the cops, we'll do everything we have to, but I'm not ruining this wedding."

"You being in danger and being harassed is not

going to ruin this wedding. Sophia will understand. I don't want anything to happen to you."

I can't lose you.

I fucking love you.

But I didn't say the words. How could I say the words. Because I didn't know what was going to happen next. I didn't know where this thing between us would go.

And it scared me to death. But not as much as it scared me that something could happen to her because some asshole was obsessed with her.

"I'll deal with it after the wedding. We'll call the cops now, and we'll deal with it. I don't know what he's playing at, but I'm not going to let him ruin this wedding. I'm not going to let him ruin my life," she spat.

And there was the fire and anger I loved about her. Not the fearfulness that had been in her tone before.

And that was the only reason I nodded. "Fine. We tell Aston, and we tell Blakely." She opened her mouth to object and I shook my head. "Someone else in your group needs to know."

"There's going to be a woman there named Daisy tonight, she's connected to the family and owns a security company. We could tell her."

"Damn straight we will," I said, liking this idea

slightly better. "I don't want the world to touch you, Bella," I said, my voice low, cupping her face.

"I don't want anything to happen either. We'll be safe. He's not here. He's in Wyoming."

"I'd rather just keep you safe in Cage Lake forever," I whispered, not meaning for the words to slip out.

She froze before she took a step back. "We should call them now. Get everything ready. We don't have a lot of time."

And with that she walked to her bag that she had dropped when we had first walked in, and I couldn't help but notice she hadn't remarked on Cage Lake.

And the fact that perhaps she didn't want to stay forever.

And that meant nothing was set in stone, except the fact that somebody wanted to hurt her.

And I would do anything to stop that.

Even if it meant hurting us both in the end.

Chapter Fourteen

ISABELLA

For once, my chest didn't ache when I woke up. I still rubbed my fist over my heart absently and realized that I hadn't needed to. Even with the letter that surely had to have come from William, I hadn't had a panic attack.

I had gone out with the girls for our bachelorette party, with both Daisy, our friend who happened to own a security company, and Blakely looking out for me. But we hadn't let on that there was a worry. Because Sophia deserved the best wedding we could possibly give her. After all, she was the first Cage of our generation to get married. Which sounded surreal to me.

My baby sister was getting married. And from the way that she spoke about Cale, and every time he looked at her, I knew that their love match was something to aspire to. He fit in with my brothers so easily. In fact, I'd been worried that he had been a little too passive since the Cages tended to have big personalities. But instead he listened politely, and quietly added jokes when nobody suspected it. He was just a nice guy who made my sister happy. What more did I need?

"Why are you thinking off in the distance?" Emily asked, and I reached out and patted my sister's hand. It was the night before the wedding, and we were having a calm and soothing evening with just the girls before we headed to our hotel rooms. Most of the wedding party was staying at the hotel that way we could enjoy a little more time together, while people like Weston's family were still staying at their relative's homes. I could have stayed at my apartment with Weston, but as the maid of honor, Sophia had wanted me here.

And now we had champagne, decaf tea, and little cakes and desserts just to unwind for the evening. No male strippers as Dorian had threatened.

"Nothing's wrong," I finally answered Emily. "Honestly I'm just thinking about the fact that we're going to have a married sister soon."

"I'm getting married!" Sophia said as she held up both hands and did a pirouette in the center of the groupings of chairs where we all sat.

I clapped, my chest tightening in a whole different way watching my sister dance.

She had always been so graceful, elegant. With her long neck and longer legs, she was the exact embodiment of a ballerina. She had put her body through hell in order to make that happen, and when she had hit her pinnacle, she had retired. But I knew she routinely danced in her studio to keep in shape—and because she loved dancing.

"Any special dance you have with Cale for the wedding?" I asked.

Sophia waved me off, smiling.

"We're having a small wedding. No group dances." She pointed at Emily and Phoebe. "And no flash mobs."

"That was so ten years ago," Phoebe said pointedly, and she and Emily burst out into laughter.

My mother sat next to Sophia, her eyes on her knitting project as she worked on what was possibly a blanket. I didn't know exactly what she was working on, but I was striving to be a stronger person. I didn't know what my mother had been thinking in lying to us for so long. But all of this hate and resentment wasn't going to get me anywhere. In fact, it just proved to me that leaning into that worry and emotion just added to my stress.

"What are you making, Mom?" Sophia asked, following my gaze.

My mother looked up, her cheeks pinking. "Oh, it's just a blanket."

"It better not be a baby blanket," Sophia said quickly, and I choked on my wine.

"Oh. Really?" I asked, surprised she was the one who brought it up.

Sophia snorted. "Cale and I are getting married quickly because we love each other. And we'd rather spend our money on buying a home and going on a trip rather than a long and tedious wedding. But no, I'm not pregnant. Hence the champagne in my hand." She held it up to the light.

"It could be non-alcoholic for all we know," Blakely said, fluttering her eyelashes. "But it's not like we're going to ask."

"Seriously. If you were pregnant, you could have just told us when you wanted to. It is none of our business until it's time for us to be aunties," Emily said with a grin.

"It's a marriage blanket. And at the rate I'm going, I should be done by the time you get back from your honeymoon."

I swallowed hard, tears pricking my eyelids.

"Really Mom?" Sophia asked as she reached forward and gripped my mother's hand.

"Really. You and Cale are just so happy together,

and it's a tradition in my family, at least with my grandparents, to have a blanket for the marriage bed. And no, it's not for good tidings and luck with babies and fertility," she said with a small laugh as Emily and I gave each other a look. We really didn't want to think about fertility when it came to our mother. However, it seemed that being fertile was not a problem when it came to my parents and even Dad's other wife. And I wasn't going to think about that anymore then I already had.

"My mother never made one for me for obvious reasons. And no, we don't need to talk about that at all. However, I wanted to continue the tradition. So, you don't have to use it or put it near your bedroom. But it'll be for your home."

Sophia's face pinked as tears slid down her cheeks.

"Oh Mom. I love it already. Thank you."

"You're so welcome. You and Cale are going to be happy, and I cannot wait to see what you have in store for the rest of us. Between the dance studio, your new home, and your wedding, you are such a bright light for your future."

Phoebe cleared her throat. "Well, now that I'm crying, does anybody want another glass of champagne?" she asked, moving around quickly. I knew Phoebe would be next, and then most likely Blakely, even though she wasn't technically my sister. But she would be when she married Aston. Everything was coming full circle.

And I wasn't going to let panic attacks that hadn't happened in a while or letters from a man who scared me to no end ruin it.

"Is something wrong?" Blakely asked, muttering under her breath.

"No, why would you think that?" I asked, only partially lying.

"Because I know you better than anyone in this room, even your sisters. What's going on? Beyond that letter."

I looked sharply around the room, afraid someone had heard, but Blakely only squeezed my hand.

"Nothing's wrong. I'm just excited for the wedding."

"I keep thinking about what would happen and what would I say if Aston asked me."

"Really?" I asked, a small smile playing on my face. "He wouldn't just order you?"

Blakely laughed, and I squeezed her hand right back. "He might order, but it's still my choice. And of course I would say yes. I never really thought I would get married."

My brow shot up. "Why?"

"Because I sucked at relationships. However, I realized that those poor dating experiences and exhaustion from them had nothing to do with me, rather than me not picking the right person. And Aston's my right person."

"When do you think he's going to propose?" I asked.

"You know, he is your brother. I could have you ask for me."

"There is not enough champagne in the world for me to ask my brother anything along those lines," I said dryly.

"True. Though maybe I should be the one to propose to him," Blakely teased.

"Please do it. When you're ready, please get down on one knee and just startle him."

Blakely threw her head back and laughed. "As if he would let me get away with that."

"He might," I said softly.

"I don't know, I think he has a plan. He's being secretive, but in a fun way."

"I'm so happy for you. And Phoebe, and Sophia. My family keeps growing."

"If our family continues to grow, we're going to run out of room even at Aston's place," Emily said dryly. "As it is, the new big brothers haven't even been to my apartment. Our immediate family can't even fit in my apartment," she said with a laugh.

"You're just starting out," Mom said, clucking her tongue. "And do not compare yourself to the others. They had a different upbringing." Mom went back to her conversation with one of Sophia's friends, as if she hadn't just dropped another bomb, reminding us of everything that had happened.

I drained my glass of wine, knowing that no matter what happened next, I was going to have to find a way to get along with my mother. Because I loved her, even if I didn't like her in that moment.

"So, what is this I hear you're dating a man from Cage Lake?" my mom asked, and I froze, wondering how on earth she could have heard that. Of course, the rehearsal had been that day so it wasn't as if I had hidden my relationship. But I had barely seen him all day. I'd had wedding things to do, and he had hung out with my brothers. Cale had his own set of friends, so none of them were in the wedding party. But they had taken Weston and his siblings in as their own.

So while I wasn't hiding it, I hadn't come out and said I was dating anyone to my mother.

And we were dating. He was my boyfriend. Which sounded like such a trivial word because I didn't know what I was doing. We had been so good at not talking about labels, that we had foregone the idea of a label altogether. I didn't know where we were going in the future, because it wasn't as if we lived similar lives. They were parallel to the point I wasn't sure when else they could cross.

But panicking like I had in the past wasn't going to help anything, so I let out a slow breath, allowing Blakely's hand on mine to anchor me.

"His name is Weston. We knew each other from before," I said, hoping my voice sounded pleasant, and not as if I was on the verge of another panic attack. Because I wasn't going to be. Damn it.

"And what does he do?" Mom asked, and I wanted to narrow my gaze, wondering exactly why she was asking. It wasn't as if I talked to my mom anymore.

"He owns his own mechanic shop. It's a family business."

My mom studied my face, and I was ready for some judgment. "Caldwell's. He's Weston Caldwell?"

I froze, those in my family going silent as others in the room talked amongst themselves.

"You know Caldwell's?" I asked, my voice pleasant.

Mom set down her knitting and nodded. "Yes. Your father took me to Cage Lake a couple of times. But it was long before Weston would have owned it. I probably met his father then when I had a flat tire."

"You went to Cage Lake. With Dad." I hadn't

known my voice could be so emotionless while anger, despair, and confusion warred beneath the surface.

My mom's eyes tightened. "Yes. Your father and I loved each other very much. And we had five beautiful children from that love. We might not have had our marriage blanket or wedding, but we loved each other, Isabella. Much like I hope you love Weston."

I had wanted to ask her why she wanted to compare us. Why she would allow herself to be the other woman. But I didn't understand my mother. Perhaps she had the relationship she wanted, and it had worked well with Melanie. I didn't know the ins and outs of that. The only thing in this moment that I cared about was her lies. That she had hidden so much from us. But then I looked over at Sophia, at the way she swallowed hard, and I knew I wasn't going to ruin today.

No matter the tightening in my chest that returned.

"Cage Lake is stunning. It's relaxing there. The view of Champagne Peak alone takes your breath away. I've enjoyed staying at your house, Blakely," I said, putting on a smile that I hoped reached my eyes.

My best friend patted my hand and looked over at Sophia. "If you don't want to use one of the rentals, you're welcome to stay at our place too," Blakely said to Sophia. "I know you have your honeymoon coming up, but I know Aston would love everybody to spend more time in Cage Lake."

"I have plans on doing so," Sophia said. "Especially because Dorian gave me a couple of ideas."

"I'm kind of afraid what ideas Dorian would have given you," I said on a laugh.

And soon we moved on to other parts of conversations, and I did not look at my mother again. I would have to find a way to make this work. For our family, and for the tightening in my chest.

But not in the moment.

By the time the evening wore down, and we decided to go to bed slightly early because of the wedding, I said my goodbyes and made my way to my hotel room. As soon as I opened the door, I nearly screamed when I realized there was already someone in there.

Weston held up both hands, his Henley's sleeves pulled up to show off his forearms, his jeans worn and fit to his body. He wore no shoes, and his hair was messy as if he had been running his hands through it over and over repeatedly.

And my heart couldn't stop racing, and it had nothing to do with being scared.

"I texted you. I'm sorry, baby." He moved forward and cupped my face even as the door snicked closed behind me. "I'm sorry."

"No, it's not your fault. You told me you would be here."

He brushed his lips against mine, and just like that, the pressure in my chest eased, and I wrapped my arms around his waist.

"You taste like champagne and strawberries." He brushed his lips against my jaw and bit down gently.

I shivered in his hold, my toes curling in my flats.

"I only had one glass, but it was a very good glass."

"Aston said he was sending along the best." Weston bit along my neck, sending quakes down my spine.

"How was dinner?" I asked. He had gone out to dinner with his siblings, a small vacation for the four of them before their lives changed once again.

"Damn good. That Thai place that Dorian suggested was perfect for us."

"He's really good at that. Though I do know that Theo offered up a spot in his reservations."

I pulled back and blinked. "It is damn hard to get into the Teal Door," I said, speaking of one of my brother's fine dining restaurants.

"I guess it helps to know the family," Weston said with a laugh.

"You should go."

"Not with my siblings. I'll take you though."

A smile crossed my face. "Yes?"

"Yes. Because it'll be fun fucking you with my fingers underneath the table when nobody's watching. A nice fine dining restaurant, when I get to have my fill."

My face heated, and I patted his chest.

"You are terrible."

"That's not what you said the last time I had my face on your pussy."

"Because I like it when I'm riding your face."

"Do you want to do that now?" he asked, and I pressed my thighs together, already wet thinking about it.

"Maybe."

"First though, I have a present."

"Is it your cock?" I asked in my most pleasant voice.

He threw his head back and laughed, then tugged me toward the large, spacious bathroom.

As soon as we walked in, I froze, my heart in my throat.

He had lit tea light candles all around the bathroom, filled the tub with still steaming hot water, with bubbles and rose petals scattered all over.

"Blakely told me when you would be heading over here, so I think I got the water temperature just right."

"You did this for us?" I asked, my voice breathy.

"I did this for you, but I can join if you want. I know you need to relax, baby. It's been a shit show recently, and I figured a hot bath before you have to deal with all of the wedding festivities tomorrow was the way to go."

I turned in his arms, went to my tiptoes, and pressed a kiss to his mouth.

"No one's ever made me a bath like this before."

He scowled. "I didn't before?" he asked, and I knew he was speaking of eight years prior.

"I had a really crappy tub at my old apartment, and there wasn't any space for even me to have a true bath."

"Well I'm glad I'm fixing this now."

"You know, I think there's enough space for you to join me," I whispered.

"If I join you, I'm going to fuck you in that tub. Are you ready for that?"

"Weston, haven't you realized by now that I'm always ready for you?" I asked, and then his lips were on mine, sweet and gentle.

We slowly stripped each other, exploring one another as we did so.

I loved this side of Weston. Yes, he could be rough, grouchy, and overbearing, and I loved that part of him too. The gentle side of him, the one who wanted to ensure that these panic attacks went away and I had someone to lean on, that part scared me.

Because I was falling so head over heels in love with

Weston Caldwell, that I could barely hold on to what was in front of me.

"Oh that's hot," I hissed as I dipped one foot into the tub, then the other. Weston held on to my hand, ensuring I didn't slip, as he followed me into the tub, me with my back to him. His rock-hard erection pressed against me, and I wiggled slightly, unable to keep still.

"You keep doing that, we're going to have a problem before we even start," he said, nipping at my shoulder.

I smiled, leaning against him. "Okay. We could do that."

"First though, we relax."

And so I took him to heart, resting my head against the warmth and sturdiness of his chest, as the water covered my breasts, and he just held me.

When his hands began to lazily draw over my skin, I moaned, my eyes closed as he explored. He traced circles over my nipples, and they pebbled beneath the water. My breath caught, and I leaned into the moment, just allowing myself to breathe.

When his fingers dipped lower, over my stomach, and between my legs, I widened for him, needing him. That was the problem. I always needed this man and Isabella Cage Dixon didn't need anyone. I'd long learned that lesson in order to protect those I loved.

"So eager," he whispered, his warm breath sending

shivers down my spine. "Let's see exactly what we have here." And in that moment, he slowly explored my lower lips before spreading me with two fingers.

"Weston," I panted.

"That's it, take me."

He slid his middle finger inside, the thick digit already stretching me. With one hand on my breast, he rocked into me, nearly sending me over the edge with just one finger.

Then he inserted two fingers, and I let out a shocked gasp.

"How are your fingers so big?"

"And my cock is bigger. I'm going to stretch you, baby. Are you ready for that?"

I swallowed hard, my throat dry. "Always. For you."

"Damn straight."

He kissed the side of my neck, before he moved quickly. Water sloshed over the side of the tub, but I didn't care. Instead he somehow moved me quickly onto the bench on the side of the bath, my back to the window as he went onto his knees in the bathtub and spread my thighs.

"There it is. That's what I've been searching for."

"Seriously?" I asked, leaning my back against the cool glass. It was clouded and tinted so nobody could see inside, but just the thought that somebody could nearly sent me over.

"Let's see exactly where you are," he whispered before he shoved three fingers deep inside me.

I couldn't think, couldn't breathe, as he stretched me wide, exploring my inner walls as he found that bundle of nerves and rubbed. My breath came in pants as my throat tightened, the feel of him inside me taking over. My eyes rolled to the back of my head, as his thumb pressed along my clit, and then I was coming, rocking my hips over his hand as he kept me steady.

"That's a good girl."

And before I could breathe, his mouth was on me, his tongue spearing me. His tongue moved inside me, licking at my inner walls, exploring. I'd never felt that sensation before Weston and hadn't thought it was possible to know the difference between tongue, fingers, and so much more. But Weston was on another level. He lapped at me before rubbing his face along my clit, continuing to explore. I knew I was swollen, tight, and all I could do was lean into him, wanting more.

"There you go. That's my girl."

When I came again, he lapped up every drop of me, and I should have been embarrassed. I was so damn wet you could hear every single slick motion echoing in the bathroom. But I didn't care.

He pulled me up to my feet, the water at my calves, and he kissed me softly. Once again, I could taste myself on him, and I loved it. But what I really wanted was to taste him.

So I went to my knees before he could say anything, more water sloshing over the edge of the tub, and took him into my mouth. He was far too big for me to swallow him whole, so I used two hands at the base of him, squeezing and tightening so I could bob my head. The piercing slid along the roof of my mouth, and I flattened my tongue, taking more of him.

"Bella," he groaned. He wrapped my hair in his fist, keeping me steady as he slowly worked his way in and out of my mouth. "That's it, swallow against me so I go deeper. You're going to take all of me. We've been practicing."

I nodded, his cock deep in my mouth. We *had* been practicing for me to deep throat, so I relaxed, flattening my tongue as he slowly went deeper and deeper until my nose pressed against the root of him, and I gagged. When he pulled out, I took in a deep breath and licked my lips.

"You're so fucking beautiful," he growled.

"More," I said, then I was there, taking him, every inch. I never knew I could do this, but with Weston I felt like I could do anything.

And when he was nearly ready to come, he pulled out and pulled me to my feet.

"I need to be inside you."

"We're going to break our necks in this tub," I said with a laugh.

"Exactly."

We found ourselves against the bathroom counter, and I went to tiptoes on one foot, and lifted my leg to straddle the counter with the other.

We faced the mirror, and I met his gaze as he slammed into me from behind, his hands hard on my hips.

I let out a gasp, but I couldn't think. I just watched his face as he moved in me, fucking me hard from behind, and I wanted more. My breasts bounced, and I couldn't help but move with each motion, knowing at this angle he was deeper than he ever had been before.

He pulled out of me and twisted me around before sitting me on the edge of the counter. "I need you to watch me as I fill you. Look at my cock filling this pussy. Whose pussy is this?" he asked as he slammed into me over and over again, using the motion to emphasize each word.

"Yours. It's your pussy."

"That's my Bella."

He fucked me on the counter, both of us reaching

for one another in a way that we hadn't been before. And when I came again, clamping around him, he groaned my name against my lips as he filled me. He pulled out and pressed his hand to my pussy, keeping his cum inside.

"What does that say about me that you filled with my cum is the hottest thing I've ever seen?"

I bit my lip and looked down between us. "You know, I'm a strong, independent woman. And yes, it's the hottest fucking thing."

He laughed before pulling his hand away and sticking one finger in my mouth. I licked the taste of us before he kissed me again, his hand on the back of my neck.

"I like it when we go soft, when we go this hard, I just like being with you, Bella."

And I held on to him, knowing I wanted more.

Because somehow, I had fallen truly in love with Weston Caldwell.

And I didn't know what he wanted.

Chapter Fifteen
WESTON

Bella thrashed in my arms, and my eyes popped open, my breath coming in pants to match hers.

"Bella. Baby. Wake up. It's just a nightmare. Wake up." She punched out, and I caught her fist, grateful that I had been watching for it.

This wasn't the first time she had punched out in her sleep, but I still held her close, hoping she wouldn't hurt herself. I didn't care if I ended up bruised because of her bad dream, or panic attack, I just cared about her.

"Bella, wake up."

Her eyes shot open, and she sat up, heaving for breath.

"I've got you. I've got you."

"Weston? What happened?"

"You were having a nightmare, and it turned into a panic attack. Let me get you some water."

Her hand shot out and she clutched my forearm, her nails digging in. "No. I'm fine. I just, I haven't had one of those dreams in a while. I'm sorry. Did I wake you?"

I looked toward the darkened window, and then at the alarm clock at the side of the hotel bed. "No. I was dozing in and out since the alarm goes off soon and, no, I never sleep through it if I can help it."

"Did I hurt you?" she asked. We were both sitting up at that moment, and she turned slightly to cup my face. She studied my body, and my cock noticed, standing at attention. With the day that we had planned, he wasn't going to get any attention anytime soon, so he was just going to have to deal with it.

"I'm fine. You didn't hurt me. Are you okay?"

She nodded tightly, and I scowled.

"Don't lie."

"I will be okay. How's that for an answer?"

"I'm not quite sure I believe you."

"I seriously am okay. It was a weird dream that I've had often. But it at least ended a little bit differently."

"The one on the cliff?"

She nodded, and once again I was reminded of how we had met up after so many years apart. Because she had almost died.

She ran her thumb in between my eyebrows, scowling right back at me. "You're going to end up with a permanent wrinkle there."

"I'm a man. It'll be distinguished."

She rolled her eyes. "Yes, and I'm a woman, therefore I'll have to go make sure I add extra face creams and retinols to it."

"It's okay, I'll still like you with whatever wrinkles you get."

I kissed that spot between her eyebrows, knowing that that was as close as I was going to get to telling her I loved her in that moment. It didn't feel like the right time yet. Or maybe I was just being a chicken shit. That seemed more likely.

I wasn't ready to tell her because I didn't have any answers to what it would mean in the end. Just because you loved somebody didn't mean it was going to work out. Hell, I had loved her the first time, and I had been forced to leave.

But now the kids were grown, and the only thing holding me back was my home.

A home that seemed to be telling me that I was allowed to leave it. That's what Ms. Patty and the rest had been saying after all. They might like Bella, but they also kept mentioning the fact that I was going to have an empty house.

And yet I couldn't help but let my mind wander in a million different directions.

And the reason I had had that scowl on my face in the first place.

"I still can't believe you fell off a cliff."

She winced. "Do you realize that I haven't actually told anyone in my family that?"

I froze. "Seriously?"

"I told Blakely because she knows everything. And I was going to tell Kyler one night at a family dinner. But then I told him about William instead, and I glossed over the whole falling off a cliff thing."

"Well, you're not allowed to go hiking alone again."

"I wasn't even hiking. I was walking a paved path to a tourist destination. You know me. I don't hike. It was like that one time I fell down a sand dune and I couldn't get back up without somebody practically dragging me. I don't hike."

My lips twitched at her telling me that story.

"Wasn't it Kyler that dragged you up?"

"Yes, with Sophie doing her best. She was rail thin at that point, and while she was all muscle from dancing, she couldn't really lift me and drag me through the sand. The younger girls just laughed and laughed, and I still haven't forgiven them for that."

"It's okay, if we ever roll down a sand dune, I'll carry you up."

"The way that you can say that so easily tells me you haven't been to a real sand dune."

"I haven't." I pause. "I haven't really seen much outside of Colorado."

"We used to do road trips as a family. Especially when we were younger, and Dad could sometimes come with us. I didn't realize it back then that he was using that time as a way to get away from his original family. I still don't know how he was able to juggle it all. There had to be some people at work that knew about it, because they had covered for him apparently with work trips. Maybe his old team that's no longer there. And the moms knew about it, so that helps. But he came with us on some road trips. And we got to see the U.S. And I've been to a few shows of Kyler's around the country, and when Sophie went on tour, I got to see her in New York, in Chicago. Once in L.A."

"Your family is damn talented."

"I know, right? I was decent at field hockey and can sometimes play piano if I really focus on it, but Kyler's a genius with his guitar, and drums, and just his voice. And Sophia is still a beautiful dancer even though she doesn't do it professionally anymore."

"I'm sad I didn't get to see it."

"I'll show you recordings. And maybe sometime when she does her amateur shows at her dance studio for her older kids, we can go watch. It is quite something."

"Oh yeah? That could be fun."

She had tensed as she said it, but I couldn't help but notice that she was talking about a future. Visiting Denver. That didn't necessarily mean I'd be leaving Cage Lake forever. But I wasn't sure where the two of us were going to end up. Because from what I could tell, this was her first panic attack in a long while. Was it because she was back in Denver? Or because of the stress of the wedding? She had come to Cage Lake for a reason. And when would that reason not be enough for her to stay? I had a lot of thinking to do. As in planning my entire life once I had an empty nest.

"Again, that furrow between your brows..."

"I'm just thinking about the fact that I can't fuck you hard into the bed before the alarm goes off."

She rolled her eyes, and the alarm did indeed go off. She shifted to the side, and I couldn't help but smack her ass. It was right there in my face.

She let out a little yelp and glared at me over her shoulder. "Really?"

"It was right there."

"I'm going to spank your ass next time."

"You're welcome to. But once you do, I'm going to have to fuck your ass. That's just the way it goes."

She froze, and I couldn't believe I'd said that out loud. "You want to?"

"Are you offering?"

"Stop answering my questions with questions."

"I'm game for whatever you want. I like having sex with you, Bella. I love it. I like touching you and just being with you. No matter what happens that's what I like to do."

She turned slightly, leaned forward, and kissed me gently on the lips.

"Let's get through this wedding, and then maybe we'll see if I let you."

"Well, now I know what I'll be thinking about for the entire wedding." I scowled, then looked at my dick.

She winced, and went to pat it, but I held her wrist.

"Don't. Or you're going to be late helping your sister get ready for the wedding."

"And on that note, I'm out." She smacked a kiss to my lips, and I reached for her as she scurried away to go get ready.

With a sigh, I leaned back on the pillows, cradling my head in my hands.

I was in damn trouble, but then again, I knew I would be from the moment I had seen her on that cliff.

The same cliff that I knew had been in that dream of hers. The one that centered around her dad, and William, and the attacker.

I hated the fact that she was still scared. It didn't matter that William was still in Wyoming. He had hurt her. And now he kept harassing her. The cops were handling it. But I didn't know what handling it meant. So that meant I had to be the bigger person and not freak the fuck out.

The shower went on, and I pulled out my phone knowing it would be a few minutes before I got in.

The family text chat had blown up, and my lips twitched.

SAM:
Seriously, this house is amazing.

SYDNEY:
Do you think we can get a walk-in shower like this?

LANCE:
Once you make a million, sure. But you're going to have to marry someone who's handy.

SYDNEY:
I'm handy.

SAM:

And I can learn.

LANCE:

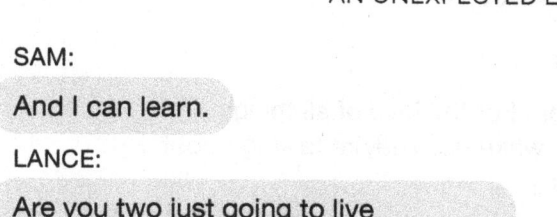

Are you two just going to live together? Twin life forever.

SYDNEY:

If it helps save on a mortgage.

SAM:

Wait, did I say yes to this?

LANCE:

I wonder when big brother's going to wake up.

SYDNEY:

He's with Isabella. Give them time.

SAM:

I really like her.

SYDNEY:

Same. And we wear the same size shoe. That has to mean good things.

SAM:

I also wear the same size shoe as you.

SYDNEY:

But Isabella has better shoes.

SAM:

I'm not going to argue with that.

> **LANCE:**
> Weston. For the love of all things Cage, wake up. They're talking about shoes.

It continued like that for a little while, and I just shook my head before finally answering back.

> **ME:**
> Once again. It is six a.m.

> **SYDNEY:**
> We've been up since five. We're excited for this wedding.

> **LANCE:**
> I still don't know how we got invited, but have you seen the venue? I like to pretend we're living the high life. So don't let Isabella go, okay?"

I rubbed my hand over my chest, trying not to think too hard about that or the fact that Bella was now naked in the shower.

> **SAM:**
> Don't stress him out. We don't want to startle him.

> **SYDNEY:**
> Yes, you just need to hold out your hand flat so that way he'll come to you with what you need very, very quietly.

LANCE:

You're not breaking a horse.

SAM:

You might as well be. He's skittish.

ME:

You know I can see all of these texts, right? You're not in the side group chat.

SYDNEY:

Of course. This way you are forced to listen to us. We like Isabella. Don't let her go. We don't care if we have to move to Denver and all live in a tiny little apartment with you because you've decided to change your entire life. We're in.

LANCE:

Way to just put it right out there, sister.

SAM:

I don't know if a tiny apartment would be good. I'm sure we can pool our resources for something a little bigger. But we're in. Don't let her go. Or the Cages. I really like the Cages. And not just the shoes and this house.

LANCE:

Same, big brother.

ME:

Get out of my love life.

> **SYDNEY:**
> He said love!
>
> **SAM:**
> Love, love, love, love, love.
>
> **LANCE:**
> See what you did? Just tell her you love her already and then we'll make plans. We've got you, bro. It's your time.

And with that, they quit texting, and I knew they had gone off to their own side chat.

I swallowed the hard lump in my throat. It was easy for them to say. They were so willing to uproot their lives and tell me I was allowed to live mine. And maybe it wasn't too much of an uproot since they were all starting over in new phases, but what was I supposed to do? I was a fucking mechanic. Sure, I could maybe start up my own business like I was planning to before everything changed. But it was different now. Everything was different now.

And while Isabella kept mentioning things in the future. Like dinners and weddings. We weren't talking about us.

And she was so damn special. She had this entire life with her family up here. With so many changes between the wedding and the new Cages. Her time in

Cage Lake was temporary. So when would she wake up and realize that it was time for her to move on and leave me behind like I had been forced to do the first time?

The shower went off, and I made sure my phone wasn't on so she couldn't read the texts. Not that Bella would, but I didn't want her to inadvertently realize that the kids were planning my future.

I paused, that startlingly crisp reality hitting. Because graduation was coming up in a week. They weren't kids anymore. They were adults.

Making new decisions and growing up and moving on.

And I was stuck in the same place I had been my entire life.

And I hated the fact that I had just used the word stuck to talk about a town that I actually liked. And loved.

"The bathroom's all yours. You could have come in when I was in the shower. We do know how to restrain ourselves."

I got out of bed and walked naked toward the bathroom. She stood there in a towel, and her gaze went straight to my very hard cock.

"We both know that I can't handle myself when I'm around you."

"And I don't have time to handle that." She pointed to my dick. "But later?"

"Are you telling me I'm getting wedding sex?"

"Maybe. If you're good."

"You don't have to be good. I'll still take you." I leaned forward and took her lips, my dick pressing against her towel. But with Herculean restraint, I pulled away so that way she could get ready, and I started my day knowing I was about to go to a wedding for the sister of the woman that I loved. And I had no idea how the hell I was going to make it throughout the day without her brothers realizing that I loved her.

"That's how all weddings need to be. Short and to the point and right to the party," Dorian said as he lifted his drink to his lips.

I had somehow found myself with every single Cage brother. Before this moment I hadn't even met them all, let alone at once. My siblings were on the dance floor, as were the Cage women, Cale, and a few other guests I didn't know. And all the Cage men had decided to sprawl on the side tables, enjoying their drinks.

"The wedding was pretty nice though."

I looked over at Aston, as Hudson just grunted at my other side.

"Thinking about going next?" Dorian asked.

Aston looked at us but didn't say anything. However, the sly smile on his face told me all that I needed to know.

"Well then," Flynn said after he whistled through his teeth. "Are you going to go simple or big? Knowing Mom, she's going to want you to go big."

Aston just scowled. "You'll notice she wasn't invited to this."

"Because she's not Sophia's mom," James muttered.

"No, Mom has nothing to do with the wedding that may or may not happen," Aston said casually.

"Either way, you're going to have to do a rotation on best men. I mean, Ford's was a little different since it was a poly marriage and they stood for each other, but maybe we can pick a name out of a hat and take turns."

Kyler snorted. "Wait, am I included on your list or should I have been included in my sister's list?" he asked.

"Oh, you're one of us. Sorry," Theo said but paused. "And Luke would be my best man."

James threw a napkin at him. "Seriously?"

"Luke's my best friend. He gets to be my best man.

You know, when somebody finally tackles me down to marry me."

I rolled my eyes, enjoying the way the Cages interacted. Kyler hadn't grown up with them, but they had easily taken him under their wing. I knew he was one of the younger ones, and the most famous person in this room. But nobody seemed to pay that much mind. If anything, people treated him as the younger brother they needed to care for. I wasn't sure that Kyler liked it.

Dorian frowned. "Wait. That means Joshua's my best man. Sorry, everybody."

"You and Amy then?" I asked, and Dorian just shrugged.

"I really like her. But I don't know if we're there yet." Then he gave me a hard look and I winced. "So should we ask you what your intentions are with our little sister?"

"Hey, that's my line, except she's my older sister and we don't use the word *old* in our family," Kyler said as he used his fingers to use air quotes on the word old.

"Seriously though, I have questions," Flynn said as he narrowed his gaze at me.

I opened my mouth to say something, and realized I had no idea what I was supposed to say.

Because I fucking loved her, but because I didn't

have answers for the most analytical woman that I knew, I wasn't about to talk to her brothers about it.

"Why don't you step off his nuts for a second?" Hudson said, surprising me. "Because if we fuck this up for Isabella, she's going to kick our ass. And then one of the Caldwell twins is going to kick our ass because those girls are feisty, and it's going to be a whole thing. Just let them figure it out. And if he fucks up, then we can kick his ass."

I stared at my friend, grateful and a little concerned. "Do you think Sam or Sydney would be the one to kick your ass?" I asked, grateful for the intervention.

"Honestly, you would think it would be Sydney at first, but Sam is a lot more sly," Hudson said with a grin that surprised me because it actually reached his eyes.

"Oh, she's been like that since birth. And when I had to be the one to figure out how to braid their hair and get them braces and all that? Sam might look like the quiet, gentle one sometimes, but then she would scare the hell out of you."

"I do not know how you raised three of them on your own," Aston said with a shake of his head.

"Lance was an adult, sort of, and I wasn't really on my own. I had the town."

"Well, I'm glad to see that the town that we own and

lord over like the oligarchs that we are helped," Dorian said, breaking the odd tension that had settled in.

I snorted. "Oh yes, you guys lorded over us. None of you are the mayor."

"Like we would allow anything to harm Ms. Patty's position as Ms. Mayor," Aston said dryly, and I snorted into my drink as I watched Sophia dance with the love of her life, and Bella dance with Lance.

I loved that woman.

And I wanted this.

And that meant I was going to have to make a change to ensure it happened. And maybe that wasn't expected, but it was everything.

Chapter Sixteen

ISABELLA

Coming back to Cage Lake oddly felt as if part of me was coming home. I wasn't sure exactly what I was supposed to feel about that because this wasn't home. Was it?

"Oh, Isabella. Thank you so much for helping me with my computer," Ruth, one of the caretakers at the local nursery said. I smiled at her as I stood on Main Street, the flower beds on each block blooming with their summer buds and colors. They had decorated the entire main street for graduation. Tonight would be the full-on event, with the small grouping of seniors walking across the stage, with apparently the entire town in attendance to watch. I had gone to a high school with at least eight hundred in my graduating class. There hadn't been enough tickets for an entire family to show up.

Meaning, each student had two tickets. My father hadn't come, he'd been on a work trip. Or perhaps he'd been with the other Cages. I tried not to think about that, but then again, one of my brothers maybe would have graduated that same day and he had chosen them instead. I didn't want to think it hurt anymore, and perhaps it didn't. Because I got my brothers out of the deal, and they weren't that bad.

Cage Lake however was showing up in force, and I felt like a local. Even if I still didn't have my own place. However, most of my things were at Weston's anyway. I didn't want to think too hard about that though.

"You're so welcome, Ruth. You had it down. It's just with the new update, they changed where the function was."

"Why do they have to keep updating things? And then they add these programs to make it seem smarter and all it does is make me feel dumb."

I reached out and squeezed her hand, something I wouldn't normally do. But it just felt right. "Believe me. I understand. And I work with spreadsheets for a living."

"You are just so good at what you do. Not that I know exactly what you do. But when your brother James was here last week to fill out some paperwork with you and Hudson, he just gushed over how much he appreciates you being part of the company."

My cheeks heated, and a small smile played over my face. "He said that, did he?" I shook my head. "He was only here for a couple of hours."

"And I'm pretty sure he went to every business he could, including the resort, just to sing your praises. I have a feeling he wants you to take over Hudson's job. You are much easier to work with than that grumpy cuss."

"I think Hudson would want me to take over that part of his job. Grumpy sort of is his middle name."

"Oh, it didn't take you long to realize that. I'm just so happy that you Cages seem to be getting along. I hate what that despicable man did, and though it's wrong to speak ill of the deceased, I'm still happy that you got to come here. We're just so happy to have you. And you've made Weston just light up from the inside out."

"Now, Ruth, please stop taking all our dear Isabella's time. She has a few things to pick up before we all head to graduation. And it's such a lovely day before it gets too hot in the summers. So why don't we take a walk?"

Ruth patted my hand and giggled at Ms. Patty. "You're right. Look at me, gossiping again. Thank you so much. And I hope to see you soon."

Ms. Patty met my gaze and rolled her eyes before she took Ruth away, leaving me slightly stunned.

She threw so much out there without even thinking, and yet it felt like she was reading my mind.

"Oh, Isabella!" Harper said as she came forward, her hands full of bags from her bakery.

"Oh, Harper, let me help you with that." I reached forward and took a few from her hand, and nearly fell over. "What do you have in here?"

"Every single baked good I could possibly think of," Harper said with a grin. "Joshua was supposed to meet me here to help, but he got stuck in traffic at the Bend." The Bend was the main part of Cage Street that branched off of the highway. It had the only main bridge to get into the area without having to come from one of the other smaller roads. With Aspen Creek River on the west side against the mountains, and the main peak on the east side, Cage Street was really the best way to get into the town. The resort itself was by the main peak, right at the edge of Cage Lake. While it was technically in the town zone, therefore taxes and other incomes could help with the town, it was almost a different town all on its own. I knew that the Cages owned it, but I had never even been there. The town spoke of it like it was one of the multiple towns that fed into each other, but it was like it was a whole different species.

"Anyway, I'm handing these over to the graduation committee, that way they can do what they need to. And then I have to go back to the cafe, set things up for the afternoon off, and then go get ready for the walk."

"I really love how each of you guys are taking time out to be part of this."

We walked over to the admin center that was situated next to the welcome building right when you entered the town on Main Street. There seemed to be a large drop-off for everyone to put their donated or purchased goods and the administrators and committee members would bring it over to the school area. It seemed that they had everything well in hand, very efficient, and had been doing this for years.

The fact that I was starting to learn people's names, and they knew me as well, startled me. I didn't even know all of my neighbors back in my apartment, let alone saying hello to them other than with a small smile. But no, walking down Main Street was an event in itself.

I recognized many people as they were helping with the committee, and there were still a few tourists walking through the streets. I knew some of the businesses would be closed during the graduation time, but others would be catering to the tourists themselves. Such as the gift shops, but all in all, it was starting to feel so familiar I wasn't sure what I was going to do when I went back home.

I ran my hand over my chest not liking that feeling. Because home didn't really feel like a true word anymore.

Because Weston wasn't there. But he hadn't asked me to stay, and we hadn't discussed what would happen next. So I wasn't quite sure what I was supposed to say at all.

A man with a dark beard and wide shoulders bumped into me, and I nearly fell into Harper.

"Sorry," the man grunted as he kept moving, and I blinked.

"Who was that?" I asked Harper, but she shrugged.

"He's one of the off-gridders," Hudson answered, and I jumped, not having realized he was there.

"Where did you come from?"

"I was at the hardware store," he said, pointing across the street. "Don't worry about him though, he is grumpy, but he at least apologized."

"You have off-gridders?" I asked.

"Yes, they live off the grid, down the trail near Hudson's place actually," Harper said with a grin.

"And contrary to what Dorian says, I'm not joining the camp."

"There's a camp?" I asked, convinced I was being played.

"You learn something new every day about Cage Lake, don't you? Don't worry. The camp's nice. They just tend to do things on their own without wanting to deal with people."

"The fact that Jefferson is walking down the street means he's probably headed to the graduation."

I blinked. "Really?"

"Hey, Cage Lake is Cage Lake. You sort of just assimilate." And with that, Hudson went to his truck, leaving me standing there next to Harper.

"I really don't understand him," I said after a moment.

"Nobody does. That's why we love him."

I raised a brow, and Harper blushed.

"Not like that. Plus, Joshua would kill me if I ever dated a Cage. They're off limits."

"You know, if he says that, it only makes it worse."

"I know right? One day I'm going to go on a fake date with one of them and just annoy the hell out of my brother. Because it's fun."

"I used to annoy Kyler just for fun, and now I have more brothers to do so."

"I thought you were the responsible one."

"That's just what she says, but she has a mischievous streak."

I jumped once again at Weston's words and scowled at him. "Really? You couldn't have stomped or something to let me know you were behind me?" I asked, even as my heart raced.

He leaned forward and brushed his lips against mine, and my shoulders eased. "I'm sorry, Bella. I didn't mean to scare you."

"You guys are so sweet. I hate it," Harper said, even as she sighed happily. "Okay, I have to get back to work, alone. Without a man of my own. But it's okay, you go off and be happy and ride into the sunset."

"You know, I do have single brothers," I teased.

"Ooh, like the rock star?" Harper asked, and Weston scowled.

"Joshua would kill them," he said, sounding serious.

"Why am I killing people?"

This time I didn't jump, because I'd seen Joshua walk forward, and Harper just blushed.

"No reason." She dashed off toward the bakery, and Joshua raised a brow.

"Do I want to know?"

"No," I said.

"Not even in the slightest," Weston put in.

Joshua shook his head and followed his sister to the bakery.

I slid my hand into Weston's and smiled up at him. "So. Are you ready to watch the girls graduate?"

Weston cringed. "How are they adults now? It doesn't make any sense."

"It's okay. They're brilliant girls who know what they're doing. They're going to be fine."

"You say that, and yet all I think about is the fact that they're going to be off in college. Living in dorms. Dealing with boys."

"They both have boyfriends."

"Yes," he growled. "I like Mason though. Even though he and Sam are going off to college together."

"And staying in separate dorms. And they're both eighteen. Breathe."

"I do not have to breathe." He paused. "You know what I mean."

My lips twitched. "Whatever you say. You've done a great job with them." My heart stopped, thinking about how scared he must've been all those years ago. Even when he had made a decision that had changed both of our lives forever.

"Sometimes I feel like I've done such a shitty job that nothing makes sense."

"You didn't do a shitty job. Lance is in business

school, and he already has offers for positions at amazing companies, including Cage Enterprises."

"I can't believe Aston just asked him like that at the wedding."

"You know he already had his resume on his desk."

"I swear, Aston, Flynn, and James are like spiders in their own webs, deciding who they can use and help not only the company, but themselves."

"And in a not-so-asshole way like your dad." He paused, and once again it was like a kick to the chest. "Sorry. I didn't mean to bring him up."

"Everybody keeps doing it today. I'm getting used to it I guess."

"Do you want to talk about it?"

There were so many things we needed to talk about, and my father was not one of them. However, I didn't bring that up.

Instead I went to my tiptoes, kissed his chin, and shook my head. "I'm okay. Let's get back to the house. Sam and Sydney wanted to show me what they were wearing."

"It's underneath a huge gown, does it matter?"

"Really? The girls are eighteen and you're still asking these questions."

"I knew it was stupid as soon as the words left my lips."

I grinned and hopped into my car with Weston getting into his truck a few spots down.

We made our way back to his place, and I noticed there were a couple of other cars there. I squinted at them and recognized one as Mason's, Sam's boyfriend, and the other as Steve's, Sydney's.

"They better not be in their bedrooms," Weston growled, and I shook my head.

"They're adults. But let's get inside," I said, imagining exactly what eighteen-year-olds on their own with their boyfriends could do.

Except when we walked in, the shouts reached me first.

"Get out!" Sydney screamed.

"I don't know why you're acting like this. It wasn't like we were going to make it. Fuck, you know the plan. This was always our plan."

"Oh really? Our plan was for you to sleep with Haylee and Kaylee?"

"It wasn't like it was at the same time."

"And that makes it better? So you cheated on me twice?"

"You're a fucking asshole," Sam put in as she stomped right in front of Steve.

"Stay out of this. I swear to God, dating a twin was the worst fucking thing I ever did. It's never just one of you. It's always the both of you. If I do one little thing wrong, I have to deal with two bitches."

"Fuck you," Mason put in as he stepped forward. I should have expected the punch, but I still let out a gasp as Mason's fist connected with Steve's jaw.

Mason, still growing into his height, packed a mean punch as Steve took two steps back, staggering before he nearly fell.

"You're going to pay for that, little dweeb."

"That's enough," Weston snapped as he came forward and gripped Steve by the neck of his shirt.

"Get your hands off of me. You can go to jail for touching me."

"That's the thing, you're an adult. In my house. So why don't you get the fuck out and I'll never see you again. Because if you ever come near one of my sisters or anyone that I care about again, they're not going to be able to find your body."

"Don't you dare threaten me," Steve spat.

I moved forward then, my brow raised.

"You're going to want to be really calm."

"Oh? You're just a fucking Cage. You don't own this town. You're a bastard just like the rest of them."

Weston shook Steve ever so slightly, even as Sam wrapped her arms around Sydney. Tears streamed down both of their faces, and Mason was there, shaking out his fist before he hugged them both as well.

"First off, you're an idiot if you think that it's smart to degrade me or anyone else in this house when Weston has you by the throat."

"He can't touch me."

"I can do whatever the fuck I want. Now, you're going to apologize or I will bury your body."

"You can't do that," he said, but he didn't sound as forceful as he had.

"I am a Cage. And like you said, I own this town. And between my brothers and the Caldwells here, we know a lot of places that nobody's ever going to find you. But you know what the best part is, it's not even the threats of physical force. You're going to the same college that Aston Cage went to. You know, the one that he's on a few boards for?" Steve's entire face paled, and I just smiled. "And, though I'm just a bastard, I also have a few connections with your department. Because you did want to go into that high-end field, didn't you?"

"You can't do anything."

"That's wrong again. I know exactly who your advisor's going to be. And with one call, I can ruin your life forever."

It wasn't that simple, but he didn't know that. He was just some dumbass kid, and I was tired of bullies.

"Fuck you."

"Wrong answer," Weston growled, and I truly saw death on his face.

"Stop it," Sydney said, and she moved forward, mascara running down her cheeks. "The only thing I regret right now is that I didn't wear waterproof mascara," she snapped. "Just get out, Steve. Don't threaten my family, don't say a word. Because if you do, I am better at the gossip network than you ever were. I never want to see your face again."

"You're just a frigid virgin." Then he wrestled out of Weston's hold and practically sped out of the house. I knew that Weston had let go of him, because that was the only way that Steve could have found his way out of that hold.

"I can still kill him for you," Weston said softly.

Sydney raised her chin before wiping her face.

"He wasn't worth it. We were going to break up anyway. We're going to two schools far away, and it only made sense that our lives would diverge. It wasn't going to be forever. He had his life, and I had mine. But apparently if you don't put out in high school, he'll find someone else that will."

"If Weston doesn't murder him, I can. And I learned how to dissolve a body."

We all looked over at Mason, who shrugged innocently. "It was for a school project. Not an actual body, but I learned things."

"You scare me, and I love you," Sam said softly, and Mason beamed as if his whole world was right in front of him.

And at eighteen, maybe that was the case.

"I love you too, boo bear."

"Boo bear?" Sam said with a laugh.

Mason winced. "You won't let me give you a nickname. So I'm trying. Also, my hand really hurts."

"Let me get you some ice." I moved past him before gently kissing his cheek.

He blushed innocently, his glasses practically fogging, and I swallowed hard. I couldn't help but think about Sydney's words. The fact that they were moving far away. That it was never going to work out. That their paths were diverging.

I couldn't help but remember exactly that feeling when Weston had left the first time.

We needed to talk. To figure out what we were doing. Because I wasn't sure I could be as strong as Sydney. Not for the second time in my life.

Pushing those thoughts from my mind, I grabbed the ice and gave it to Mason as both Sam and Sydney took care of him. The twins seemed to be on the same wavelength, not even speaking to each other as they soothed each other's hurts and Mason's as well.

Weston wrapped his arm around my shoulders and sighed. "I'm going to kill him."

Damn it. I loved this man. "You aren't. You've raised two beautiful and strong girls that can handle anything. And one of them has great taste."

"Mason's okay."

"We heard that, and thank you," Sam shouted, and I pressed my lips together, holding back a laugh as Weston just scowled.

"Well then. That's one way to begin graduation day."

"I'm sure there have been worse days out there." I paused. "Not much worse."

I shook my head and went to grab something off the counter when I realized that there was a letter with my name on it on the counter.

"What's this?" I asked, my throat tightening.

"It was from the lawyers. Hudson dropped it off earlier."

"He didn't say anything," I said softly. "Is it from him?"

"It's not from William."

With a shaky hand, I reached out and broke the seal,

wondering why it felt like this was something I should burn.

Isabella,

You were always my favorite. At least of the girls. You always did exactly what I needed you to.

And I will always be grateful for that. But you have to make sure you keep your heart and your choices on the right path.

I made wrong choices over my life, but it was because they were the choices I needed to make at the time.

You are decent at what you do. Mediocre at best. However, I know that you can achieve certain things.

You will always strive to be better than you are, and that is why I never let you be one of the other Cages. The ones that I put in positions of power. Because I knew you would fail.

You were always good at taking care of your siblings. So find a way to be a good mother. A good homemaker.

Because that is what you will be best at.

Loren Cage.

I blinked at the letter, remembering that Aston, Phoebe, and Ford had each gotten one as well. Each with nonsensical rambling words of an asshole who was a narcissistic prick.

"Are you fucking kidding me?" Weston shouted as he moved closer.

I held up my shaking hand, trying to let the rage leave my body. Weston immediately froze, and I wasn't sure how I was supposed to deal or think in this moment. It was as if the man had seen beyond the grave and found the exact moment I had let the doubts of my future seep in. He'd always been good at that and now he'd done it again.

My father had never respected me. Had never truly thought much of me.

He wanted me to be a homemaker. To walk away from the career I had wanted. And to make the choices he had given me. And I wasn't even sure I had the capability to figure out what choices that he had wanted for me versus the ones I wanted for myself.

Because I loved Weston Caldwell. And if that meant defying my father, changing how I focused on my career, and leaning into the man that I loved, then so be it. I just needed to hope to hell that Weston wouldn't leave again. That he loved me back.

And that I wasn't doing this all to spite the father who never loved me at all.

Chapter Seventeen
WESTON

Bella had been quiet ever since her father's letter, and I had no idea what I was supposed to do to make it better. *There was no making this better.* Her father had always been an asshole. Everybody in town had known it, we just hadn't known the full depth of his assholeness until he'd finally died. And with every newly unveiled secret, he just got even worse.

How he could attack Bella from the grave with nearly the exact thing she was worrying about, tore at me. The man had known exactly where to tear her down, highlighting the insecurities she tried to overcome —and the ones that plagued my mind when it came to a future together. Bella had a whole career, a life down in Denver. And I was in love with her. In love with Isabella Cage Dixon.

I was at my kid sister's high school graduation. The ties that bound me here in the first place were slowly leaving. So I could find a way to live in Denver or any of the surrounding suburbs. If Bella wanted to work full-time at Cage Enterprises, I would find a way to make it work.

I wasn't about to let her think that she had to give up one thing for another. Not like I had the first time without talking to her. I wasn't going to make that stupid mistake again.

"Bruh, you paying attention?"

I looked over at Lance, shaking myself and my thoughts "What?"

"It's almost the girls' time. Aren't you going to record this?"

I cursed under my breath and pulled out my phone as the principal called out their names.

"Samantha Robin Caldwell."

Samantha skipped across the stage, tears sliding down her face. However, with the wide grin there, I knew it wasn't about terror like what was running in my veins. She dashed off the stage after smiling and waving and I held up my phone, trying not to let my hands shake in excitement. And then she jumped into Mason's arms since he had been two ahead of her. The crowd cheered, and I rolled my eyes.

"Seriously?" I mumbled.

Bella leaned into me, clapping along with the others. "He punched somebody for her. And though violence is never the answer, she probably thought it was hot."

"Please don't say things like that. Especially because I'm recording this," I said.

Bella let out a laugh. "Oops." And for the first time since the kitchen I saw humor in her gaze. Not the confusion and downright despair that had been etched over her features before.

"Sydney Anastasia Caldwell."

Sydney lifted her chin but had no smile on her face. Instead she prowled across the stage as if she would be queen and these were her subjects. And when she took the diploma from her principal, she finally smiled.

Then she turned to the crowd and held up both hands.

"The Caldwells did it!"

The crowd roared.

This time I truly rolled my eyes.

"I love her," Bella whispered.

Another kick to the gut.

It was so easy to say things like that, the fact that she loved my family.

Well why couldn't I say the damn words that meant everything.

I nearly opened my mouth to say something, but we were drowned out by shouts and calls from other family members. I slid my phone into my pocket and inhaled deeply through my nose.

"We should talk after this."

She looked up at me, startled. "You're right. We do need to talk."

My stomach fell, and I swallowed hard. Was she going to take her father's words to heart? This couldn't be over. We weren't going to let another damn note ruin us.

I somehow made it stoically through the rest of the graduation, but I wanted to be anywhere but there. The girls were going to meet us later, and Lance was headed off with Joshua and Hudson for something. I wasn't sure what they were planning, but all I could do was focus on what I needed to say to Bella.

I was ready to leave. Leave this town that I loved, the people who had somehow become my family.

Because Bella was my future. She was going to be my family.

Only I had no idea if she even wanted that. She had a whole damn life without me. I'd left her once before and I wasn't sure she wanted or *could* take me back beyond what we had. We'd never made any promises, and for all I knew, this was temporary.

She was ready to walk away.

I knew it.

And I could only blame myself.

"You want to go for a walk?" I asked, gesturing toward the edge of the lake. The Cages held most of the property and rented out homes to residents who wanted to live there permanently. So we wouldn't be trespassing no matter where we went.

"Okay. A walk would be good."

She sounded as distracted as I felt, so I squeezed her hand, and we made our way down the path. The trees surrounding us were at full bloom, the allergies scratching my eyes. The lake itself shown bright blue underneath the sunlight, and in the distance the sound of the river winding through the passage filled the canyon.

"We're only a couple of miles from where I first saw you again," I said after a moment, realizing that we were indeed close to the mountain that she had nearly fallen down. It wasn't exactly Champagne Peak, but it had been tall enough to terrify me.

"It seems like so long ago the ground literally gave way under my feet. And yet sometimes it feels like it's constantly doing that."

"I hate how we met again, but I'm glad for it."

"Me too. Really glad for it."

"Bella," I began, not sure what to say.

"I need to go back to the city," she blurted.

I blinked, feeling as though I'd been kicked in the gut, my hands shaking. "What?"

"I've been here for a couple of months now. Far longer than I was planning. And I love it here. I truly do."

"Are you serious?" I whispered, my voice cold.

"I left so many things unsettled at home. I came here to breathe, to try to find my peace. I had had panic attack after a panic attack, especially after the mugging. And I can finally breathe again."

"So just like that, you're going to leave Cage Lake. You're going to leave me."

Her brow furrowed. "No. Not *just* like that."

I wasn't listening. Not really. No, I could only hear the fact she was leaving even while something inside screamed for me to tell her the truth. "I'm glad you're telling me this. So you're not even going to ask me to go with you?"

She took a step back. "That's not what I'm saying at all."

"So you just made this decision? You're going to listen to your dad and you're not even going to talk to me about it?" I knew I needed to stop talking but I just blurted words that didn't make any sense.

"I'm trying to talk to you about it."

I shook my head, bile coating my tongue. "Is this payback? Because I left you with a note? You're at least going to leave me with a kind word? Are you serious? Just like that, you're going to leave?"

"I need to fix a few things. Weston. It's not like that." She fisted her hands at her side, not reaching out. She couldn't touch me. Didn't want to. No wonder she was ready to leave.

"Just go. If all of this was so you could breathe, I'm glad you can. But if there's no reason for you to stay, no reason for you to ask me to go? Then just leave."

Tears filled her eyes, and she took a staggered step back. "That's not what I meant at all. But if you aren't even going to give me the decency to tell you what I was thinking, then fine. Stand in your self-righteousness. But I fucking love you, Weston Caldwell. And I wasn't leaving you."

I blinked, the roaring in my ears intensifying. "You love me?"

"Of course I love you. Or at least I thought I did."

I was a fucking idiot. Why the hell did I have to keep ruining things? "Bella. I'm sorry, I..."

"No. You can stand there, and you can treat me like shit, but I don't have to take it. I'm leaving tonight. I have a few things to take care of."

"Bella."

"No. I'm so angry right now, I can't even listen to you."

And with that, she stormed away, and I realized I had once again made one of the worst mistakes of my life.

I had broken Bella's heart.

Again.

And this time I'd done it on purpose to save myself.

Like a fucking coward.

I STOOD THERE FOR WAY TOO LONG BEFORE THE sound of approaching footsteps made me whirl. A familiar face nearly calmed my heart, but the relief was short lived. "Hudson. You scared the shit out of me."

"You're lucky I don't beat the shit out of you." From the glare in his eyes, I had a feeling that mine and Bella's shouts had echoed over the lake.

"It's not what you think."

"What, that my best friend is an idiot who doesn't realize that if he actually uses his words, he won't be an asshole?"

"That's an odd thing for you to say. Since you never speak," I snapped back.

"No. We're not going to talk about me. You're going to go after Bella and you're going to tell her how you feel. Because if you would have listened to what she said, because the whole fucking lake heard it, you would have heard her saying she needed to fix a few things. Not leave forever."

I opened my mouth, and then closed it again. She hadn't said she was leaving forever. I had just steamrolled right over her. Like her father.

"Oh shit."

"Fucker. You know that she's been working for Cage Enterprises this whole time, right? And she's been taking over the parts of the job that I hate. That I'm not even trained to do. Hell, I got a business degree so I could do some of that shit when I lived at the lake, but it's not my job. Her living here would fix so many things. And maybe if you would just let her speak, you wouldn't be in this predicament."

I knew all this. I knew it. But I'd been too scared to see the truth. I'd been ready to tell her I loved her, but was so fucking afraid she wouldn't love me back that I pushed her away before she could do it first. What the hell was wrong with me? I deserved a punch to the face. Even from my best friend. "I should go after her."

"No shit. I'm only letting you go with a warning once because if you show up to her with a bloody nose and cut lip because I beat the shit out of you, she will be angry with me. And I don't know if you heard this, but the Cage women are feisty. They could take any one of us."

"That's what I hear. I should go."

"Off with you. Don't make me be matchmaker again."

And with that, I ran toward where Bella had gone. We had walked a couple of miles into the forest from the school. And the path she had taken was in the opposite direction, ironically toward Aston and Blakely's home. Although most of her stuff was at my place.

And she hadn't packed that morning. Meaning she didn't have a plan to fully leave.

What the hell was I thinking?

I kept running, annoyed that I wasn't in my work boots, since I had dressed for the damn graduation. But Bella had been in nice flats and not hiking boots, so why was she so far ahead of me?

I finally made it to the edge of the clearing where the long winding driveway to Aston's place was, and saw her standing underneath the sunlight, her face tilted up underneath the fading light. I followed her gaze and realized storm clouds had settled in when I hadn't been looking. A breeze slid through the trees as the first drops of rain began to fall.

"Perfect," I growled, knowing the weather suited my mood.

Bella turned to me. "Go away, Weston. I don't want to talk to you."

"Bella. Please." Thunder cracked, and the rain fell in earnest. In an instant we were both drenched, and I cursed again. "Let's go inside. I've got a key if you don't."

She shook her head, staring at me as if I'd lost my mind. She wasn't wrong. "Of course I have a key. This is my best friend's home. Where I've been staying when I wasn't with you. And of course it's raining now. My dress is going to look ridiculous soon."

It already clung to her, and I could see every single angle of her. But I tore my gaze from her body, and up to her face.

"I'm sorry. I was so damn scared that I was going to mess it up, that I made up a scenario where you were messing it up."

"I wasn't leaving for good, you asshole. You wouldn't let me finish my sentence. My dad used to do that and I hated it. Don't you ever do that to me again, okay? I don't like fighting about things like that."

"So are you going to give me another chance to be an idiot?"

"I told you I love you and you didn't say anything back. You told me to leave."

"I love you so fucking much, Bella. I've loved you for eight years." The wind billowed, throwing more rain in our faces. But I didn't care how drenched we were, or the fact that we were both probably going to catch a cold, I just needed to tell her what I felt.

"I'm sorry. I've spent the past few weeks trying to figure out how I was going to live my life in Denver, to maybe franchise the business or start over in some way. Because the kids are going to be fine on their own, and I can start over there."

"And you didn't even ask?" She shook her head. "But then again, I didn't either. I love this town, Weston. I love the way that everybody seems to care about one another and talk about one another at the same time. I love the fact that I feel more connected to my entire family here than I did when surrounded by them in Denver. I know that it makes no sense and it's far too fast, but I love it here. And I know you just said you love me, but if you're still telling me to go, I will. But across the lake. I'll stay in one of the many homes my family owns, and figure something out. I'll figure out how to breathe and walk next to you in this small town when I can't have you."

"I want you. I want you by my side. I want to walk down Main Street and have Ms. Patty guess what we're thinking. I want the whole town to talk behind our backs about what the hell we're doing. I want Sam and Sydney to tell me they told me so. I'm sorry."

"You can't get scared again. I'm so used to doing everything by myself. From making sure that Phoebe and Emily and Sophia had what they needed. To making sure Kyler didn't go off the deep end because our parents didn't understand what he wanted to do with his life. I've been so worried about trying to make sure that we keep the will the way that it needs to be so we don't lose this town, or my family doesn't lose everything that they've worked for in these past years. But with you I'm not that person. I can just be me. Figuring out what I want, and finally breathing."

"I love you," I whispered as I cupped her face in my hands, the rain slicking down our bodies. "I don't know how to just be Weston. I've been the pseudo dad for so long. And I hate myself for having to leave that first time."

"So you tried to push me away this time. It's not going to work, Weston Caldwell. I'm much bitchier than you."

I threw my head back and laughed before leaning forward and taking her mouth with mine.

She wrapped her arms around my waist, deepened the kiss, and I knew I was a damn fool.

"I don't know what happens next, but I swear, I'm going to tell you things from now on."

"You better. Because I can't read your mind," Bella said with a laugh.

"And I can't even pretend to read yours."

I brushed my lips against hers, needing her, when lightning cracked again.

Only, the sound of thunder didn't echo, instead it was a car engine.

I wrenched my mouth from hers, headlights nearly blinding me, and in the next moments, it was all I could do to shove Bella out of the way.

And then, there was only pain as the car clipped me at the side, and I rolled up to the windshield, then down again. The sound of brakes grinding filled my ears even as I tried to cough, my lungs seemingly not wanting to work.

I lay there underneath the beam of the headlights, trying to crawl toward Bella where I had shoved her to the ground.

Only my gaze and focus went in and out.

Blink. Bella trying to stand.

Blink. A stranger moving forward.

Blink. A scream.

And then nothing.

Chapter Eighteen
ISABELLA

Blood filled my mouth as I slowly opened my eyes and tried to move. I spit out the copper taste, grateful I didn't appear to be bleeding more. At least from that wound. Everything ached. The last thing I remembered was a car coming at us, headlights nearly blinding me, and Weston pushing me to the ground. I had screamed for him, trying to get up from the now muddy side of the road, but then somebody had been standing over me. It wasn't Weston. It couldn't be. Because whoever it was had moved their arm quickly, something slamming into the side of my head.

And now here I was, shaking, trying to figure out what just happened.

"I told you I would find you."

That voice. I knew that voice.

"William," I said through chattering teeth. I blinked, trying to realize where I was, and a sick icy chill slid through me.

When William had knocked me out, he had dragged me deeper into the forest surrounding Cage Lake away from the Cage homes. And now I was tied to a thick tree, rain still sliding down through the canopy, and I couldn't break free. My wet clothes stuck to my body, and I was shaking even though I didn't know if it was from fear, adrenaline, or being so cold.

But I had to get out of this. I needed to get to make sure Weston was okay. Was he alive?

Oh God. Had William killed him?

Everything came into my brain in a split second, one thought after another, as the man in front of me moved from the shadows and smiled.

It was still daylight, the slight light shifting through the leaves, but the cloud cover was enough that it felt like midnight. Or maybe that was just my mind playing tricks on me. I wasn't seeing double, but I had been knocked out. Meaning I probably had a concussion.

I didn't think anything else was broken, but my hands were bound in front of me, the rest of me tied to a damn tree.

And I didn't know how I was going to get out of this.

Nobody knew where we were. It wasn't as if they could hear us.

And I didn't know what I was going to do.

"I'm so glad that you remember me." William smiled at me then, and I tried to figure out who this man was in truth.

I hadn't wanted to date him. I had been polite in rejecting him. But he hadn't agreed with that. Instead, he ignored my pulling away and decided I was for him.

He had slammed my head into a wall, threw me down to the ground, kicked at my side, and nearly broke my jaw. I ended up bruised, cut, and had almost lost my spleen.

Kyler and my sisters had been so worried about me, that they had stayed overnight in the hospital despite being told that they weren't all allowed to stay there. My mother had cried at my bedside, and I had pulled away from all of them, telling them that I was fine. That it was only a few cuts and scrapes and I would be okay.

But I hadn't been.

Nor had the woman that William attacked later before he had been finally caught.

He had done so much worse to that woman. So much worse.

And now he was out of jail. Far away from his parole officer.

And he wasn't going to get out of this. Not this time.

William then stood in front of me and tilted his head. His blond hair was slicked back, wet from the rain. He had on a gray button-down tucked into dark pants. He looked like any parent going to graduation. But he wasn't. He was a monster.

"I'll forgive you for running from me that one time. I know I scared you." He bent down in front of me, and my pulse raced. When he reached out and slid his finger along my jaw I shied away, cringing.

"Don't. Don't look away from me." He gripped my jaw in a fierce hold and forced my gaze to him.

"Don't do this William. Please."

"Oh. You'll beg. But later. For now I just want to know if you read all my letters? Or just the ones that your family let you see?"

"Please. You don't have to do this." The rain finally began to subside, but I couldn't hear anything other than the droplets falling from the tall trees hitting leaf by leaf before they hit the ground beside us.

I wanted to scream, to ask for help, but I had no idea what William would do.

"It took me a while to find you. It shouldn't have really. But your family is a little annoying. You own so many things. And you hid them from me before. I thought you were just a little accountant. A sad woman with a broken heart who needed a firm hand. But it turns out you're some rich bitch who thought you were better than me. But don't worry, I'm going to make sure you know exactly who I am." He tilted his head, studying my face as I tried to work the ropes at my wrist. I would not be a victim. I would not let him hurt me. I needed to get out of this and check on Weston.

While the ropes on my shoulders and chest were tight, my wrists weren't that well done. If I kept his attention on my face maybe I could get my arms outstretched and try to do something. I just didn't know what.

"Now, once I'm done with you, I'm going to find that bitch I left behind in Wyoming and finish what I should have done. But don't worry, she's only scared because she heard what happened to you. You on the other hand I sent a special gift. Did you like my friend?"

I froze, bile filling my throat.

He smiled softly, his eyes darkening. "Oh yes. All I had to do was convince a friend of a friend back in prison to have a little chat with you. He was dumb about it though. He should have waited until the others weren't around. But we weren't aware you had so many brothers. Maybe once I'm done with you and I make sure that bastard on the ground back there is truly dead,

I'll work on those too. You have sisters, don't you?" he asked, grinning.

"Fuck you. Don't you dare hurt them."

"Tut-tut. I would be careful about how you speak to me."

I twisted my wrists, loosening the rope around them, and smashed my fist into his face.

"Screw you."

I thrashed against the ropes binding me to the tree, and somehow they loosened. The man didn't know how to tie knots thankfully, and I wiggled from beneath them, crawling across the ground as I tried to get up.

"You bitch!" he spat as he reached for me. He pulled at my hair, shoving me to the ground. I kicked out, punching.

"You're going to pay for that."

"You are," a low voice growled from the side, and then Weston was there, shoving himself at William.

Relief slammed into me even as horror filled me. Because William had a knife, the one he'd just slid out of his pocket as he tried to shove it into Weston's shoulder.

"She's mine!" William screamed.

"Weston!" I called as I leapt toward the two of them, shoving the man that I loved out of the way. Fiery pain slid across my arm as the knife glanced over my skin, and I let out a shocked gasp before Weston was there again, his leg broken even as he crawled and slammed his fist into William's face. Again. And again.

I kicked the knife away as Weston continued to hit William in the face, in the side, anything to keep him down.

"Don't kill him," I said through choked sobs. "Just don't kill him."

Before I could do anything, to try to stop the bleeding on my arm or blink away the black dots in front of my vision, two other people ran toward us.

I flinched as someone touched my uninjured arm, and realized it was Dorian.

"Isabella," my brother whispered, and then I burst into tears as Dorian tried to stanch the blood on my arm and held me close.

I looked over to see Hudson pinning William to the ground and tying him up with such ease that I had to wonder where he had learned that. But it didn't matter. All that mattered was Weston was still breathing.

"Weston," I whispered as I reached out for him.

He sat there, chest heaving, blood covering his side, his face, his hands, and I was so grateful that he was alive, that the man that I loved was safe, but I couldn't hear his voice in full as I finally succumbed to the darkness threatening my vision and passed out in Dorian's arms.

"You should still be in the hospital," Hudson warned.

I shook my head, immediately regretted the action, and reached out to hold Weston's hand. "I *am* in the hospital. But I'm not leaving Weston's side." I was still in my hospital gown, though no longer attached to an IV. I was still technically admitted, but Hudson had helped me break out of my room to sit by Weston's bed. He was still sleeping after dealing with the doctors and nurses and I had no plans to leave his side.

My brother let out a deep breath. "Fine. But sit down and don't wear yourself out. The family will be in the waiting room soon. You know they'd have been here sooner if there wasn't that logging accident on I70, blocking the highway for a few hours. Not to mention the subsequent brush fires."

I nodded along, knowing Hudson was trying to explain why it was only the two of us when I knew the rest of the Cages would be here en masse.

He patted my shoulder before leaving to talk to

someone, I wasn't sure who as I was only barely listening.

"Weston. I...I love you so much. You saved me. You saved *us*. And I hate that you were hurt. I'm not leaving, Weston. You're mine. I'm sorry about that. Meaning you're going to have to deal with *all* the Cages. And if you think I'm overbearing when it comes to making sure you rest and heal, just wait until you get to know the rest."

"I am pretty sure I can handle them," he whispered, his voice low.

I looked up into those light eyes and finally let the tears fall. "You're awake."

"You should be in bed, Bella."

I snorted even as I moved closer to him. If I wouldn't hurt his broken leg, I'd have gotten into bed next to him, just to feel his warmth. To remind us *both* that we were alive after everything that had happened.

"Everyone keeps telling me that, but I'm sitting down. I'm fine."

"You're not fine, and you're going to get your ass kicked."

I jumped at the sound of Dorian's voice, wincing at the sharp movement to my ribs. Apparently, I wasn't *that* rested. "I'm fine."

He rolled his eyes. "You're not. Neither of you are.

But thankfully it's a small town and we Cages happen to know how to pull strings." He moved to the side and my angry nurse walked into the room.

"Ms. Cage Dixon. You *will* get into the second bed in this room and rest. We'll move all of your information and items here. And if you don't rest, I have been told I can stick the others on you to make that happen."

Weston let out a rough chuckle and I just blinked as the twins poured into the room, Lance and the sheriff on their tail. "Seems like we have a full house."

"Yes, we do and now you're going to have to deal while we take care of you," Sam said with a tight nod, her eyes filled with tears.

I opened my arms and both twins moved toward me, hugging me softly as to not hurt me. "We're okay, girls."

"I see where I stand," Weston grumbled next to me, but I saw Lance and the sheriff go to his side.

Before the girls could respond, the nurses and their teams moved me to the empty bed in the room since there was only so much space in the small hospital that serviced multiple small towns—including Cage Lake.

"We'll take care of what we can here," Sheriff Brothers said after we were all settled. "I'll be talking to you both soon, but for now, just rest."

"That's exactly what they'll be doing," Aston

ordered as he came into the small room, Blakely pushing past him to run toward me.

"Isabella!"

Tears fell in earnest as she took me in her arms, the twins holding us both. And somehow the room continued to fill with Cages and friends. I knew the hospital staff wasn't happy, but right then, I didn't care. I held out my arm, grateful they'd pushed the beds together enough so I could reach for the man I loved. Weston held my hand, and I met his gaze.

"I love you," he mouthed, and I swallowed hard.

"I love you too," I whispered back.

The others spoke around us, discussing the next family dinner, after graduation plans, and upcoming Cage family builds and businesses. And when my mother arrived, my heart nearly burst. But I didn't say anything I would regret. Instead I let my mother hold me. Then watched as she spoke kindly with the twins and my siblings. The Caldwells had lost their caring and loving parents and there was no coming back from those broken bonds.

While my father was gone and I knew I would never truly find the peace he never let us have, I could move on from what he'd done and try to find forgiveness for the woman who had raised me under a life I never understood. Perhaps it would never be my place, but in the end, I'd nearly lost everything I loved, and I wasn't sure I could stand to hold on to the pain to lose it again.

"Did someone say baked goods?" Harper asked, pulling me out of my thoughts as she and her brother walked into the very cramped room.

"Oh thank the sugar gods," Dorian exclaimed as he helped gather bags of food and pastries from the siblings.

"We also brought burgers, fries, and nothing healthy," Joshua explained. "We also bribed the staff to let us come back, but apparently Dorian here had already used his Cage charm to make that happen."

Weston squeezed my hand and I sat back, watching my family blend with Weston's and the town of Cage Lake.

I didn't know what would happen next or how we'd get through the next few weeks, but I knew we wouldn't do it alone. They were my family—unexpected, large, rambunctious, and full of trouble.

And I knew I'd found my place.

As a Cage. And as Weston's.

Just like he was mine.

Chapter Nineteen
WESTON

"Welcome to another Cage family dinner, this time in stereo."

I raised a brow at Dorian's words and shook my head from my spot on the couch.

In the month since our world had shifted, some things remained the same while other things were vastly different.

Now I sat in Aston and Blakely's home down in Denver, my booted leg on a pillowed ottoman, with the woman I loved sitting at my side.

When I slept, I could still hear Bella scream for me, could still feel the impact of the car against my leg.

We all had been damn lucky that William had slowed down around the curve in the rain and the only thing I had broken was my leg. It could have been anything else, including my neck. But I did my best not to think too hard on that. When I had finally woken up from the first impact, I had crawled my way toward William's voice. I would never be able to get the sight of Bella tied to a tree and fighting for her life out of my mind. Though, I knew that she had similar nightmares. For all that work we had done against her panic attacks in Cage Lake, we were right back to where we started and yet completely different. Because William was behind bars and would be for a hell of a long time. Now it was two counts of attempted murder in addition to his stalking charges and breaking his parole. There would be no more William in our lives, and for that I could be grateful.

However, I just truly wished none of that had happened.

"Are we taking a photo for the lawyer?" Emily asked as she walked into the large living room, a platter in her hand. Phoebe and Ford were right behind her, more platters in their hands.

We had a full house today, and I was still surprised that everybody could fit inside these walls.

"Yes, everyone move in closer for the photo," Dorian ordered, holding up his phone.

"Do you think if all of us are in this one, it can count

for like two or three dinners?" Flynn asked as he pushed James and Theo into the room.

"I'm pretty sure the will doesn't work that way, but I can ask," Bella said from my side, and I leaned over to kiss her temple.

"I honestly don't mind coming to dinner because people cook for me. I'm lazy like that."

The woman I loved rolled her eyes. "Yes, because we totally need more food with the number of casseroles we have at home in Cage Lake."

My heart swelled at that comment because she said home.

We didn't have everything worked out yet, but we were working on it. Because Bella would be working remotely full-time. She would go down into the city if she needed to for certain things, but now she would be the full-time forensic accountant for Cage Enterprises because she would be able to do things from our home or in an office that she could have on Main Street if she needed space. And she was also the go-between for the businesses in town and Cage Enterprises.

All in all, it was working out, and I still couldn't quite believe our luck. Not that being run over by a car and attacked by a psychopath was lucky, but I was doing my best not to think too hard about certain things. It only made the stress of nearly losing her too much.

"Everybody say cheese!" Dorian said as he snapped the photo, and I leaned into Bella. "I'll send this over to the lawyer, and then we can actually eat and not have to deal with this crap."

"Tell me how you really feel, brother of mine," Sophia said as she kissed his cheek, and then went to sit on her husband's lap. They had come back from their honeymoon early, everybody worried about Bella and me. And somehow in a matter of moments, we were all closer than ever.

The twins had been distraught, and Lance was still having issues leaving town. He wanted to keep an eye on us, however, we were all doing okay. Or at least as okay as we could be while dealing with everything that had happened.

"So what are we having for dinner?" Dorian asked, grinning.

"Italian. Tons of different kinds of Italian because I think we're past the point of having just one lasagna," Bella said at my side.

"And I did not help because apparently when I'm in the kitchen, even though I'm allowed to put some weight on my boot, I get yelled at," I said with a laugh.

"Damn straight you get yelled at," Bella said as she pinched my thigh gently.

"You're the one who had stitches in your arm. Don't get me started."

I swallowed hard, remembering the sight of all that blood, and kissed her gently on the mouth.

"You two are disgustingly sweet. We get it, you both love each other. But will you please stop making out in public?"

"I think it's sweet," Amy said as she wrapped her arms around Dorian's waist. "You don't want to make out with me in public?" she asked, fluttering her eyelashes.

"Well, if you insist." Then Dorian dipped Amy into a deep kiss, and I rolled my eyes.

"Don't worry, bro, you'll be able to do this once the cast and boot come off."

"You know, we could probably find a way to break his leg. Just to annoy him," Bella said with a laugh.

"Oh, I can probably make that happen," Kyler drawled as he walked into the room.

"Kyler. You're back." Bella left me and ran across the room to go hug her brother. Kyler had been able to come to Cage Lake and check on us after the attack but had been forced to go on tour once again. I knew Kyler hadn't been happy about it, but we had all understood. Life had to go on. Hell, I was still working at my shop, and we all had jobs to do. Kyler's just took him out of the country.

"I couldn't miss the Cage family dinner." He had cleared his throat. "And I brought a guest."

I raised a brow, expecting a date, and froze when I realized it was Constance.

"Mom," Bella breathed before she hugged her mother tightly. The other siblings came over to hug their mother, and I met Hudson's gaze.

When Constance had heard about the attack, she had dropped everything and returned to the small town she swore she would never go back to. And she had sat by her daughter's side until they had run out of room with all of the Cages there.

I knew the family still had a long road to go in acceptance, but in the end, there was really only one person to blame.

Their father, the original Cage.

But he was gone, and this family was rising from the ashes. One complicated connection at a time.

While everybody moved around to start serving themselves for dinner, having a thousand different discussions at once, Hudson came to my side.

"You ready to get that boot off?" he asked, gesturing toward my leg.

"Still have a little while to go. I probably would have healed quicker, but I'd put too much weight on it."

"I'm just glad that Dorian and I were showing up to annoy the hell out of you." He shook his head. "I would like to think that you guys would've been okay on your own, but I'm glad we were there."

I swallowed hard, doing my best not to let the worst case scenarios slide through my mind for the umpteenth time. There was no use dwelling on what I couldn't change. After all, we had a hell of a lot more to think of and focus on when it came to our families and future. And that's all I wanted to deal with for the moment.

The group of us took two different rooms in order to fit all of us for dinner, and I found myself beside Bella and Emily. Cale and Sophia were across from us, both of them whispering to each other and looking so damn in love it was a little sickening.

"How are you feeling?" Bella asked as she gripped my hand.

I threaded my fingers with hers and leaned down to kiss her temple. "I'm good. It just always surprises me that I'm here. With all of you."

"This isn't what our life was even a year ago. But I don't think I would know what to do with myself without all of these annoying brothers."

"I heard that," Dorian said as he went back to his conversation with Flynn.

"Are you sure you're okay coming up to Cage Lake? We can find a way to make it work here."

Bella gave me an odd look before reaching forward to push my hair back from my face. "I love that small town. I love those people, and I love the fact that your siblings are going to have a home to come back to. And it's not like I will ever run out of siblings to come and visit and stay with."

"That is true, you will always have us to deal with," Flynn said with a sly wink.

"I really did get outnumbered quite quickly."

"And I was the one outnumbered by Caldwells up in the mountains. So you're just going to have to deal with it."

"You two are adorable," Constance put in.

I smiled at Bella's mom before leaning down and capturing Bella's lips again. "I love you. Just in case I haven't said it recently."

"You said it like ten minutes ago, but I don't mind hearing it too," Emily said with a laugh.

Ignoring how the others laughed at our sentimental expense, I tilted my head to kiss Bella again.

"You guys are ridiculous," Sophia replied primly

before she kissed Cale, and everybody threw rolls at the four of us.

I pulled Bella into my lap, ignoring the way her brothers groaned, and held up my glass.

"To the Cages. All twenty of you. May you forever be annoying in that small town, take over everything in your limits, and remind me that it's okay to take a chance every once in a while."

"When did you get so sappy?" Hudson grumbled before we each clinked our glasses, and I took a sip of my beer.

Bella wiggled off my lap, and I was grateful she did that since having a hard on in front of her family wasn't the greatest idea. "You're ridiculous, but I love you anyway. Now, we need to look at the spreadsheet for the next few dinners because I know there's some traveling going on, and I feel like we don't have the color-coding set."

"Well, I see that Bella's back to herself," Aston said dryly.

I glared at the man before my lips twitched, and Bella just shrugged.

"I am who I am. It's not like it's unexpected."

But she was. In everything that she did, she constantly surprised me. And I would forever be grateful for the moment the ground fell beneath us, and we fell into each other.

Because I had fallen in love with a Cage. Twice in my life. And I would continue to do so every day until our last breaths.

And I couldn't wait to finally do something that I'd yet to do.

Surprise her.

Because the ring I had picked out would look damn fine on her finger. As soon as she expected the unexpected.

Chapter Twenty
DORIAN

"It kind of worries me that I'm so easily persuaded to get in this thing."

My best friend just beamed at me as we looked over at the Cessna Skyhawk. "Isn't she gorgeous? I realize she's not mine, however, my boss lets me borrow her."

"When you say borrow, do you mean *borrow*, or are you stealing this from your boss?" With Joshua, one never knew. It wasn't that Joshua was reckless, far from it. But we had been in our fair share of scrapes throughout the years.

I had many friends throughout my life. Some that I worked with now, some that I had gone to school with. Joshua was the only one I had met on a summer vacation that had turned into a full semester vacation when my father hadn't wanted me to come back to town. That wasn't a time in my life that I liked to think of, but throughout all the pain and rejection, including neglect, I found my best friend.

Joshua worked with me sometimes at the various clubs and businesses that I owned, but he also worked with a billionaire who liked to have his hands in every single pot he could find.

When I had been shipped off to Cage Lake to stay with my mother in one of the various houses that the family owned, dear old mother had been too busy to pay attention to me for many hours of the day, so I had strolled the small-town streets and found my best friend. Seriously, we had clicked just like that and got in enough scrapes together that the local sheriff and deputy probably still had our pictures as teenagers up somewhere.

We'd grown up, of course, and quit doing stupid things that could get us sent to jail, however, I needed to be a little clear on this.

"Who do you take me for? Of course I'm not stealing a damn plane. Adam wants me to fly it, because he just got his new baby, and he wasn't sure if he wanted to sell this or not. So I get to take it out after they work on maintenance, just to make sure she's doing good."

"That still doesn't fill me with confidence," I said dryly.

"I've had enough flying hours solo that I could be a pilot if I wanted to. You know this is what I've always wanted to do."

"Why weren't you a pilot?" I asked, interested. He met my gaze, and I got it. "Harper."

"Yes and no. When Mom and Dad died, flying didn't feel like an option. We were spiraling trying to deal with custody and what I'd do for school. Then when the grandparents died and Harper was getting out of school, I didn't want to leave my baby sister alone all the time flying back and forth. You know that pilots don't get to spend as much time with their families as they'd like. And I couldn't do that to Harper. Plus, I liked working with you and Adam. And a business degree isn't anything to laugh at. Hell, I'm making more money now than I would have as a pilot. Which means I can have a hobby now, instead of having to fly from one place to another."

"I guess the glass is half full in your case."

"Damn straight."

"So where are we going in this thing? Vegas?" I teased.

"No, I'm not taking you to Vegas in a piston single engine aircraft. This baby has six hundred nautical miles of range, can seat up to four, has over an eight-hundred-pound useful load, and needs a little over fifteen hundred feet of takeoff distance. It's the best training plane out there."

"Did you read that in the manual?" I asked dryly.

"You know I did. I know every inch of this baby. It's going to suck when he sells her."

"You really think Adam's going to sell her."

"Probably. He got a green Caravan which seats up to fourteen, and I don't know if he wants this tiny plane."

"Maybe he doesn't want to waste that much fuel, or deal with that many people. He won't give up your baby easily."

"I hope not because I love her. So get in, and I'm going to do my normal preflight checks. You just sit there and look pretty."

I batted my eyelashes. "It doesn't take much."

I got into the co-pilot seat and did what I did best. Nothing. At least that's what my father had said.

I frowned, pushing those thoughts from my head. Why the hell was I thinking of my dead father today? He truly didn't matter. He was gone, and while his sharp talons of control were still dug in deep in some of us, I didn't really care about him. He had never liked me, pretty sure he had never loved me, and so I wasn't going to give him the time of day.

AN UNEXPECTED EVERYTHING

My phone buzzed and I looked down at the readout as Joshua did his preflight checks.

> **FLYNN:**
> Are you heading to town this weekend? Hudson isn't answering my calls.

I rolled my eyes because those two might be twins, but they sure didn't have that twin-speak like others did.

> **ME:**
> Probably. We were just there, but Amy liked the place. Plus, it's always good to check on Harper.

Harper was Joshua's little sister. Eight years younger than us, barely out of college, and owned her own business that was doing damn well in town. Yes, she rented from us and had taken a loan from the Cages, but it was better us than the bank. At least, that's what my father had said.

I frowned, annoyed he was in my head once again.

> **FLYNN:**
> Get him to call me. I have paperwork to go over, and I don't have time to head out to the lake this weekend.

> **ME:**
> I thought you had to work on whatever the mayor had asked of you?

While our family owned and operated much of the town, Flynn was the one who took care of many of the businesses in Cage Lake. With Hudson being his proxy, as our brother was the only one who lived there full-time. Of course, that would change in the future since Isabella was moving there for most of the year to be with Weston. And wasn't that a change? I had known Weston for as long as I had known Joshua, though he had been a couple of years older than us. It was a damn small world it seemed. But that was small towns for you. Even though I didn't live there, I stayed there enough that I got the idea of it.

> **FLYNN:**
> I have a meeting that I can't get out of. And I need Hudson's help.

> **ME:**
> I'll take care of it if he can't. Maybe he's working.

Considering Hudson got lost in his work when he was painting, it made sense.

But I knew we were both worried about the unsaid

things. That maybe Hudson was in another spiral. Neither of us wanted that to happen.

> ME:
> I'll check on him, and whatever business things you need me to do. I don't mind.

> FLYNN:
> You're a lifesaver. And please check on my twin for real. He's scaring me.

> ME:
> I've got it.

I nearly put my phone away when it buzzed again, and I smiled down at who was calling. I picked up and wiggled my brows over at Joshua.

"Hello Harper darling."

Joshua curled a lip at me, and I just laughed.

"Hey, is my lovely brother with you?" she asked, her voice all soft and happy. She also sounded a little tired, but considering what hours she worked at the bakery, that made sense.

"He's right next to me. We're about to take off, though."

"Hand me your phone," Joshua grumbled, and I did as he ordered, grinning.

When their parents had died, Joshua hadn't been able to get full custody of Harper. She had been shipped off to her grandparents, since she had been a minor and Joshua had just turned eighteen. It had been a huge fight for custody with only partial visitations. My best friend had done his best by Harper, but I knew he didn't feel like it was enough. Then their grandparents had passed right when Harper had graduated high school, so she had come back to Cage Lake, at least for the summers while she finished school. I didn't know exactly what it had done to Joshua to lose out on being with his baby sister for so long. But they made it work. They were all each other had now.

"Yes yes. I'll bring home milk too, how's that?"

I rolled my eyes at the two, though I didn't know what they were talking about, and held out my hand when he hung up.

"We ready to go?"

"Almost. Your girlfriend texted when I was on the phone. Sorry."

I frowned and looked down at the readout.

> **AMY:**
> I miss you. Are you coming over tonight?

> **ME:**
> Yes. As soon as I'm done with Joshua. Need me to bring something for dinner?

> **AMY:**
> I think I can be dinner. What do you think?

Then she sent a photo that made my eyebrows raise, and Joshua whistled through his teeth. "Well then. That's an invitation."

"Hey, eyes on the runway and not on my girlfriend."

"I didn't see much. Although you should probably put a screen on your phone or something if she's going to send so many of those."

I made a note to do just that and was grateful I didn't have to adjust myself. Flying with a hard on didn't sound like a picnic. "My girlfriend likes me. And she's hot."

"Well that is true," Joshua said dryly. I said my goodbyes to Amy, as Joshua did the rest of his checks, and soon we were going down the runway, and in the air.

Despite my joke to my best friend earlier, I loved flying. It didn't matter what kind of plane. I loved being in it. I also liked bungee jumping, skydiving, and just anything that gave that little burst of adrenaline. And Joshua always did it right with me. My best friend had had his license forever, and I was thinking maybe it was time to get mine. Everything just felt right. After so many years of bullshit and stress, things were finally coming together.

"I'm thinking of asking Amy to move in with me," I blurted.

We spoke through our headsets, the sounds of the engine loud within the small compartment. But even with sunglasses on, and that huge headset, I saw the way Joshua's eyes widened with his eyebrows lifting. "Really? I didn't think she was really your type."

I frowned. "What the hell do you mean by that?"

My best friend winced. "Sorry. I just, well, I thought you guys were just having fun? I didn't know it was serious."

"I think it is."

"Do you love her?" Joshua asked.

Surprised, I just blinked at my friend. "I don't even know what love is really. But I like being with her. And she makes me happy."

"Okay, so that's a no."

"Why are you acting like this? I figured moving in with each other was just the next thing to do right? I suck at dating. We both know this."

"Considering Amy's your fourth girlfriend in how many years?"

"In a year." I swallowed hard, ignoring that familiar sliver of doubt that always threatened when it came to settling down. "Which seems like a lot in retrospect, but Amy's great."

"I'm sure she is."

I glared at my best friend. "I'm not a player like some people think. I just can't find the right person."

"And Amy's that right person?"

Unsettled, I shrugged. "Maybe."

Jousha fiddled with a few things on the dash. "Okay, if that's what you think."

"That doesn't sound very helpful."

The other man let out a breath. "I'm not trying to be helpful. I'm trying to be your friend. I mean, you were there for me when Harper needed me. When my parents died and the grandparents were hell-bent on trying to split us apart. *You* were there for her to open up her shop. To make sure I knew what I was doing in each of our businesses. You're the *best*, man. Fuck whatever your daddy thought. And fuck the fact that your mom thought that she was going to mold you into a perfect pawn."

I swallowed hard at that diatribe, wondering exactly how long Joshua had been holding on to this particular rant. "Why does that make me sound weak?"

"No, it makes you sound like you had family issues. Believe me. I know what you mean."

"This is about me and Amy. Not my past."

"Okay then. Ask her to move in. If she says yes, I'll

be right there with boxes and tape to help. I promise. But Amy—"

"But Amy *what*?" I bit out, annoyed now. I thought Joshua would be happy for me finally trying to settle down. Joshua didn't have a serious girlfriend, but he had one at one time. And he was still looking for that perfect person. They didn't have to be perfect, just perfect for him. That's what I thought I was doing with Amy.

Once again, Joshua was quiet. "I love you, Dorian. You're my best friend. And I'm sorry if I'm off base. If I'm wrong, then you can punch me in the face later. But I don't know if you're truly seeing what we see."

"Who is we?"

"I misspoke," he said quickly, and I didn't believe him. "But Dorian? Amy likes Fun Dorian. Club Owner Dorian. Cage Money Dorian."

"That's a fucking lie." I practically spat the words into the headset.

"If that's what you think. But I think it's the truth."

"Just because you can't get a woman to actually love you doesn't mean you have to shit on my relationship."

I didn't even realize the words were out of my mouth until they filled the small cabin. And they were such a goddamn lie, that I hated myself.

"Well, good to know how you really feel, Dorian."

"Joshua. I'm sorry. I didn't mean that. Seriously. I

don't think that. At all. I love you, damn it. Just like one of my brothers. I didn't mean it."

"Whatever. Shit." There was an odd sound, and I swallowed hard, realizing we were descending faster than we had been before. Joshua had started the descent for our landing earlier, but now, everything got oddly quiet.

"What's going on?"

"The engine stalled." Joshua cursed again. "Mayday, mayday, mayday. November-niner-seven-eight-Charlie-Papa. We have engine failure upon descent and request immediate landing. Mayday, mayday, mayday."

He continued to say a few other words, and I swallowed hard, panic rising. I knew Joshua trained for something like this, but the ground was coming up really fucking fast.

"What can I do?" I asked, bile coating my tongue.

"Just breathe. Tighten your seatbelt. And hold on." He let out a slow breath, his entire body focused as he worked. "We've got this, Dorian. I've got you."

He met my gaze for a bare instant before turning to once again to speak to the control tower, his gaze on the runway. The engine sputtered once and started again, and my heart leapt out of my chest.

"I trust you," I repeated.

"I know, buddy. I know."

And then there was nothing.

Next in the series? Dorian finally takes a chance in:
If You Were Mine.

AND IF YOU'D LIKE TO READ A BONUS SCENE YOU CAN FIND IT HERE! I LOVE THIS SCENE SO MUCH!

If you'd like to read the next Generation with the Montgomery Ink Legacy Series:
Bittersweet Promises

In the mood for more small town romance? Check out the Ashford Creek series with LEGACY. Or as I like to call it "The Small Town of Single Dads".

A Note from Carrie Ann Ryan

Thank you so much for reading **An Unexpected Everything.**

These Cages have my heart! Writing a mix of small town vs the big city has been thrilling and I love figuring out more secrets of Cage Lake.

The next story is all about figuring out who you are and what you want. Dorian needs a change in this best friend's little sister, age gap romance: If You Were Mine!

In case you'd like to read Phoebe's romance, you can read about her and Kane in His Second Chance!

And Ford finds his match with Greer and Noah in Best Friend Temptation!

The Cage Family
Book 1: The Forever Rule (Aston & Blakely)

Book 2: An Unexpected Everything (Isabella & Weston)
Book 3: If You Were Mine (Dorian & Harper)

Next in the series? Dorian finally takes a chance in:
If You Were Mine.

AND IF YOU'D LIKE TO READ A BONUS SCENE YOU CAN FIND IT **HERE**! I LOVE THIS SCENE SO MUCH!

If you'd like to read the next Generation with the Montgomery Ink Legacy Series: Bittersweet Promises

In the mood for more small town romance? Check out the Ashford Creek series with LEGACY. Or as I like to call it "The Small Town of Single Dads".

If you want to make sure you know what's coming next from me, you can sign up for my newsletter at www.CarrieAnnRyan.com; follow me on twitter at @CarrieAnnRyan, or like my Facebook page. I also have a Facebook Fan Club where we have trivia, chats, and other goodies. You guys are the reason I get to do what I do and I thank you.

Make sure you're signed up for my MAILING LIST so you can know when the next releases are available as well as find giveaways and FREE READS.

Happy Reading!

From One Way Back to Me
ELI

When my morning begins with me standing ankle-deep in a basement full of water, I know I probably should have stayed in bed. Only, I was the boss, and I didn't get that choice.

"Hold on. I'm looking for it." East cursed underneath his breath as my younger brother bent down around the pipe, trying his best to turn off the valve. I sighed, waded through the muck in my work boots, and moved to help him. "I said I've got it," East snapped, but I ignored him.

I narrowed my eyes at the evil pipe. "It's old and rusted, and even though it passed an inspection over a year ago, we knew this was going to be a problem."

"And I'm the fucking handyman of this company. I've got this."

"And as a handyman, you need a hand."

"You're hilarious. Seriously. I don't know how I could ever manage without your wit and humor." The dryness in his tone made my lips twitch even as I did my best to ignore the smell of whatever water we stood in.

"Fuck you," I growled.

"No thanks. I'm a little too busy for that."

With a grunt, East shut off the water, and we both stood back, hands on our hips as we stared at the mess of this basement.

East let out a sigh. "I'm not going to have to turn the water off for the whole property, but I'm glad that we don't have tenants in this particular cabin."

I nodded tightly and held back a sigh. "This is probably why there aren't basements in Texas. Because everything seems to go wrong in these things."

"I'm pretty sure this is a storm shelter, or at least a tornado one. Not quite sure as it's one of the only basements in the area."

"It was probably the only one that they had the energy to make back in the day. Considering this whole place is built over clay and limestone."

East nodded, looked around. "I'll start the cleanup with this water, and we'll look to see what we can do with the pipes."

I pinched the bridge of my nose. "I don't want to have to replace the plumbing for this whole place."

"At least it's not the villa itself, or the farmhouse, or the winery. Just a single cabin."

I glared at my younger brother, then reached out and knocked on a wooden pillar. "Shut your mouth. Don't say things like that to me. We are just now getting our feet under us."

East shrugged. "It's the truth, though. However much you weigh it, it could have been worse."

I pinched the bridge of my nose. "Jesus Christ. You were in the military for how long? A Wilder your entire life, and you say things like that? When the hell did you lose that superstition bone?"

"About the time that my Humvee was blown up, and when Evan's was, Everett's too. Hell, about the time that you almost fell out of the sky in your plane. Or when Elliot was nearly shot to death trying to help one of his men. So, yes, I pretty much lost all superstition when trying to toe the line ended up in near death and maiming."

I met my brother's gaze, that familiar pang thinking about all that we had lost and almost lost over the past few years.

East muttered under his breath, shaking his head.

"And I sound more and more like Evan these days rather than myself."

I squeezed his shoulder and let out a breath, thinking of our brother who grunted more than spoke these days. "It's okay. We've been through a lot. But we're here."

Somehow, we were here. I wasn't quite sure if we had made the right decision about two years ago when we had formed this plan, or rather *I* had formed this plan, but there was no going back. We were in it, and we were going to have to find a way to make it work, flooded former tornado shelters and all.

East sighed. "I'll work on this now. Then I'll head on over to the main house. I have a few things to work on there."

"You know, we can hire you help. I know we had all the contractors and everything to work with us for some of the rebuilds and rehabs, but we can hire someone else for you on a day-to-day basis."

My brother shook his head. "We may be able to afford it, but I'd rather save that for a rainy day. Because when it rains, it pours here, and flash flooding is a major threat in this part of Texas." He winked as he said it, mixing his metaphors, and I just shook my head.

"You just let me know if you need it."

"You're the CEO, brother of mine, not the CFO. That's Everett."

"True, but we did talk about it so we can work on it." I paused, thinking about what other expenses might show up. "And what do you need to do with the villa?"

The villa was the main house where most things happened on the property. It contained the lobby, library, and atrium. My apartment was also on the top floor, so I could be there for emergencies. Our innkeeper lived on the other side of the house, but I was in the main loft because this was my project, my baby.

My other brothers, all five of them, lived in cabins on the property. We lived together, worked together, ate together, and fought together. We were the Wilder brothers. It was what we did.

I had left to join the Air Force at seventeen, having graduated early, leaving behind my kid brothers and sister. After nearly twenty years of doing what we needed to in order to survive, we hadn't spent as much time with one another as I would have liked. We hadn't been stationed together, so we hadn't seen one another for longer than holidays or in passing.

But now we were together. At least most of us. So I was going to make this work, even if it killed me.

East finally answered my question. "I just have to fix

a door that's a little too squeaky in one of the guestrooms. Not a big deal."

I raised a brow. "That's it?"

"It's one of the many things on my list. Thankfully, this place is big enough that I always have something to do. It's an unending list. And that the winery has its own team to work on all of that shit, because I'm not in the mood to learn to deal with any of the complicated machinery that comes with that world."

I snorted. "Honestly, same. I'm glad there are people that know what the fuck they're doing when it comes to wine making so that didn't have to be the two of us."

I left my brother to this job, knowing he liked time on his own, just like the rest of us did, and went to dry my boots. I was working by myself for most of the day, in interviews and other "boss business," as Elliot called it, so I had to focus and get clean.

I wasn't in the mood to deal with interviews, but it was part of my job. We had to fill positions that hadn't been working out over the past year, some more than others.

Wilder Retreat was a place that hadn't been even a spark in my mind my entire life. No, I had been too busy being a career military man—getting in my twenty, moving up the ranks, and ending up as a Lieutenant Colonel before I got out. I had been a commander of a squadron, and yet, it felt like I didn't know how to command where I was now.

When my sister Eliza had lost her husband when he was on deployment, it had been the last domino to fall in the Wilder brothers' military career. I had been ready to get out with twenty years in, knowing I needed a career outside of being a Lieutenant Colonel. I wasn't even forty yet, and the term retirement was a misnomer, but that's what happened when it came to my former job.

East had been getting out around that time for reasons of his own, and then Evan had been forced to. I rubbed my hand over my chest, that familiar pain, remembering the phone call from one of Evan's commanders when Evan had been hurt.

I thought I'd lost my baby brother then, and we nearly had. Everett had gotten hurt too, and Elijah and Elliot had needed out for their own reasons. Losing our baby sister's husband had just pushed us forward.

Finding out that Eliza's husband had been a cheating asshole had just cemented the fact that we needed to spend more time together as a family so we could be there for one another.

In retrospect, it would have been nice if Eliza would have been able to come down to Texas with us, to our suburb outside of San Antonio. Only, she had fallen in love again, with a man with a big family and a good heart up in Fort Collins, Colorado. She was still up there and traveled down enough that we actually got to get to know our sister again.

It was weird to think that, after so many years of always seeing each other in passing or through video calls, most of us were here, opening up a business. And all because I had been losing my mind.

Wilder Retreat and Winery was a villa and wedding venue outside of San Antonio. We were in hill country, at least what passed for hill country in South Texas, and the place had been owned by a former Air Force General who had wanted to retire and sell the place, since his kid didn't want it.

It was a large spread that used to be a ranch back in the day, nearly one hundred acres that the original owners had taken from a working ranch, and instead of making it a dude ranch or something similar, like others did around here, they'd added a winery using local help. We were close enough to Fredericksburg that it made sense in terms of the soil and weather. They had been able to add on additions, so it wasn't just the winery. Someone could come for the day for a winery tour or even a retreat tour, but most people came for the weekend or for a whole week. There were cabins and a farmhouse where we held weddings, dances, or other events. We had some chickens and ducks that gave us eggs, and goats that seemed to have a mind of their own and provided milk for cheese. Then there was the main annex, which housed all the equipment for the retreat villa.

The winery had its own section of buildings, and it was far bigger than anything I would have ever thought that we could handle. But, between the six of us, we did.

And the only reason we could even afford it, because one didn't afford something like this on a military salary, even with a decent retirement plan, was because of our uncles.

Our uncles, Edward and Edmond Wilder, had owned Wilder Wines down in Napa, California, for years. They had done well for themselves, and when we had been kids, we had gone out to visit. Evan had been the one that had clung to it and had been interested in wine making before he had changed his mind and gone into the military like the rest of us.

That was why Evan was in charge of the winery itself now. Because he knew what he was doing, even if he'd growled and said he didn't. Either way though, the place was huge, had multiple working parts at all times, and we had a staff that needed us. But when the uncles had died, they had left the money from the sale of the winery to us in equal parts. Eliza had taken hers to invest for her future children, and the rest of us had pooled our money together to buy this place and make it ours. A lot of the staff from the old owner had stayed, but some had left as well. Because they didn't want new owners who had no idea what they were doing, or they just retired. Either way, we were over a year in and doing okay.

Except for two positions that made me want to groan.

I had an interview with who would be our third wedding planner since we started this. The main component of the retreat was to have an actual wedding venue. To be able to host parties, and not just wine tours. Elliot was our major event planner that helped with our yearly and seasonal minute details, but he didn't want anything to do with the actual weddings. That was a whole other skill set, and so we wanted a wedding planner. We had gone through two wedding planners now, and we needed to hire a third. The first one had lied on her résumé, had given references that were her friends who had lied and had even created websites that were all fabrication, all so she could get into the business. Which, I understood, getting into the business is one thing. However, lying was another. Plus, we needed someone with actual experience because we didn't have any ourselves. We were going out on a limb here with this whole retreat business, and it was all because I had the harebrained idea of getting our family to work together, get along, and get to know one another. I wanted us to have a future, to be our own bosses.

And it was so far over my head that I knew that if I didn't get reliable help, we were going to fail.

Later, I had a meeting with that potential wedding planner. But first, I had to see what the fuck that smell was coming from the main kitchen in the villa.

The second wedding planner we hired was a guy with great and *true* references, one who was good at his job but hated everything to do with my brothers and me. He had hated the idea of the retreat and how rustic it was, even though we were in fucking South Texas. Yes, the buildings look slightly European because that was the theme that the original owners had gone for. Still, the guy had hated us, hadn't listened to us, and had called us white trash before he had walked away, jumped into his convertible, and sped off down the road, leaving us without help. He had been rude to our guests, and now Elliot was the one having to plan weddings for the past three weeks. My brother was going to strangle me soon if we didn't hire someone. And this person was going to be our last hope. As soon as she showed up, that was.

I looked down on my watch and tried to plan the rest of my day. I had thirty minutes to figure out what the hell was going on in the kitchen, and then I had to go to the meeting.

I nodded at a few guests who were sipping wine and eating a cheese plate and then at our innkeeper, Naomi. Naomi's honey-brown hair was cut in an angled bob that lit her face, and she grinned at me.

"Hello there, Boss Man," she whispered. "You might need to go to the kitchen."

"Do I want to know?" I asked with a grumble.

"I'm not sure. But I am going to go check in our next guest, and then Elliott needs to meet with the Henderson couple."

"He'll be there." I didn't say that Elliot would rather chew off his own arm rather than deal with this, considering we had a family event coming in, one that Elliot was on target with planning. The wedding for next year was an important one, so we needed to work on it.

Naomi was a fantastic innkeeper, far more organized than any of us—and that was saying something since my brothers and I knew our way around schedules, to-do lists, and spreadsheets. Naomi was personable, smiled, and kept us on our toes.

Without her, I knew we wouldn't be able to do this. Hell, without Amos, our vineyard manager, I knew that Evan and Elijah wouldn't be able to handle the winery as they did. Naomi and Amos had come with the place when we had bought it, and I would be forever grateful that they had decided to stay on.

I gave Naomi another nod, then headed back to the kitchen and nearly walked right back out.

Tony stood there, a scowl on his face and his hands on his hips. "I don't understand what the fuck is wrong with this oven."

"What's going on?" I asked as Everett stood by Tony. Everett was my quiet brother with usually a small smile on his face, only right then it looked like he was ready to scream.

I didn't know why Everett was even there since he was part responsible for the financials side of the company and usually worked with Elliot these days. Maybe he had come to the kitchen after the smell of burning as I had after Naomi's prodding.

Tony threw his hands in the air. "What's going on? This stove is a piece of shit. All of it is a piece of shit. I'm tired of this rustic place. I thought I would be coming to a Michelin star restaurant. To be my own chef. Instead, I have to make English breakfasts and pancakes with bananas. I might as well be at a bed and breakfast."

I pinched the bridge of my nose. "We're an inn, not a bed and breakfast."

"But I serve breakfast. That's all I do these days.

That and cheese platters. Nobody comes for dinner. Nobody comes for lunch."

That was a lie. Tony worked for the winery and the retreat itself and served all the meals. But Tony wanted to go crazy with the menu, to try new and fantastical items that just weren't going to work here.

And I had a feeling I was going to throw up if I wasn't careful.

"I quit," Tony snapped, and I knew right then, it was done for. I was done.

"You can't quit," I growled while Everett held back a sigh.

"Yes, I can. I'm done. I'm done with you and this ranch. You're not cowboys. You're not even Texans. You're just people moving in on our territory." And with that, Tony stomped away, throwing his chef's apron on the ground.

I was thankful that the kitchen was on the other side of the library and front area, where most of the guests were if they weren't out on one of the tours of the area and city that Elliott had arranged for them. That was the whole point of this retreat. They could come visit, and could relax, or we could set them up on a tour of downtown San Antonio, or Canyon Lake, or any of the other places that were nearby.

And yet, Tony had just thrown a wrench into all of

that. I didn't know what was worse, the smell of burning, Tony leaving, the water in the basement that wasn't truly a basement, or the fact that I was going to smell like charred food and wet jeans when I went to go meet this wedding planner.

"You're going to need to hire a new cook," Everett whispered.

I looked at my brother, at the man who did his best to make sure we didn't go bankrupt, and I wanted to just grumble. "I figured."

"I can help for now, but you know I'm only part-time. I can't stay away from my twins for too long," Sandy said as she came forward to take the pan off the stove. "I wish I could do full time, but this is all I can do for now."

Sandy had come back from maternity leave after we had already opened the retreat. She had been on with the former owners and was brilliant. But she had a right to be a mom and not want to work full time. I understood that, and I knew that Sandy didn't want to handle a whole kitchen by herself. She liked her position as a sous chef.

I was going to have to figure out what to do. Again.

"I'll get it done," I said while rubbing my temples.

"You know what we need to do," Everett whispered, and I shook my head.

"He'll kill us."

"Maybe, but it'll be worth it in the end. And speaking of, don't you have that interview soon? Or do you want me to take it?" His gaze tracked to my jeans.

I shook my head. "No, help Sandy."

Everett winced. "Just because I know how to slice an onion, it doesn't mean I'm good at cooking."

"I'm sorry, did you just say you could slice an onion? Get to it," Sandy put in with a smile, pointing at the sink. "Wash those hands."

"I cannot believe I just said that out loud. I just stepped right into it," Everett said with a sigh. "Go to the interview. You know what to ask."

"I do. And I hope we don't get screwed this time."

"You know, if we're lucky, we'll get someone as good as Roy's wedding planner, or at least that woman that we met. You know who she is." Everett grinned like a cat with the canary.

I narrowed my eyes. "Don't bring her up."

"Oh, I can't help it. A single dance, and you were drawn to her."

"What dance? You know what? No, I don't have time. We have to work on lunch and dinner. Tell me while you work," Sandy added with a wink.

Everett leaned toward her as he washed his hands.

"Well, you see, there was this dance, and he met the perfect woman, and then she got engaged."

Sandy's eyes widened. "Engaged? How did that happen? She was dating someone else?" she asked as she looked at me.

I pinched the bridge of my nose. "It was at Roy's place when we were looking at the venue to see if we wanted to buy the retreat here." I sighed, I knew if I just let it all out, she would move on from this conversation, and I would never have to deal with it again. "Somehow, I ended up at a wedding there, caught the garter. This woman caught the bouquet, and she happened to be the wedding planner. We danced, we laughed, and as she walked away, her boyfriend got down on one knee and proposed."

"No way!" She leaned forward with a fierce look on her face, her eyes bright. "What did she say?"

"I have no clue. I left." I ignored whatever feeling might want to show up at that thought. Everett gave me a glance, and I shook my head. "Enough of that. Yes, the wedding that she did was great, but I honestly have no idea who she is, and she has a job. She doesn't need to work here." And I didn't know what I would do if I saw her again or had to work with her. There had been such an intense connection that I knew it would be awkward as hell. But thankfully, she had her own business and wasn't going to come to the Wilder Retreat for a job.

I left Sandy and Everett on their own, knowing that they were capable, at least for now. And I knew who we would have to hire if she said yes, and if my other brother didn't kill me first.

I washed my hands in the sink on the way out, grateful that at least I looked somewhat decent, if not a little disheveled, and made my way out front, hoping that the wedding planner who came in through the doors would be the one that would stick. Because we needed some good luck. After the day we've had, we needed some good luck.

I turned the corner and nearly tripped over my feet.

Because, of course, fate was this way.

It was her.

Of all the wedding planners from all the wedding venues, it was her.

In the mood to read another family saga? Meet the Wilder Brothers in One Way Back to Me!

From Bittersweet Promises

LEIF

"Not only did you convince me to somehow go on a blind date, it became a double date. How on earth did you work this magic on me, cousin?" I asked Lake as she leaned against the pillar just inside the restaurant.

Lake grinned at me, her dark hair pulled away from her face. She had on this swingy black dress and looked as if she were excited, anxious, nervous, and happy all at the same time. Considering she was bouncing on her toes when usually Lake was calm, cool, and collected, was saying something. "I asked, and you said yes. Because you love me."

"I might love you because we're family, but I still think we're making a mistake." I shook my head and pulled at my shirt sleeves. Lake had somehow convinced me to wear a button-up shirt tucked into gray pants, I even had on shiny shoes. I looked like a damn banker. But if that's what Lake wanted, that's what I would do.

Lake might technically be my cousin, even though we weren't blood-related, but we were more like brother and sister than any of my other cousins.

I had siblings, as did Lake, but with the generational gap, we were at least a decade older than all of our other cousins. That meant, despite the fact that we had lived over an hour apart for most of our lives, we'd grown up more like siblings.

I loved my three younger siblings and talked to them daily. Unlike some blended families, they *were* my brothers and sister and not like strangers or distant family members. I didn't feel a disconnect from the three of them, but Lake was still closer to me.

Probably because we were either heading into our thirties or already there, where most of our other cousins were either just now in their early twenties or still teenagers in high school. With how big we Montgomerys were as a family, it made sense that there would be such a widespread age group. That meant that Lake and I were best friends, cousins, practically siblings, and sometimes the banes of each other's existences.

We were also business owners and partners and saw

each other too often these days. That was probably why she convinced me to go on a blind double date. But she had been out with Zach before. I, however, had never met May. Lake had some connection with her that I wasn't sure about, and for some reason Lake's date had said yes to this double date.

And, in the complicated way of family, I had agreed to it. I must have been tired. Or perhaps I'd had too many beers. Because I didn't do blind dates, and recently, I didn't do dates at all.

Lake scanned her phone, then looked up at me, all innocence in her smart gaze. "You shouldn't have told me you wanted to settle down in your old age."

I narrowed my eyes. "I'm still in my early thirties, jerk. Stop calling me old."

"I shouldn't call you old since you're only a few years older than me." She fluttered her eyelashes and I flipped her off, ignoring the stare from the older woman next to me. Though I was a tattoo artist, I didn't have many visible tattoos. Most of mine were on my back and legs, hidden from the world unless I wanted to show them. I hadn't figured out what I wanted on my arms beyond a few small pieces on my wrists and upper shoulders. And since tattoos were permanent, I was taking my time. If a client needed to see my skin with ink to feel comfortable, I'd show them my back. My body was a canvas, so I did what I could to set people at ease.

But I still had the eyebrow piercing and had recently taken out my nose ring. I didn't look too scary for most people. But apparently, flipping off a woman, growling, and cursing a time or two in front of strangers probably made me appear too close to the dark side.

"Yes, I want to settle down, but this will be awkward, won't it? Where the two of us are strangers, and the two of you aren't?" I wanted a life, a future, and yeah, one day to settle down with someone. I just didn't know why I'd mentioned it to Lake in the first place.

"If it helps, May doesn't know Zach, either. So it's a group of strangers, except I know everybody." She clapped her hands together and did her version of an evil laugh, and I just shook my head.

"Considering what you do for a living and how you like to manipulate things in your way, this makes sense. Are you going to be adding a matchmaking company to your conglomerate?"

Lake just fluttered her eyelashes again and laughed. Lake owned a small tech company that made a shit ton of money over the past couple of years. And because she was brilliant at what she did, innovative, and liked pushing money towards women-owned businesses, she owned more than one company at this point and was an investor in mine. I wouldn't be surprised if she found a way to open up a women-owned matchmaking company right here in town.

"It might be fun. I can call it Montgomery Links." Her eyes went wide. "Oh, my God. I have to write that down." She pulled out her phone, began to take notes, and I pinched the bridge of my nose.

"You know I trust you with my actual life, but I don't know if I trust you with my dating life."

Lake tossed her hair behind her shoulder as she continued to type. "Shut up. You love me. And once I finish setting you up, the rest of the family's next."

"Oh, really? You're going to get Daisy and Noah next?" I asked, speaking of two more of our cousins.

"Maybe. Of course, Sebastian's the only one of the younger group that seems to have a serious girlfriend."

I nodded, speaking of our other familial business partner. Sebastian was still a teenager, though in college. He had wanted to open up Montgomery Ink Legacy with me, the full title of our company. There was a legacy to it, and Sebastian had wanted in. So, though he didn't work there full-time, he was putting his future towards us. And in the ways of young love, he and his girlfriend had been together since middle school. The fact that my younger cousin was better at relationships than I was didn't make me feel great. But I was going to ignore that.

"You're not going to start up a matchmaking service, are you? Or maybe an app?"

"Dating apps are ridiculous these days, they practically want you to invest in coins to bid on dates, and that's not something I'm in the mood for. But maybe there's something I can try. I'll add it to my list."

Lake's list of inventions and tech was notorious, and knowing the brilliance of my cousin, she would one day rule the world and might eventually cross everything off that list.

"Oh, here's Zach." Lake's face brightened immediately, and she smiled up at a man with dark hair, piercing gray eyes, and an actual dimple on his cheek.

Tonight was not only about my blind date, but me getting the lay of the land when it came to Zach. I was the first step into meeting the family. Oh, if Zach passed my gauntlet, he would meet the rest of the Montgomerys, and we were mighty. All one hundred of us.

"Zach, you're here." Lake's voice went soft, and she went on her tiptoes even in her high heels as Zach pressed a soft kiss to her lips.

"Of course, I'm here. And you're early, as usual."

Lake blushed and ducked her head. "Well, you know me. I like to be early because being on time is late," she said at the same time I did, mumbling under my breath. It was a familiar refrain when it came to us.

"Zach, good to meet you," I said, holding out my hand.

The other man gripped it firmly and shook. "Nice to meet you too, Leif. I know you might be the one on a blind date soon, but I'm nervous."

I chuckled, shaking my head. "Yeah, I'm pretty nervous too. Though I'm grateful that Lake's trying to look out for me."

My cousin laughed softly. "You totally were not saying that a few minutes ago, but be suave and sophisticated now. Or just be yourself, May's on her way."

I met Zach's gaze and we both rolled our eyes. When I turned toward the door, I saw a woman of average height, with black straight hair, green eyes, and a sweet smile. I didn't know much about May, other than Lake knew her and liked her. If I was going to start dating again after taking time off to get the rest of my life together, I might as well start with someone that one of my best friends liked.

"May, I'm so glad that you're here," Lake said as she hugged the other woman tightly.

As Lake began to bounce on her heels, I realized that my cousin's cool, calm, and collected exterior was only for work. She was bouncing and happy when it came to her friends or when she was nervous. I knew that, of course, but I had forgotten how she had turned into the mogul that she was. It was good to see her relaxed and happy.

Now I just needed to figure out how to do that for myself.

May stood in front of me, and I felt like I was starting middle school all over again. A new school, a new life, and a past that didn't make much sense to anyone else.

I swallowed hard and nodded, not putting out my hand to shake, thinking that would be weird, but I also didn't want to hug her. I didn't even know this woman. Why was everything so awkward? Instead, I lifted my chin. "Hello, May. It's nice to meet you. Lake says only good things."

There, smooth. Not really. Zach began to move out of frame, with Lake at his side as the two went to speak to the hostess, leaving May and me alone.

This wasn't going to be awkward at all.

The woman just smiled at me, her eyes wide. "It's nice to meet you, too. And Lake does speak highly of you. Also, this is very awkward, so I'm so sorry if I say something stupid. I know that your cousin said that I should be set up with you which is great but I'm not great at blind dates and apparently this is a double date and now I'm going to stop talking." She said the words so quickly they all ran into one breath.

I shook my head and laughed. "We're on the same page there."

"Okay, good. It's nice to meet you, Leif Montgomery."

"And it's nice to meet you too, May."

We made our way to Lake and Zach, who had gotten our table, and we all sat down, talking about work and other things. May was in child life development, taught online classes, and was also a nanny.

"I'm actually about to start with a new family soon. I'm excited. I know that being a nanny isn't something that most people strive for, or at least that's what they tell you, but I love being able to work with children and be the person that is there when a single parent or even both parents are out in the workforce, trying to do everything."

I nodded, taking a sip of my beer. "I get you completely. With how my parents worked, I was lucky that they were able to get childcare within the buildings. Since they each owned their own businesses, they made it work. But my family worked long hours, and that's why I ended up being the babysitter a lot of the times when childcare wasn't an option." I cleared my throat. "I'm a lot older than a lot of my cousins," I added.

"Both of us are, but I'm glad that you only said yourself," Lake said, grinning. She leaned into Zach as she spoke, the four of us in a horseshoe-shaped booth. That gave May and me space since this was a first date and still awkward as hell, and so Lake and Zach could cuddle. Not that that was something I needed to be a part of.

"Oh, I'm glad that you didn't judge. The last few dates that I've been on they always gave me weird looks because I think they expected a nanny to be this old crone or someone that's looking for a different job." She shrugged and continued. "When I eventually get married and maybe even start a family, I want to continue my job. I like being there to help another family achieve their goals. And I can't believe I just said start a family on my first date. And that I mentioned that I've been on a few other dates." She let out a breath. "I'm notoriously bad at dating. Like, the worst. Just warning you."

I laughed, shaking my head. "I'm rusty at it, so don't worry." And even though I said that, I had a feeling that May felt no spark towards me, and I didn't feel anything towards her. She was nice and pleasant, and I could probably consider her a friend one day. But there wasn't any spark. May's eyes weren't dancing. She wasn't leaning forward, trying to touch my hand across the table. We were just sitting there casually, enjoying a really good steak, as Lake and Zach enjoyed their date.

By the end of dinner, I didn't want dessert, and neither did May, so we said goodbye to the other couple, who decided to stay. I walked May to her car, ignoring Lake's warning look, but I didn't know what exactly she was warning me about.

"Thanks for dinner," May said. "I could have paid. I know this is a blind date and all that, but you didn't have to pay."

I shook my head. "I paid for the four of us because I wanted to be nice. I'll make Lake pay next time."

May beamed. "Yes, I like that. You guys are a good family."

"Anyway," I said, clearing my throat as I stuck my hands in my pockets. "I guess I'll see you around."

May just looked at me, threw her head back, and laughed. "You're right. You are rusty at this."

"Sorry." Heat flushed my skin, and I resisted the urge to tug on my eyebrow ring.

"It's okay. No spark. I'm used to it. I don't spark well."

"May, I'm sorry." I cringed. "It's not you."

"Oh, God, please don't say that. 'It's not you. It's me. You're working on yourself. You're just so busy with work.' I've heard it all."

"Seriously?" I asked. May was hot. Nice, but there just wasn't a spark.

She shrugged. "It's okay. I'll probably see you around sometime because I am friends with Lake. However, I am perfectly fine having this be our one and only. You'll find your person. It's okay that it's not me." And with that, she got in the car and left, leaving me standing there.

Well then. Tonight wasn't horrible, but it wasn't great. I got in my car, and instead of heading home where I'd be alone, watching something on some streaming service while I drank a beer and pretended that I knew what I was doing with my life, I headed into Montgomery Ink Legacy.

We were the third branch of the company and the first owned by our generation. Montgomery Ink was the tattoo shop in downtown Denver. While there were open spots for some walk-ins and special circumstances, my father, aunt, and their team had years' worth of waiting lists. They worked their asses off and made sure to get in everybody that they could, but people wanted Austin Montgomery's art. Same with my aunt, Maya.

There was another tattoo shop down in Colorado

Springs, owned by my parents' cousins, who I just called aunt and uncle because we were close enough that using real titles for everybody got confusing. Montgomery Ink Too was thriving down there, and they had waiting lists as well. My family could have opened more shops and gone nationwide, even global if they wanted to, but they liked keeping it how it was, in the family and those connected.

We were a branch, but our own in the making. I had gone into business with Lake, of course, and Sebastian, when he was ready, as well as Nick. Nick was my best friend. I had known him for ages, and he had wanted to be part of something as well. He might not be a Montgomery by name, but he had eaten over at my family's house enough times throughout the years that he was practically a Montgomery. And he had invested in the company as well, and so now we were nearly a year into owning the shop and trying not to fail.

I pulled into the parking lot, grateful it was still open since we didn't close until nine most nights, and greeted Nick, who was still working.

Sebastian was in the back, going over sketches with a client, and I nodded at him. He might be eighteen, but he was still in training, an apprentice, and was working his ass off to learn.

"Date sucked then?" Sebastian asked, and Nick just rolled his eyes and went back to work on a client's wrist.

"I don't want to talk about it," I groaned.

The rest of the staff was off since Nick would close up on his own. Sebastian was just there since he didn't have homework or a date with Marley.

"Was she hot at least?" Sebastian asked, and the client, a woman in her sixties, bopped him on the head with her bag gently.

"Sebastian Montgomery. Be nice."

Sebastian blushed. "Sorry, Mrs. Anderson."

I looked over at the woman and grinned. "Hi, Mrs. Anderson. It's nice to see you out of the classroom."

She narrowed her eyes at me, even though they filled with laughter. "I needed my next Jane Austen tattoo, thank you very much," the older woman said as she went back to working with Sebastian. She had been my and then Sebastian's English teacher. The fact that she was on her fifth tattoo with some literary quote told me that I had been damn lucky in most of my teachers growing up.

She was kick-ass, and I had a feeling that she would let Sebastian do the tattoo for her rather than just have him work on the design with me as we did for most of the people who came in. He had learned under my father and was working under me now. It was strange to think that he wasn't a little kid anymore. But he was in a long-term relationship, kicking ass in college, and knew what he wanted to do with his life.

I might know what I want to do with my work life, but everything else seemed a little off.

"So it didn't work out?" Nick asked as he walked up to the front desk with the clients after going over aftercare.

"Not really," I said, looking down at my phone.

The client, a woman in her mid-twenties with bright pink hair, a lip ring, and kind eyes, leaned over the desk to look at me.

"You'll find someone, Leif. Don't worry."

I looked at our regular and shook my head. "Thanks, Kim. Too bad that you don't swing this way."

I winked as I said it, a familiar refrain from both of us.

Kim was married to a woman named Sonya, and the two of them were happy and working on in vitro with donated sperm for their first kid.

"Hey, I'm sorry too that I'm a lesbian. I'll never know what it means to have Leif Montgomery. Or any Montgomery, since I found my love far too quickly. I mean, what am I ever going to do not knowing the love of a Montgomery?"

Mrs. Anderson chuckled from her chair, Sebastian

held back a snort, and I just looked at Nick, who rolled his eyes and helped Kim out of the place.

I was tired, but it was okay. The date wasn't all bad. May was nice. But it felt like I didn't have much right then.

And then Nick sat in front of me, scowled, and I realized that I did have something. I had my friends and my family. I didn't need much more.

"So, you and May didn't work out?"

I raised a brow. "You knew her name? Did I tell you that?"

Nick shook his head. "Lake did."

That made sense, considering the two of them spoke as much as we did. "So, was it your idea to set me up on a blind date?"

"Fuck no. That was all Lake. I just do what she says. Like we all do."

I sighed and went through my appointments for the next day. "We're busy for the next month. That's good, right?" I asked.

"You're the business genius here. I just play with ink. But yes, that's good. Now, don't let your cousin set you up any more dates. Find them for yourself. You know what you're doing."

"So says the man who dates less than me."

"That's what you think. I'm more private about it.

As it should be." I flipped him off as he stood up, then he gestured towards a stack of bills in the corner. "You have a few personal things that made their way here. Don't want you to miss out on them before you head home."

"Thanks, bro."

"No problem. I'm going to help Sebastian with his consult, and then I'll clean up. You should head home. Though you're doing it alone, so I feel sorry for you."

"Fuck you," I called out.

"Fuck you, too."

"Boys," Mrs. Anderson said, in that familiar English teacher refrain, and both Nick and I cringed before saying, "Sorry," simultaneously.

Sebastian snickered, then went back to work, and I headed towards the edge of the counter, picking up the stack of papers. Most were bills, some were random papers that needed to be filed or looked over. Some were just junk mail. But there was one letter, written in block print that didn't look familiar. Chills went up my spine and I opened it, wondering what the fuck this was. Maybe it was someone asking to buy my house. I got a lot of handwritten letters for that, but I didn't think this was going to be that. I swallowed hard, slid open the paper, and froze.

"I'll find you, boy. Oops. Looks like I already did. Be waiting. I know you miss me."

I let the paper hit the top of the counter and swallowed hard, trying to remain cool so I didn't worry anyone else.

I didn't know exactly who that was from, but I had a horrible feeling that they wouldn't wait long to tell me.

**Read the rest in Bittersweet Promises!
OUT NOW!**

Acknowledgments

After writing nearly 150 romances, I still cannot believe I get to do this for a living. This book wouldn't have happened without my team, my family, and frankly, without my Nespresso. (Not sponsored haha.)

Brandi - thank you for catching this one. For standing up when we figured all was lost. And one day we will have a giant spreadsheet of spreadsheets and fall into a heap. But for now, thank you for rocking it with the whole people thing. And the edit thing.

Fedora and Lillie - thank you for being the best proofers! I'm so lucky to have you on my team!

LB - You're the best buddy read around and frankly, the best at reading my mind to make sure I got this book done and pretty. I can't wait to see what we do soon!

Ann - Thank you for understanding my rambling words and I truly truly admire you. You're a force. You're brilliant. And I'm honored to learn from you daily.

Ashley and Brianna - Thank you for helping me

take time "off". Or at least not work until 2 am anymore. Y'all are so helpful!

Lasheera - Thank you for loving the Cages and helping them soar!

The Ryans - thank you for being my bests friends. And yes, I should probably get a few more best friends lol. But I love you three.

Thank YOU dear readers. I wouldn't be here without you. I love writing romance and I get to do so because of YOU.

Happy Reading!

~Carrie Ann

Also from Carrie Ann Ryan

The Montgomery Ink Legacy Series:
Book 1: Bittersweet Promises (Leif & Brooke)
Book 2: At First Meet (Nick & Lake)
Book 2.5: Happily Ever Never (May & Leo)
Book 3: Longtime Crush (Sebastian & Raven)
Book 4: Best Friend Temptation (Noah, Ford, and Greer)
Book 4.5: Happily Ever Maybe (Jennifer & Gus)
Book 5: Last First Kiss (Daisy & Hugh)
Book 6: His Second Chance (Kane & Phoebe)
Book 7: One Night with You (Kingston & Claire)
Book 8: Accidentally Forever (Crew & Aria)
Book 9: Last Chance Seduction (Lexington & Mercy)

ALSO FROM CARRIE ANN RYAN

The Cage Family

Book 1: The Forever Rule (Aston & Blakely)

Book 2: An Unexpected Everything (Isabella & Weston)

Book 3: If You Were Mine (Dorian & Harper)

Ashford Creek

Book 1: Legacy (Callum & Felicity)

Clover Lake

Book 1: Always a Fake Bridesmaid (Livvy & Ewan)

The Wilder Brothers Series:

Book 1: One Way Back to Me (Eli & Alexis)

Book 2: Always the One for Me (Evan & Kendall)

Book 3: The Path to You (Everett & Bethany)

Book 4: Coming Home for Us (Elijah & Maddie)

Book 5: Stay Here With Me (East & Lark)

Book 6: Finding the Road to Us (Elliot, Trace, and Sidney)

Book 7: Moments for You (Ridge & Aurora)

Book 7.5: A Wilder Wedding (Amos & Naomi)

Book 8: Forever For Us (Wyatt & Ava)

Book 9: Pieces of Me (Gabriel & Briar)

Book 10: Endlessly Yours (Brooks & Rory)

The First Time Series:
Book 1: Good Time Boyfriend (Heath & Devney)
Book 2: Last Minute Fiancé (Luca & Addison)
Book 3: Second Chance Husband (August & Paisley)

Montgomery Ink Denver:
Book 0.5: Ink Inspired (Shep & Shea)
Book 0.6: Ink Reunited (Sassy, Rare, and Ian)
Book 1: Delicate Ink (Austin & Sierra)
Book 1.5: Forever Ink (Callie & Morgan)
Book 2: Tempting Boundaries (Decker and Miranda)
Book 3: Harder than Words (Meghan & Luc)
Book 3.5: Finally Found You (Mason & Presley)
Book 4: Written in Ink (Griffin & Autumn)
Book 4.5: Hidden Ink (Hailey & Sloane)
Book 5: Ink Enduring (Maya, Jake, and Border)
Book 6: Ink Exposed (Alex & Tabby)
Book 6.5: Adoring Ink (Holly & Brody)
Book 6.6: Love, Honor, & Ink (Arianna & Harper)
Book 7: Inked Expressions (Storm & Everly)
Book 7.3: Dropout (Grayson & Kate)
Book 7.5: Executive Ink (Jax & Ashlynn)
Book 8: Inked Memories (Wes & Jillian)
Book 8.5: Inked Nights (Derek & Olivia)

ALSO FROM CARRIE ANN RYAN

Book 8.7: Second Chance Ink (Brandon & Lauren)

Book 8.5: Montgomery Midnight Kisses (Alex & Tabby Bonus(

Bonus: Inked Kingdom (Stone & Sarina)

Montgomery Ink: Colorado Springs

Book 1: Fallen Ink (Adrienne & Mace)

Book 2: Restless Ink (Thea & Dimitri)

Book 2.5: Ashes to Ink (Abby & Ryan)

Book 3: Jagged Ink (Roxie & Carter)

Book 3.5: Ink by Numbers (Landon & Kaylee)

The Montgomery Ink: Boulder Series:

Book 1: Wrapped in Ink (Liam & Arden)

Book 2: Sated in Ink (Ethan, Lincoln, and Holland)

Book 3: Embraced in Ink (Bristol & Marcus)

Book 3: Moments in Ink (Zia & Meredith)

Book 4: Seduced in Ink (Aaron & Madison)

Book 4.5: Captured in Ink (Julia, Ronin, & Kincaid)

Book 4.7: Inked Fantasy (Secret ??)

Book 4.8: A Very Montgomery Christmas (The Entire Boulder Family)

The Montgomery Ink: Fort Collins Series:

Book 1: Inked Persuasion (Jacob & Annabelle)

Book 2: Inked Obsession (Beckett & Eliza)

Book 3: Inked Devotion (Benjamin & Brenna)
Book 3.5: Nothing But Ink (Clay & Riggs)
Book 4: Inked Craving (Lee & Paige)
Book 5: Inked Temptation (Archer & Killian)

The Promise Me Series:
Book 1: Forever Only Once (Cross & Hazel)
Book 2: From That Moment (Prior & Paris)
Book 3: Far From Destined (Macon & Dakota)
Book 4: From Our First (Nate & Myra)

The Whiskey and Lies Series:
Book 1: Whiskey Secrets (Dare & Kenzie)
Book 2: Whiskey Reveals (Fox & Melody)
Book 3: Whiskey Undone (Loch & Ainsley)

The Gallagher Brothers Series:
Book 1: Love Restored (Graham & Blake)
Book 2: Passion Restored (Owen & Liz)
Book 3: Hope Restored (Murphy & Tessa)

The Less Than Series:
Book 1: Breathless With Her (Devin & Erin)
Book 2: Reckless With You (Tucker & Amelia)
Book 3: Shameless With Him (Caleb & Zoey)

ALSO FROM CARRIE ANN RYAN

The Fractured Connections Series:
Book 1: Breaking Without You (Cameron & Violet)
Book 2: Shouldn't Have You (Brendon & Harmony)
Book 3: Falling With You (Aiden & Sienna)
Book 4: Taken With You (Beckham & Meadow)

The On My Own Series:
Book 0.5: My First Glance
Book 1: My One Night (Dillon & Elise)
Book 2: My Rebound (Pacey & Mackenzie)
Book 3: My Next Play (Miles & Nessa)
Book 4: My Bad Decisions (Tanner & Natalie)

The Ravenwood Coven Series:
Book 1: Dawn Unearthed
Book 2: Dusk Unveiled
Book 3: Evernight Unleashed

The Aspen Pack Series:
Book 1: Etched in Honor
Book 2: Hunted in Darkness
Book 3: Mated in Chaos
Book 4: Harbored in Silence
Book 5: Marked in Flames

The Talon Pack:

Book 1: Tattered Loyalties
Book 2: An Alpha's Choice
Book 3: Mated in Mist
Book 4: Wolf Betrayed
Book 5: Fractured Silence
Book 6: Destiny Disgraced
Book 7: Eternal Mourning
Book 8: Strength Enduring
Book 9: Forever Broken
Book 10: Mated in Darkness
Book 11: Fated in Winter

Redwood Pack Series:
Book 0.5: An Alpha's Path
Book 1: A Taste for a Mate
Book 2: Trinity Bound
Book 2.5: A Night Away
Book 3: Enforcer's Redemption
Book 3.5: Blurred Expectations
Book 3.7: Forgiveness
Book 4: Shattered Emotions
Book 5: Hidden Destiny
Book 5.5: A Beta's Haven
Book 6: Fighting Fate
Book 6.5: Loving the Omega
Book 6.7: The Hunted Heart

ALSO FROM CARRIE ANN RYAN

Book 7: Wicked Wolf

The Elements of Five Series:
Book 1: From Breath and Ruin
Book 2: From Flame and Ash
Book 3: From Spirit and Binding
Book 4: From Shadow and Silence

Dante's Circle Series:
Book 1: Dust of My Wings
Book 2: Her Warriors' Three Wishes
Book 3: An Unlucky Moon
Book 3.5: His Choice
Book 4: Tangled Innocence
Book 5: Fierce Enchantment
Book 6: An Immortal's Song
Book 7: Prowled Darkness
Book 8: Dante's Circle Reborn

Holiday, Montana Series:
Book 1: Charmed Spirits
Book 2: Santa's Executive
Book 3: Finding Abigail
Book 4: Her Lucky Love
Book 5: Dreams of Ivory

ALSO FROM CARRIE ANN RYAN

The Branded Pack Series:
(Written with Alexandra Ivy)
Book 1: Stolen and Forgiven
Book 2: Abandoned and Unseen
Book 3: Buried and Shadowed

About the Author

Carrie Ann Ryan is the New York Times and USA Today bestselling author of contemporary, paranormal, and young adult romance. Her works include the Montgomery Ink, Redwood Pack, Fractured Connections, and Elements of Five series, which have sold over 3.0 million books worldwide. She started writing while in graduate school for her advanced degree in chemistry and hasn't stopped since. Carrie Ann has written over seventy-five novels and novellas with more in the works. When she's not losing herself in her emotional and action-packed worlds, she's reading as much as she can while wrangling her clowder of cats who have more followers than she does.

www.CarrieAnnRyan.com